Mass Moralizing

Mass Moralizing

Marketing and Moral Storytelling

Phil Hopkins

LEXINGTON BOOKS
Lanham • Boulder • New York • London

Published by Lexington Books
An imprint of The Rowman & Littlefield Publishing Group, Inc.
4501 Forbes Boulevard, Suite 200, Lanham, Maryland 20706
www.rowman.com

Unit A, Whitacre Mews, 26-34 Stannary Street, London SE11 4AB

British Library Cataloguing in Publication Information Available

Library of Congress Cataloging-in-Publication Data
Hopkins, Phil, 1958–
Mass moralizing : marketing and moral storytelling / Phil Hopkins.
pages cm.
Includes bibliographical references and index.
ISBN 978-0-7391-8851-4 (cloth : alk. paper) — ISBN 978-0-7391-8852-1 (electronic)
ISBN 978-1-4985-1357-9 (pbk: alk. paper) 1. Mass
media—Moral and ethical aspects. 2. Communication—Moral and ethical aspects. 3. Marketing. I. Title.
P94.H658 2015
175—dc23
                                                                              2015000455

♾ ™ The paper used in this publication meets the minimum requirements of American National Standard for Information Sciences Permanence of Paper for Printed Library Materials, ANSI/NISO Z39.48-1992.

Printed in the United States of America

Contents

List of Figures

Acknowledgments

I want to thank the students in my many Media and Ethics classes for bringing a number of the ads and commercials analyzed in this book to my attention, and my daughter, Rebecca, for first calling my attention to the Lancôme and French McDonald's ads. I want to thank her in particular for all the years of watching, analyzing, and discussing marketing together with me, and my son, Isaac, and wife, Lisa, for their tireless review of this work in progress and equal patience with my constant deconstructions of whatever we happened to be watching together. Some material in this book was originally published in different form in the chapter "Mass Moralizing" in Amir Hetsroni, *Advertising and Reality* (New York: Continuum Press, 2012) and is used with permission of Bloomsbury Academic. The American Century advertisement is used with permission of American Century Investments Inc., American Century Services. All other advertising material is used under the Fair Use Clause, Section 107, of the Copyright Act of 1976, which protects the unlicensed reproduction of media for the purposes of criticism, commentary, and education.

Introduction

"What are the . . . implications of our whole form of life? Is the confusion about 'values' and the absence of larger meanings that seem to characterize many Americans the result of life contexts that produce more confusion than clarity?"[1]

It is a well-established and much discussed fact that each of us encounters a great deal of mass media every day in what many refer to as our "consumer culture." There is what amounts to a subsidiary industry whose primary task is reflecting upon media and our consumption of it. Since Marshall McLuhan famously informed us that the medium is the message, many others have addressed this powerful force in our lives, often decrying its vast influence and predicting no good to come of it.[2]

One such alarmist, Jeffrey Scheuer, in *The Sound Bite Society*, warns that our "electronic culture fragments information into isolated, dramatic particles and resists longer and more complex messages." These characteristics work against "ambiguity and non-binary thinking" and "reasoning that appeals to causal, contextual, or environmental considerations," he argues. Scheuer believes that our "sound bite culture in fact reinforces a contrary vision: one that focuses on the immediate and the obvious; the near-term and the particular; on identity between appearance and reality; and on the self rather than larger communities." "Above all," he believes, it has created a "society that thrives on simplicity and disdains complexity."[3] Later in the same work he claims: "TV excels at changing the subject . . . likes action and dislikes thought. It favors conflict and spectacle, and disfavors ambiguity [and] irony."[4] While his specific conclusions about political party "control" of mass media discourses are indeed questionable, this analysis of its larger structural character is not wrong.

1

Richard Adler has similarly argued: "The TV set has become the primary source of news and entertainment for most Americans and a major force in the acculturation of children. Television has transformed the country's political process. It is a fundamental component of the corporate marketing structure that underlies our consumer economy. Television, in short, pervades and alters the contemporary American environment."[5] Adler argues that it does this by being a *mediator*, and not just a medium, "a mediator between our individual lives and the larger life of the nation and the world; between fantasy and fact; between old values and new ideas; between our desire to seek escape and our need to confront reality."

In the now vast literature on media studies, though, what goes almost unnoticed, or at least largely unremarked, is how much mass media now operates in an explicitly moral register. It is virtually impossible to go through a day that includes any mass media (and for most of us, that means any given day) without hearing some mention of moral values or ethics, either explicit or implied. In the television programming we watch, both for entertainment and for information, the music we listen to, even the video games we play, and, finally, the great deal of marketing that we consume, we hear the constant refrain of "values," are quite explicitly invited to judge the actors in the narrative dramas we watch (both fictional and journalistic), and are repeatedly reminded that our choices have moral and ethical significance. Morality, as subject matter, has never been limited to sermons, either from the pulpit or from our parents and teachers, and certainly not to some specialized discourse, either in the academy or politics; but the explosion of mass media as a narrative force in our world has both magnified the occasions for and in significant ways altered how we engage the topic of morality as a set of central questions about what it means to be a human being in society.

The central role and power of storytelling both in our cultures and as a fundamental human dynamic has also been recognized by many thinkers, although not often with respect to its impact upon and use of moral motifs and questions. Richard Rorty has noted the connection, however. Rorty believes that television and newspapers are two of the main channels of "moral progress" in the contemporary world because they have become our dominant storytellers. He argues that it is in story rather than theory that we can most directly learn about ourselves, our impulses and capacities, and how to think about "others" and the world. For that reason, he believes "the novel, the movie, and the TV program have, gradually but steadily, replaced the sermon and the treatise as the principal vehicles of moral change and progress."[6]

This book is about the relationship between three interrelated dynamics – the power of narrative in the construction of identity and world, the truth-telling pretenses of marketing (and also, in briefer compass, related discourses in journalism and education), and the growth of moralizing as a primary moral discourse practice in contemporary consumer culture. In it, I will examine in particular how marketing speaks to us in explicitly moralistic terms, significantly influencing how we think about ourselves and our moral possibilities. Marketing and related mass media voices have become primary cultural storytellers. As sources, or at least mirrors, of cultural myths about ourselves and the world, they articulate and shape our possibilities of identity and obligation. This book examines how those media stories that purport to tell us about the world—primarily in marketing, but also in journalism and education—interact with our cultural ideas about morality in ways that deeply affect our sense of ourselves and our relations to each other. I analyze the way that these practices have cooperated, not always intentionally, to fundamentally delimit possibilities for moral discourse; that is, to simply change what we mean by "moral" and how we go about meaning it, often in ways that are in tension with themselves and other cultural narratives about moral judgment and behavior.

There has been work, in philosophy and other disciplines, that examines the "culture industry" and its impact on society broadly, but this work is often itself moralistic, frequently offering critique and judgment about media practices from a particular moral standpoint. There is work that explores the ethics of mass media practice, particularly in journalism and marketing, but this work is a kind of applied ethics, asking and addressing questions about ethical standards and practices (or the absence thereof). These analyses focus on questions about the morality *of* the various mass media, asking about the limits of ethical practice, the moral responsibility of the press or advertising, the moral character of the content. There has also been more limited attention given to mass media as providing models for moral and ethical ideals.

My analysis is largely unrelated to these sorts of questions. I am not concerned with the moral character of the media, but with the interplay of media and morality itself, the influence of media moralizing, and even of media practices not explicitly moralistic such as more systematic journalistic and marketing discourse structures, on popular conceptions of morality and on public and popular moral discourse. There has not been a sustained and focused examination of the ways in which these new "truth-telling" mass media narratives intentionally inhabit moralistic rhetoric as a means of accomplishing their primary goals: informing us about the world or themselves, and selling us things; nor has there been close analysis of the impact of those practices on our ways of thinking about moral and ethical possibilities and choices. That is the examination which this book seeks to develop.

My primary approach is philosophical, i.e., a critical inquiry that attempts to clarify the contours of the phenomenon as it is both experienced and expressed in consumer culture. I will move from what is more obvious—the surface moralism of consumer culture narratives—toward what is less obvious and more structurally concealed—the close and often complex interaction of those narratives with our popular ideas about ethics and morality, and, moreover, our larger cultural notions of self and world. My analysis is grounded in a phenomenology of narrativity which understands storytelling to be a central and essential human activity, the primary means by which we make sense of ourselves and our world. I explore the ways in which mass-mediated stories interact with broader cultural and our own personal narratives in ways that profoundly influence each other.

While I seek to understand the changes produced by the phenomena I analyze, my analysis is not alarmist or, itself, moralistic. I do not adduce some general moral threat wherein we might imagine corporate mass media spoon-feeding us the morality they would like us to have, or think we'd like to have, or experiment with in case any of us would like to have it, in ways that benefit them but work to the detriment of some pure or, at the very least, more rationally preferable moral system or deliberative process. Rather I argue that we have entered into a phase of popular moral heuristics wherein our moral concepts and their integral symbols are mirrored at us as consumer culture, creating new moral dynamics. We participate in that mirroring, of course, both knowingly and not, helping to create an evolving moral patter that shapes our fundamental ideas about ourselves and our relations with each other in multiple and even conflicting ways. I argue that as a result, we find ourselves, more and more, both morally unsure and adventurous at the same time, both uncertain and too certain, and so ever more ready to adopt a distancing skepticism or take a position on the front lines of the new moral holy wars.

I believe that we have always engaged in a fairly sharp public debate about morality, about what is right and wrong, about how to see the world and what to believe, about which beliefs should guide our practice. I'm certainly not nostalgic for some (perhaps largely imagined) earlier age in which this debate happened in some possibly better way. I'm interested in the shape this debate takes now, and, in particular, the influence upon this debate of important changes provoked by a rapidly developing and ubiquitous mass media. I believe we are still talking about what we have always talked about, but we are talking about it, in part, through new media that have profoundly reshaped the way we talk and think. I'm interested in thinking about how a society which has come to be so dominated by mass media whose primary dynamics are so thoroughly consumerist, while simultaneously moralistic, may have altered our very sense of that debate.

There are new and powerful storytellers in our culture. It is important to look closely at how these new stories work, how they are themselves shaped and by what forces and structures and desires, and how these stories shape us and the ways we tell our own stories. I believe the critical tools and categories of philosophy are particularly useful for illuminating and explaining the dynamics of these dominant discourse practices. The book hopes to provide readers with some of those critical tools for analyzing the dynamics of both these new narrative practices and their own media consumption as those relate specifically to how we all think about morality.

The book is divided into two parts, in which the first and more theoretical part seeks to prepare the reader for the central analysis of the moralistic discourses of much contemporary marketing, in part II. In part I, I will present and argue for the claim that narrative is central to any conception of morality or ethics, that questions about what kind of person we can or should be, to what groups we can or do belong, to whom we owe duty and responsibility and why cannot be separated from the metaphysical structures of self and world that flow from the stories we tell ourselves about ourselves and the worlds we inhabit. As Plato recognized, any conception of morality is grounded in some conception of the order of things, a conception of what is related to what else and how it is related. It is the structure of things that determines the lines of relation, and thus the lines of obligation and duty. Morality, therefore, is necessarily grounded in a particular metaphysics. Metaphysics, though, I will argue, are grounded in the stories we tell. Each story constructs or configures the world in which it can be told, shaping both its characters and its possible tellers. Stories make sense of events and of experiences. Indeed, experiences aren't experiences until they are formed within a narrative structure in which they make sense. Making sense means quite simply piecing together bits of experience such that the bits fit together into an order or pattern of relations. Human beings make sense, of the world and themselves, in narrative form, building worlds with words. Recognizing this important fact and working to understand its dynamics is essential to understanding how marketing works upon us, and not just with respect to its moralizing narratives.

The remaining chapters of part I will further this analysis by focusing on the relations of the stories we tell to the power of images and symbols in consumer culture. In chapter 2, I will offer an analysis of a particular genre of mass media storytelling that I call "truth-telling" narratives, which inhabit narrative conventions importantly different from stories we encounter as fictive. I will look at how marketing inhabits "truth-telling" narrative conventions by looking closely at the relation of those conventions to similar, if not identical, conventions in journalism and education, two dominant "truth-telling" genres in the contemporary world. I will look at the nature of the authority of such narratives, and also examine the relations of that authority to moral authority as a way of particularly attending to the relation of the primary discourse practices and structures of these conventions to our moral thinking and concepts.

In chapter 3, I will touch upon the centrality, ubiquity, and narrative power of images in our world. I will look at the relation of identity to image, and, thus, the relation to ethics, or questions about what kind of person to be, including how that question is shaped by how we see ourselves in the world, and the world itself, as spectacle. I will take up again the question of narrative authority as embodied in images. In this chapter I will also examine the conflation of worlds that is provoked by the ontological character of the high-fidelity image and the structural practices of image producers and media, a conflation between representation and reality which borrows authority *from* reality and transfers dynamics of representationality *to* reality. I will look at the conflation of self and image, and how such a conflation necessarily doubles us, at least, placing ourselves in relation to ourselves as other to ourselves, as viewed and viewer.

In both chapters 3 and 4, then, I will examine the mythologized character of our world and ourselves in it, how we create and inhabit hyperrealized experiences and possibilities through the stories and the image-stories we consume. I will begin to look at how specific marketing motifs collaborate with the dynamics of story and image just examined to offer pre-packaged narrative and symbolic identities, the opportunity to see and understand ourselves through "brands," identities *expressed* and not just represented through brands. Such opportunities are invitations to join "tribes," hyperrealized communities that cut across many other kinds of identity groupings to offer belonging as choice, and as individual fulfillment.

Part II will then offer the primary concrete analysis of this book through marketing narratives and images drawn from many media sources, but particularly from television commercials, still one of the most prominent forms of marketing, to examine how they frame us, the world, and our ideas about morality and practices of moral judgment. In chapter 5, I will look at how marketing presents "the good life" as enabled through consumer goods and consumption. In chapter 6, I will look at how marketing offers explicit or implicit moral lessons about how to live well and what values to "have," preferably through market exchange, ultimately offering morality itself as consumer product. In chapter 7, I will look at how some marketing campaigns configure market activity, the act of consumption itself, as a kind of moral activism. Finally, in chapter 8, I will directly address the question as to what morality has to already be in popular culture in order to have been configured and used within marketing in the ways analyzed. I will propose that morality must already be a kind of sociological propaganda along the lines theorized by Jacques Ellul.

Since the advent of "brand" marketing, advertisers have largely stopped telling us about the things they sell. They still trumpet generic qualities, that what they sell is "new" or "bigger" or "better." Mostly, however, marketing tells us stories instead. Brand marketing focuses on creating a "meaning system" for and emotional attachment to a brand rather than directly promoting the qualities or features of a given consumer product. It attempts to accomplish this work by co-opting and inhabiting our cultural myths about the world that they believe will resonate emotionally and that will attract and interest us because such stories speak to what we already believe is important or find valuable. They tell us stories about our dream worlds and dream selves.

Over the past few decades, many of these stories have become increasingly moralistic. When marketing takes the time to tell us about their companies or their products directly, they often do so in terms that frame what kind of company they are, what they care about, and what their "values" are. Marketing, along with journalism and education, increasingly offers its narratives as a form of moral guidance, teaching lessons about "values" and offering to remind us about what really matters in life. There is almost no sector of the consumer market that hasn't participated in this new moralistic genre. In this book, I examine how marketing draws upon and reshapes a growing moralism in popular culture that lends itself to market use because it is itself configured as commodity.

NOTES

1. Robert Bellah, "Education: Technical and Moral," in *The Good Society* with Richard Madsen, William M. Sullivan, Ann Swidler, and Steven M. Tipton (New York: Knopf, 1991), 150.

2. There are many such voices, including influential thinkers both more popular, such as Neil Postman and Noam Chomsky, and scholarly, such as Jean Baudrillard, and also others more sharply focused on the potential harms of advertising and popular culture, such as Jackson Katz, Sut Jhally, and Jean Kilbourne. I believe much of their collective analysis, if not always their arguments or conclusions, is cogent and apt.

3. Jeffrey Scheuer, *The Sound Bite Society: Television and the American Mind* (New York: Four Walls Eight Windows Press, 1999), 9–10.

4. Scheuer, 85.

5. Richard Adler, ed., *Understanding Television* (Santa Barbara, CA: Praeger, 1981), xi.

6. Richard Rorty, *Contingency, Irony, and Solidarity* (Cambridge: Cambridge University Press, 1989).

I

Self and World: Story, Image, Brand

Chapter One

The Stories We Tell

"We assume that life produces the autobiography as an act produces its consequences, but can we not suggest, with equal justice, that the autobiographical project may itself produce and determine life?"[1]

"None of us lives without reference to an imaginative singularity which we call our 'self.'"[2]

"For there are many stories of self to tell, and more than one self to tell them."[3]

Robert Sokolowski has said that philosophy is primarily about making distinctions.[4] I believe it is important to start with a few crucial distinctions in order to set the stage for and clarify the analysis that follows. The first of these is the distinction between the term "morality" or "moral" and the term "moralizing." This book concerns itself with what I will argue are predominant *moralizing* narratives in our culture. The larger term "moral" may refer to principles, behavior, actions, character, rules, values, codes, judgments, decisions; and this list is far from exhaustive. Indeed, the semiotic range of the term moral is, in popular and technical practice, quite extensive. The narrower term, moralizing, refers to the explicit practice of offering moral lessons. Moralizing always refers to some bit of language, often, I will argue, narrative language. There is one connotation of the term moral, however, that overlaps with the term moralizing in an illuminating way, and that is the sense of "moral" in the phrase "the moral of the story." In this one restricted sense, moral means the lesson to be learned from a story or event. By event, I mean not something that actually happens, but what we tell ourselves and others happened, indeed, a narrative *construction* and not mere recounting of what happens. Moralizing, then, for our purposes, and indeed, generally, means adducing or delivering the *moral*, in this last restricted sense of a lesson to be learned, in some narrative form.

The term moralizing often carries negative connotations, invoking a sense of sermonizing or lecturing, self-righteousness, or at least a button-holing or finger-wagging character. However we encounter the term, though, we are not averse to moral lessons generally. Indeed, we seem to crave them. Much literature consists of moral lessons offered in the form of heroes to emulate, characters, situations, and temptations to be shunned, scandals to avoid or learn from. It is not news that most narratives operate in such a moral register.[5] It will be the work of the main part of this book to show that register widely operating in marketing narratives. To that end, we need to think past the negative connotations of the term moralizing and focus on its central place in culture, a place that we desire and appreciate. We like to be reminded of what matters, particularly if the reminder corresponds to existing beliefs or comes by means of emotionally charged images and stories. We like our "heartstrings" pulled, and appreciate the metaphysical comfort that comes from being assured that how we see things is good and right.

Perhaps an example or two will help clarify this distinction. A magazine ad for American Century carries the label "American Values" at the top center (see figure 1.1). Beneath that we see a black and white picture of a sandwich on a lunch tray, taking up half the page. Below this we read a little story the company wants to tell us:

> Every day, our founder has the same lunch. It isn't lobster tail. — It's a true story. At noon, he sits down in the cafeteria and eats a peanut butter sandwich. When he's done, he folds up his paper sack so it can be used again tomorrow. It's a tradition around here. One of the many we've created in our 44 years of managing investments. Over time we've grown, but two things have remained constant. His lunch. And our values. Your success is still our first priority. The proof is in the peanut butter.

Another ad, this time from the website for McDonald's Australia, shows a family celebrating what may be some special event or just the pleasure of eating out together (from the television commercial from which this scene was taken we would learn the family is having dinner out after their son's soccer game). The image is captioned: "Love my family. What really makes me happy? The smile on my kids' faces." (see figure 1.2)

The first ad operates in a register that is overtly moral, in that it makes explicit reference to moral values in several ways. It trumpets "American values" at the top center of the ad, a shop-worn phrase from American political rhetoric with heavy moral implications. It unpacks that notion through reminders of the virtues of "tradition," frugality, consistency, and more figuratively, through nostalgic images that conjure notions of youth and simplicity. It slyly distances itself from connotations it fears we might attach

Every day, our founder has the same lunch. It isn't lobster tail. ========

It's a true story. At noon, he sits down in the cafeteria and eats a peanut butter sandwich. When he's done, he folds up his paper sack so it can be used again tomorrow.

It's a tradition around here. One of the many we've created in our 44 years of managing investments. Over time we've grown, but two things have remained constant. His lunch. And our values. Your success is still our first priority. The proof is in the peanut butter.

Please call 1-877-44-AMCEN or visit www.americancentury.com to obtain a prospectus with more complete information, including charges, expenses and minimums. Be sure to read it carefully before you invest or send money. American Century Investment Services, Inc. © 2002 American Century Services Corporation.

AMERICAN
CENTURY.
Investment Managers

Figure 1.1.   American Century website ad.

to the idea of an investment firm: the extravagance of "lobster tails" and a perhaps too impersonal interest in financial growth, while at the same time drawing upon any positive sensibilities we attach to the idea of "founder," a phrase that, happily for the marketing team, echoes the American political notion of founding fathers and personalizes the company for us at the same

Figure 1.2.   McDonald's website ad.

time as it locates it within a tradition of authority and iconic power. It does all of this as a way of persuading us to invest our money with them. The ad does not mention portfolio performance histories, or specific investment strategies or principles. It asks us, instead, to believe that American Century shares our values, and moreover lives those values (in a way that we, it subtly suggests, may not as fully) as a model for the rest of us. So, the ad is clearly moralistic. It offers lessons about what matters, phrased in what are commonly known as glittering generalities, words like "tradition," "values," and even "true." Such words exert emotional power without needing to be unpacked in concrete terms because of their close association with deeply held beliefs and commitments, words that are persuasive without needing to be informative or reasoned, words that remind us about what we believe to be good and right.[6]

I will insist, however, that the second ad is no less moralistic. Without any explicit mention of values or virtues, McDonald's offers just as explicitly to teach lessons about what matters. It does not operate in a register we may recognize as overtly moral since it does not use morally charged vocabulary, but it does speak to us directly and even didactically about how to parent, about "love," "family," happiness, and less explicitly, about selflessness and giving. Even if we have not seen the full television commercial with its references to the many obligations to our children in contemporary life, we are shown enough in this ad to recognize the familiar narrative of family togetherness, the truism that being a good parent means doing what makes our family happy. We will have more to say about McDonald's marketing and its many lessons on how to parent in later chapters. Here I merely want to point out that narratives (and our focus will largely be marketing narratives) can be moralistic without overtly referencing elements we recognize as moral as we usually understand that term. Certainly, lessons about how to parent are also inherently lessons about how to be a good parent, and so good generally, and therefore are moral in the broader sense.

The distinction I want to make clearly here is that moralistic narratives need not, and usually will not explicitly refer to "morality" or "ethics" in terms we would readily recognize as such. And many of them, the less clumsy of them, will be appealing. What kind of talk do we usually recognize as moral? Talk about what kind of person to be and what we owe to others: that is a good formula for encapsulating a fair bit of what we mean by the terms ethics and morality. Indeed, there is some merit for distinguishing between the terms according to these two main questions in this way: ethics can be thought of as the question of what kind of person to be, and morality can be considered to be the question of how to live together justly, what obligations we owe to others with whom we are in relation.

If you found these ads effective, though, I suspect it is because you find the references in them to be appealing, emotionally or conceptually. It is because you value the same things, family or tradition, and appreciate a congenial reminder about those values, or because the images and sentiments draw out an emotional response from you that you find pleasant, perhaps even poignant. That is what they intend to do. I suspect more of us will have found the McDonald's ad more effective and appealing simply by virtue of its more indirect moralizing. It probably feels less preachy, and thus more inclusive. You may have been more willing to be "taught" the lessons it offers as a result.

Both images are narratively rich, and both ads rely upon the narratives embedded in those images to do a great deal of the "work" of both selling the brand and "reminding" us about what is important. Both tell stories that the marketers hope will resonate and involve us fully, calling to mind our own complex mix of memories and emotions around the nexus of family and eating, in and out of cafeterias, and also ambiguously signified moments of triumph or tradition. Neither ad's image is merely some visual aid to its more expansive linguistic message. Much of the narrative is presented and not merely illustrated by the image. The apple and the milk carton do not need the linguistic reference of "cafeteria" to register that meaning in our consciousness and call to mind important associations with simpler times. Indeed, I would argue (as do many semiologists such as Barthes or Bourdieu) that the word almost always serves to reinforce the image in these pairings (to anchor and relay it, in Barthes' terms), rather than the reverse.[7]

Still, the ads work for and on you, or they don't. You found them appealing and even, perhaps, edifying, or you didn't. What is important to see is that when they work, they work by means of a moralizing narrative, rather than by means of some more direct claims for the product ostensibly being offered for purchase, such as an investment strategy or a burger and fries. For much of this book I will offer analysis of the moralistic character of much marketing narrative, and I will explain how images no less than and often more fully than spoken or written language work as narratives presenting moral lessons. I am not going to argue that marketers offer moralistic narratives because they believe we need such lessons. They are not, I believe, concerned about any moral deficiency on our part; nor do they think, I believe, that encountering moral lessons generally makes us want to buy things. If they offer to be our moral guides, it is not because they think themselves particularly or uniquely qualified or have experienced an altruistic urge to help us better ourselves, but because they think we like moral guides, and will feel good about their company and product as a result. I will argue that marketing offers moralistic narratives because they believe we already find moralizing appealing, if done in the right way, if grounded, I will argue, in stories that speak to our deeply emotional attachments to ideas and beliefs that matter to us. They do it because we like it, or at least they think we do.

THE NOBLE LIE

This chapter, then, is about the role of narrative in identity and morality, about stories and storytelling as central both to how we think of and indeed construct ourselves and to how we think about and enact morality and ethics. What we think is possible and desirable for us, the nature of our goals, and the character of our duties all are grounded in particular ideas about human potentiality and promise that are constructed and communicated through the stories we tell. There are two main elements I want to call to our particular attention in this claim, one most directly related to understanding our thinking about ethics and morality itself, and the second quite important to understanding mass moralizing narratives. The first is that any morality is grounded in a particular metaphysics, in particular ideas about how things are structured, ordered, related. Exploring this claim is the primary work of this chapter. The second, that our metaphysics, and so our moralities, flow from the stories we tell about ourselves and our world, and so depend upon how we tell those stories, who tells them, and what they say, will take up the remainder of the book, beginning with this chapter. Understanding this claim fully will require seeing clearly just how our ideas about what kind of thing we are or have the potential to be are propagated and shaped in our culture.

Power of narrative to determine our id.

In short, my argument is that human beings are essentially storytellers, *Such* telling stories about themselves into worlds they construct by means of stories. As we live our lives, our first and most essential work is to make sense of our experiences and of the world; and this sense-making occurs as a kind of collaborative storytelling. In the process of telling ourselves these stories about who we are and how the world works, we simultaneously and necessarily construct the metaphysics of the worlds we inhabit, such that some elements exist for us but not others, and such that all elements relate to each other in specific ways, but not others. Once we inhabit certain stories with their particular metaphysics (ways of understanding the world) rather than others, we are no longer free to simply adopt just any set of moral values. The stories we tell already delineate and configure lines of obligation and duty, possibilities of identity and character. Therefore, the stories we tell determine the moral and ethical values that are possible, and in some cases, even inevitable.

That will be my argument, in sum. Now for the longer version. I should begin by distinguishing what I am about to argue from what is usually called "narrative ethics." There will certainly be points of contact, but what I will argue is substantially different, more general and inclusive, more a theory of ethics than what is usually called narrative ethics. Hilde Lindemann Nelson offers a helpful characterization: narrative ethics is the idea that "accords a central role to stories, not merely employing them as illustrations, examples, or ways of testing our intuitions regarding moral theories or principles, but regarding them as necessary means to some moral end."[8] She recognizes that many people view stories as *illustrative* of moral ideals, presenting moral lessons or acting as moral guides or touchstones. Narrative ethics takes stories more seriously and as essential to the project of morality. In this view, stories are the means by which we learn our duties and they help make moral actions intelligible. Stories form the basis for ethical reflection and moral learning, by making intelligible the "life events" of the individual or community. The leading philosophical proponents of this view would include Martha Nussbaum, Richard Rorty, Alasdair MacIntyre, and Charles Taylor, but the idea has also achieved popularity in many therapeutic fields.[9]

This way of looking at the relation of story and morality remains grounded in traditional moral theory, particularly virtue ethics. Morality is understood to be ontologically independent, existing as something in itself, but disseminated, learned, and understood by means of stories. Narratives help us understand ourselves and morality, but both we and our morality pre-exist those narratives. I want to argue something quite a bit different from this: that morality exists nowhere else but in and through the stories we tell about how the world is. Plato lays the groundwork for thinking about morality in this way, so a little detour through Plato's *Republic* will set the stage for us.

In Book 3 of *The Republic*, after laying out the procedure and criteria by which the ultimate guardians and rulers of the *kallipolis* will be selected and trained, Socrates proposes to tell them and all the citizens a "noble lie." He frets a bit about how people will receive his story, since, in it, we are to be told that what we usually think of as what happens to us is actually a kind of dream. While we think we are undergoing the various experiences of this world we are really, we are to be told, down inside the earth, being formed and nurtured, and so should treat the land in which we live as a kind of mother to whom we owe care and advocacy. Further, we are to be told that the gods and the earth have formed us with particular characters, mixing into this one gold, into another silver, and into others iron or bronze; and that we are to take up the responsibilities and duties imposed upon us by those pre-formed characters rather than those we might select from preference.

This "lie" is necessary, Socrates argues, to provide for a stable social structure. It seeks this goal through an attempt to persuade all who hear it that there is another and more important story to tell of our lives beyond our mundane frame of reference that focuses upon the job we must get to and perform or the meal we need to prepare and eat. It would persuade us that our lives encompass more than mere events, negotiated on the basis of personal desires and interests, but rather participate in larger purposes framed by obligation and responsibility. It would privilege tradition over interest and duty over advantage in order to convince us not only to search out the best among us to take up the responsibility of safeguarding all of us, but that each of us has a role to play in that larger process. It seeks to replace a frame of reference in which relations in the world are constituted through individual agency with a frame of reference that privileges a pattern of categories and relations that are posited as natural and/or divine, as *a priori* and autochthon-ous. It is an odd story, in an odd passage, in what even the characters of the dialogue admit is an odd project of imagining an ideal state.

I relate this story because I want to argue the perhaps radical idea that all ethics take the form of Plato's "noble lie." The rhetorical strategy behind any articulation of ethical guidelines is to posit a human subject which is capable of entering into the description of human nature or world structure that it offers with the idea that such a person will then act in ways that are better for her and better for all. We may be skeptical of some or all particular ethical formulations because they foreground possible relations or behaviors on the basis of one or another specific view of human nature with which we may or may not agree. But that skepticism ignores the key point. Each ethical theory describes how one acts *once one accepts* a description of what generally matters and how the world is, regardless of whether that description has ever actually been accepted. This is to say that an ethical system will always posit a human subject which is capable of entering into it, that the posited human subject does not pre-exist the narrative frame but arises with the ethical framework which has described it into existence. Each theorist frames interactions and elements of human nature corresponding to the demands his narrative makes of the people it describes. [10]

Ethics, then, requires and is embedded in stories. We tell stories, not just about human subjects and the sort of thing being human is through stories about being a friend or being courageous or any of the character traits our stories construct as possibilities for us, but also about the way things relate in the world, the way the world itself is, such that this or that character or action is right or good. That is why, for Socrates, some story must be told, true or not, which provides the ground for specific obligations and relations that form the foundation of what matters, the character of our values. We don't know how to posit such valuations without a narrative frame within which they achieve whatever character they may possess and which provides their criteria. Our valuations emerge, moreover, not from any congruence with possible rules or immutable categories to be found in our stories (and categories and rules always exist inside stories), but within and through the narrative elements as they are coherently related by a given story as the way the world works.

In this view, narrative is not merely an aid to understanding, and it is not even a separate and distinct activity, a fictive augmentation to our usual and more real life activity. As Booth has noted, referencing Ricoeur and speaking of metaphor but informing his larger sense of story, our essentially narrative language "is not an isolable literary device . . . but the inescapable medium of our very being, the fundamental structure of our essentially 'non-literal,' symbolic grasp of an ever-elusive reality."[11] In the view I am proposing, we do not live our lives and occasionally tell stories in order to frame or clarify the meaning or significance of our "un-storied" activity. Our lives become "lives" only through a process of constructing and telling stories. Storytelling is constant and foundational, not occasional and supplementary.

Most of our cognitive activity, I would argue, those activities aimed at understanding ourselves and our world, including memory, is exercised in creating a coherent narrative that makes sense of experience. This activity, the telling of stories as a way of both experiencing and interpreting the events in our lives, makes good claim to being both a distinctive and categorical human dynamic. It is not surprising, then, for our possibilities of identity and obligation to flow from that activity. To see this clearly, we will need to more fully explore what we mean by "identity" and "self", and also the relation of the concept of "self" to narrative generally, and, then, specifically how our stories work to frame moral and ethical possibilities.

IDENTITY

In scholarship before the 1950s, and still in popular consciousness, "identity" is often used as a term for "who one is," in some true or essential sense, the atomic soul, as Nietzsche termed it.[12] My "identity" is what makes me be "me" and remain me through all of the changes I experience throughout my life. As Ricoeur notes, the question of identity is vexed by an almost un- avoidable conflation of the two primary meanings of the term: on the one hand sameness, and on the other hand selfhood.[13] This conflation shapes how we view ourselves, conditioning our character: whatever the self is, it is what makes anyone the same as themselves across time and contexts. We need not review the extensive literature across a range of disciplines that challenges this notion. A moment's reflection on our part is enough to recognize that whatever "I am," whatever self I "possess" or present to myself and to others, this "self" does not remain constant for any period of time, either at the physical, conceptual, existential, or social/political levels. As Ricoeur repeat- edly argues, selfhood is not sameness.

By the mid twentieth century, however, in sociology and psychology, and also in philosophy, the term "identity" came more usually to refer to the collective social or political features of people as groups, and as applied to individuals, such as religion or nationality, but also race, gender, or sexual- ity.[14] That our actions and desires, our "projects," will inevitably be shaped by these social and political features came to be accepted in moral thought as a fact to be dealt with. While less essentialist, perhaps, and certainly intersub- jective, in this way of thinking, such selves are still often viewed as in some sense constituted by such features, and largely static.

Noted philosopher of the social and natural sciences, Ian Hacking, means by "identity" something related to this view, but a bit looser and, I would argue, more colloquially accurate: "kinds of people."[15] For him, identities are created by labels that come into general use in social discourse, rather than by some common and salient feature of groups of people. In other words, kinds of people come into being through the creation of categories that iden- tify them as distinct.[16]

This insight echoes a great deal of metaphysical thinking tracing all the way back to Aristotle and Plato. For Aristotle, to use language was to *kata- gorein*, literally, to accuse something of being a particular thing. It is primari- ly a legal term in Greek. To name is to "indict." In Latin, to "indict" from *indicere*, means to utter or pronounce, and is related to *indicare*, "indicate," which means to make known or show. Language reveals and accuses.[17] Plato several times explored the relation of universal and particular in ways that suggest strongly that we need to know the categories of experience before and in order to parse the world of experience into the discrete and knowable objects we encounter. We do not know that some particular thing we encoun-

ter is a "bush," for instance, until we have the concept category for so identifying it.[18] Hacking's formulation is influenced by Elizabeth Anscombe's
work on intention, in which actions are conceptually shaped, in that they
operate "under descriptions."[19] Those "descriptions," which inform and influence every action, cover a broad range of territories, even for the simplest
action, and include descriptions of many aspects of the world, not least,
descriptions of the sort of thing the actor is.

A good way to illustrate the centrality of "descriptions" for self and social
understanding may be found in a beautiful tale about the fragility of identity
by Milan Kundera.[20] In his story, we meet two young people on their first
"vacation" together. They are somewhat new to their relationship, still in the
early stages of exploring each other. They stop to get gas and the young
woman wanders into the woods to relieve herself. Upon her return, she walks
down the road a bit waiting for the young man to finish and on a whim puts
out a thumb, pretending to be a hitchhiker. He stops and immediately joins
the game, pretending to be the kind of person who is eager to pick up
attractive female hitchhikers. She adopts the role of the kind of girl she
secretly fears he desires, but knows herself not to be: bolder, more provocative. He falls into a role he has played in the past, but in which he is no longer
fully comfortable: a womanizer.

As they progress through the remainder of their day together, the roles
they so casually and playfully adopted begin to shape their interactions in
ways neither of them intend nor enjoy. As each becomes uncomfortable with
one aspect or another of the game, each tries to break out of it, but they find
that the roles they have adopted are not so easy to drop. Once the "descriptions" of who they are and what they are doing which derive from those
initial choices and communications are in place, the question of which is the
"real" character, and which merely a theatrical costume becomes increasingly difficult to parse. They wind up in a restaurant/hotel far from their intended destination, and, after some unsavory interactions, lay in bed together
in the dark, shattered and lost.

As both sense that the "game" has come to an end, the young man finds
himself far removed from the self he set out with that morning, and unsure
how to recover it. The young woman, sobbing and desperate, repeats a single
refrain in the hope that she can reconnect to both herself and the relationship
she unintentionally damaged: "I'm me, I'm me . . . I'm me, I'm me, I'm me."
As a philosopher, I am fascinated by the semiological structure of that assertion of self-identity. To assert her identity, both in the sense of self-hood and
sameness, requires, grammatically, that she split herself into relational entities, subject and object. Her unity is a community. The angst-ridden refrain
suggests that our "I" exists only in reflexive relation to the "me" that it
indicates and identifies, and that it cannot do this apart from the course of
social interaction in everyday life. The story also shows, quite nicely, that

any such assertion of unity is just that, an assertion, tentative, fleeting, perhaps futile. The tale, as a whole, reveals that one cannot simply claim one's "self," one becomes oneself in interaction with others (even when the other is oneself).

It is this sense of identity as a "kind of person" we are able to choose to be, to some extent, but also in an important sense pre-configured by the narrative frames we inhabit and by current social labels, that we will use throughout the remainder of the book. Each of us is familiar with a range of identity possibilities derived from the many identity narratives we encounter and inhabit. As in the case of the young lovers, we too adopt and "wear" a number of roles as we travel through our daily lives: teacher, student, lover, parent, child, worker, friend, and many, many more, each affording a range of distinct variations. Each of these is framed by the "descriptions" dominant in our cultures. In the west, certainly, and increasingly elsewhere, those descriptions are borrowed by, sometimes transformed or re-purposed, and increasingly propagated through mass media. If ethics is about what kind of person to be, then it is fundamentally shaped as a real possibility, a human potency, by the forces at work that prescribe and construct (and constrict) the options through dominant "descriptions." Borrowing, (re)constructing, and propagating those "descriptions" is a core work of marketing.

SELF

The concept of the "self," however integral to the concept of "identity," is at least equally complex, and requires further analysis. One of the primary "descriptions" about the self prevalent in the contemporary world posits the self as autonomous and individual. The "self" is grammatically singular, after all. I have a "self," and you have a "self," and they are distinct to each of us. This story has recently been thoroughly challenged. Holstein and Gubrium argue that early twentieth-century thinkers William James and George Herbert Mead helped to instigate a transition of the idea of the self as a stable, if idealized or abstract, platform from which concepts and perceptions and judgments emanate and which transcends, or is at least more "primitive" than, society, to a self grounded and formed in society through the everyday, intersubjective activity of life, and so in large part a reflection of social participation and structures. For these early thinkers, if there is an individual "self," it arises out of a social self, both historically and genealogically.

Foucault has argued that it wasn't until the last few centuries in Western Europe that the subject was constituted as an individual.[21] Contemporary individual selves have evolved, he believes, to become a particular, and now primary, form of subjectivity. Such a subject is viewed as an agent of their own actions, for their own purposes, rather than a primarily a participant in activity that is understood to be both larger than the individual (in which he or she is a "cog in the wheel") and circumscribed by those larger structures. An individual agent is understood to make choices, however influenced or limited by social structures, and therefore is a moral agent, since, given this assumed freedom of choice, he or she needs "reasons" for acting as they do. Any such reasons are a justification (why this rather than another choice or action), and so are inherently evaluative and thereby moral. Reasons, of course, take the form of accounts, indeed, exist only within accounts, which not only spell out the grounds or motives for action, but the way the world works such that a given action or motive is possible and preferable. These accounts are the stories we tell about what we are and how the world is. They are made necessary and possible by the very constitution of the self in the modern world, understood as the prerequisite for action in society.

Even such selves-as-individual-agents, however, are understood to conduct their lives within social institutions and other social structures. The ways we live, work, eat, move through the world, build families, educate, gather for numerous and varied reasons, practical and spiritual, get sick, get well, and get old all serve to frame world and individual possibilities, and not exclusively or even primarily in terms of limits. We are individuals made possible within larger structures, and at some level understand our positive possibilities to be tied up with the shape and promise of those structures. Particular structures generate certain possibilities of individual selfhood rather than others, but it is also the case that individual framings of the self influence both the valuation and development of social structures. It is a complex, fluid, and multivalent relation.

As George Herbert Mead puts it: "The individual experiences himself . . . not directly, but only indirectly, from the particular standpoints of other members of the same social group." He "becomes an object to himself just as other individuals are objects to him." Therefore, "it is impossible to conceive of the self arising outside of social experience."[22] Michel de Certeau claims that over a century of anthropological, sociological, psychoanalytic and economic research has thoroughly challenged the story that the self is primarily individual and groups are composed of and reducible to individuals, assumed to be the primitives in and origins of social interactions. He argues that our social relations determine their terms, and that each individual is a kind of locus of a plurality of such relations, each and all of them fluidly interacting with the whole. He insists that a theory of social practice is "*indissociable*," as he puts it, from a theory of narrative, because "stories" are the condition and means of production of human social practices.[23] Paul Eakin, noted theorist of autobiography, insists: "Knowledge of the self is inseparable from the practice of language."[24]

These thinkers argue that the self, as Mead also says, is a kind of communicative act. Mead locates the foundation of the self in language. The self s not pre-exist the communicative act, nor is it merely generated or expressed by the communicative act. It is itself a kind of communication, always with others, and with oneself as another. In Kundera's story, the young woman desperately wants to tell herself, and her lover, that the "roles" she adopted that day were a kind of "mask" that her "true" self merely wore, as a "game." But this is itself a story (about the self), and one that masks, in a way, the kind of thing the self is, grounded in stories. The stories we tell aren't just frames of reference, stage settings within which we act out prefigured character roles that we merely inhabit. They generate selves *as roles*. We are who we are *in* these roles. As Mead argues, the roles we inhabit in the "games" we play have socially determined and organized structures that form the selves that inhabit them. Such selves are formed collectively, not individually.[25]

Erving Goffman was one of the first to write extensively about the self as emanating from the social by means of "roles." He argues that the "self itself does not derive from its possessor, but from the whole scene of his action"[26] He often used theatrical language to describe the self because he understood that one of its key dynamics is that the self *presents* itself to others (and to itself). It is not "given" in any social situation, but "gives off" as Goffman puts it. The self is inherently a presentation. Such a view helps us understand the prevalence and character of social media. Social media are not, as they are often presented, new and strange forms of social communication, somehow forcing us to distort ourselves to fit new categories and technologies, but merely the same dynamic of performance and presentation as always inhabiting new media forms. As Goffman argues, the self, in *all* its activity, aims at guiding and controlling the impressions others form of it.[27] The self is "dramatic" precisely in the sense that it manages and performs a number of small or larger dramas everyday in the effort to accomplish its ends. We dramatically realize ourselves by performing in a range of roles, sometimes simultaneously, each of which has a "life" or story of its own. These are the identity options mentioned above, roles we inhabit daily that come to us with completely realized dramas attached: student, teacher, spouse, parent, child, coworker.

Jerome Bruner argues "it is culture, not biology, that shapes human life and the human mind, that gives meaning to action by situating its underlying intentional states in an interpretive system. It does this by imposing the patterns inherent in the culture's symbolic systems—its language and discourse modes, the forms of logical and narrative explication, and the patterns of mutually dependent communal life."[28] He introduces the helpful notion of "folk psychology, a set of more or less connected, more or less normative descriptions about how human beings 'tick,' what our own and other minds are like, what are possible modes of life, how one commits oneself to them, and so on."[29] These folk psychologies are "noble lies," laying out the way the world is and we are such that things make sense as a basis for orienting ourselves toward the good. The organizing principle of folk psychology, like the "noble lie," is narrative rather than conceptual. It is built out of and operates by means of stories we circulate about our possibilities and character. These narratives organize our sense of selves by organizing our experiences, at the level of everyday interpretations of actions and events. They forge links between the exceptional (each unique event) and the ordinary (how we come to understand events as instances of larger comprehensible structures and patterns), and negotiate meanings we can use to locate ourselves in a world we can understand. These stories *explain* who we are and what the world is like, and configure our possibilities and promise.

STORIED SELVES, NARRATIVE IDENTITY

It may seem to the reader that such thinking moves us from a particular ontological conception of the self, as "real" or "essential," to an epistemological conception, the self as "self concept." In this view, it may appear, we seem to abandon an idea of a core self, and are indeed reduced to our "ideas" about ourselves. This may lead to some cognitive discomfort, but that discomfort would, I believe, be misplaced. Popular thought, at least, does cling to that particular ontological formulation. We desire, it seems, selves that are what Nietzsche called "soul atoms," core and essential selves that underlie and source all our various ideas about ourselves and the world, and from which we act. However, both in theoretical and popular thought, such an ontological self has proven a very illusive subject. As Nelson Goodman and others have argued, there doesn't seem to be direct experience of any such "real" self.[30] Thinkers such as Nietzsche, Gadamer, and Merleau-Ponty, to name but a few, argue that human experience is an act of interpretation, primarily of the perceptual field, which as Aristotle and Kant both recognized, is thoroughly permeated by the imaginative. The world of appearance, as we often call it, is simply our world; and we come to know it, in large part, by means of narratives. Yet, as Nietzsche has said, to get rid of the "real" is to get rid of the "apparent" at the same time. The self as understood through these thinkers, I believe, is an ontological entity still, but of a different sort.

Oliver Sacks has said: "We have, each of us, a life-story, an inner narrative—whose continuity, whose sense, *is* our lives. It might be said that each of us constructs and lives a 'narrative,' and that this narrative *is* us, our identities."[31] In an interesting new book that explores the relation of narrative and ethics through the philosopher Kierkegaard, Anthony Rudd argues that it is not merely the case that we understand ourselves (our "selves") by means of telling coherent stories about what happens and who we are, but that we become selves in the activity of narration. "The self is not something that just exists, and is then narrated (by itself or others); it only comes to exist through its being narrated."[32] He explains:

> As temporal beings, we have pasts and (we hope) futures; as temporal *agents* we act so as to project ourselves towards those uncertain futures. As *self-conscious* temporal agents we are aware of the pasts that we have and we consciously attempt to build our futures on the basis of those pasts as we understand them . . . . We live our lives forwards with an always partial and revisable sense of what they mean to us, a sense that we try to build as we live . . . this means that we live our lives as narratives.[33]

This is an ontological claim, which goes significantly beyond the epistemological claim that the self is understood narratively.

Such claims as these may strike the reader as hyperbolic. We might adopt a less radical view and consider the self as narrative in a limited sense by accepting the alternative Rudd rejects and understanding the individual to draw from experience in order to "compose" narratives about himself in the world. In this view, expressed by Holstein and Gubrium, "experience provides an almost endless supply of potentially reportable, storyable items" from which the individual composes coherent accounts to give those experiences meaning.[34] In this way of looking at our "self," the self is again figured as an individual agent, drawing from his or her environment to intentionally shape a meaningful self for oneself and also for others. Experience is an entity twice removed in this *possible story* of the self, however. It is the object of a subject which is itself abstracted from its linguistic and social world. Such experiences can only be abstractions and something that abstract selves have.

What the thinkers we have been reviewing argue, instead, is that the self is not a discrete agent, standing apart from their experiences and situations, selecting and constructing accounts. They are embedded in those situations which already come in the form of accounts. The picture emerging from contemporary research and thought is that experiences are already coherent social narratives, and the individual can neither "construct" nor even substantially modify them. This less agent-centered way of viewing the relation of self and experience does not deny our agency altogether. It recognizes a "role" for the "performer" in bringing the drama to life and presenting the self. It merely argues that, as in the theater, the performer is constrained to some degree by the "play," the "stage," and one's fellow "actors." We are not so much playwrights as actors. We do not create from raw elements provided by "experience." We inhabit roles already socially created and try to make them "personal" and individualized.

There are, of course, critiques of this emerging view. In the third chapter ' 's book, *How Our Lives Become Stories,* he begins his discussion of and self-narration by stating: "We know perfectly well that life certainly isn't a story, at least not in any simple, literary sense, and we also know that a person isn't a book"[35] He quickly complicates this observation himself, but it is worth noting that its formulation may be congenial for many readers, and participates in something like a conventional wisdom response to the fairly radical claim that our identity, in an important sense, exists in and through stories. Galen Strawson has famously argued that life, the multi-faceted and concrete being underway of living, is most certainly something *other* than story, regardless of the fact that it is something about which stories might be told.[36]

This position probably better mirrors our common and general perspective. It affirms a clear distinction between living, the going about in the world of concrete things or bodies, and any narrative description of those goings on. I would argue that this response feels right to us, in part, because it is also common to import some questionable presuppositions about what is meant by "story," primarily the supposition that story is always recognizable as such, as a distinct narrative form.[37] In this view, "stories" present themselves as such, as narratives of what might be but isn't, of what is distinctly and recognizably fictive. In my view, and those of the thinkers we have been discussing, the ubiquitous human activity of interpretation, the continuous and necessary activity of making sense of ourselves and our experiences, is thoroughly and comprehensively narrative in ways that are difficult to clearly demarcate from the "fictive."

The claim that we become selves through stories certainly doesn't make us books. Books are not the exclusive or even primary territory or mode of story performance. That we can write stories, write books that we take to be "stories" in the conventional sense, stems directly from the fact that we are essentially storytellers to begin with, busy constructing and telling stories all the time. The claim that life isn't a story falls apart under a richer interpretation of the term. For human beings, living involves being aware of their living, and that awareness is, at some level, narrative. We may be able to live without awareness, but to have "experience" awareness is required. Even if there is direct perception unmediated by reflexive consciousness, then there must be interpretation of that perception at some point for it to become apperception; and not before that point will we find a "self."

It is also common for us to make a distinction between experience and expression, content and form, but many thinkers have offered cogent critiques of this impulse.[38] Although the distinction itself is as old as thought about the self, and indeed, about "being" generally, tracing all the way back to the Greeks, so are the arguments that the distinction is exceedingly difficult to maintain under critical scrutiny.[39] The term "self-representation" itself misleadingly presupposes the distinction, positing both a subject and the reflexive activity of that subject. Nietzsche argues that this is a common error, a kind of seduction of language, leading us to posit a subject of activity where there is only activity. He comments on the silliness, forced upon us by the demands of grammar with its inevitable subject and predicate, of trying to speak of lightning as the subject of some "flashing" activity.[40] Lightning is nothing other than the "flashing." The young woman's refrain—"I'm me"— participates in this seduction, positing an *ego* as the subject of the activity of being herself. But, in the view I am advocating, she is nothing other than her activity in the roles she inhabits, roles which are themselves activity. We might advisedly adopt a similar terminological strategy with respect to the self and speak rather of "selfing," as an activity of self-making that needs no pre-existing subject to perform it, needing no "doer behind the deed," and which, like lightning, exists while it is active, and not otherwise.

After his disclaimer about what we know "perfectly well," Eakin complicates things in a similar fashion. He cites the work of Kay Young and Jeffrey Saver who have researched the relation of neurological impairments of certain brain lesions and narrative self-construction. They argue that the impairment caused by certain of the lesions they researched pointed to the "inseparable connection between narrativity and personhood . . . [since] individuals who have lost the ability to construct narrative have lost their selves."[41] If one cannot tell a story, one no longer seems to have access to a "self," and that loss indicates quite strongly that the "self" is an element of story. Eakin adds: "Narrative and identity are performed simultaneously . . . in a single act of self-narration; the self in question is a self defined by and transacted in narrative process."[42] As he says: "In this view, narrative is not merely an appropriate form for the expression of identity; it is an identity content."[43] Indeed, in his introduction, Eakin discusses how in speaking of "the self," the definite article lends too much stability and fixity to what is talked about. And what is talked about is, in important part, a process of talking, of storytelling. He suggests that he has come to think of "selves" less as entities and "more as a kind of awareness in process." He suspects that "identity formation is not available for conscious inspection as it happens." He believes that we "can never expect to witness the emergent sense of self as an observable event."[44]

Another presupposition commonly at work when thinking about stories follows Frege's famous distinction between "sense" and "reference," or connotation and denotation. We tend to view the distinction between story and life in terms of this difference: stories connote (make sense) but do not denote (refer to anything in an actual world). This is a strategy employed for keeping the two "worlds" distinct and ourselves metaphysically comfortable, as Nietzsche would say. Such a distinction is itself in the "world constructing" business, however, and begs the question as to the objective, empirical, or phenomenological difference between connoting and denoting. What form does "pointing" at an "actual" world take that demarcates it from "mere" making sense? Language does both of these operations whenever it does either. I cannot "make sense" unless my language points to something, "says something," as Plato says in the *Sophist*. The distinction between sense and reference begs the question of the real rather than locates it.

I am not arguing against the very real importance of the material, of flesh and blood, as it were, in human being; only the necessity for flesh and blood to be understood by us in order for it to *be* us, *for* ourselves and others. If it is our flesh and blood that lives in the world, unmediated, in some sense, then it is only through what we tell ourselves about that living that we *make sense* of that living. It is clearly possible to live without *making sense* of our living; but the "self" only arises when we do, or try to. It is this practice of making sense as self-generating, not a theory of the "subject," *per se*, or of non-representational or non-symbolic living, that is the key to understanding our moral and personal possibilities.

There is another way in which our lives and stories mirror each other that we all recognize: both *unfold*. In "Narrative Time," Ricoeur explains that both our lives and stories must be followed to their conclusions. In neither can the "end" be deduced or predicted.[45] Further, in both, any unity flows from the particular narrative construction of that unfolding. In the "Sixth Study" of *Oneself as Another*, he argues that if a self has any unity, it is not provided by the biological, nor by memory *per se*, nor by consciousness, but by narrative.[46] We become a unified self by telling ourselves and others stories, and, in some ways, *being told* stories about who we are, drawing together what otherwise might be discordant or at least disparate elements into a coherent whole and assigning them to a distinctive *character*. He says: "The narrative constructs the identity of the character, what can be called his or her narrative identity, in constructing that of the story told. It is the identity of the story that makes the identity of the character."[47]

This unified self need not, and usually does not remain self-identical, in the sense that all narratives about ourselves need to overlap and harmonize across time and contexts. We may have completely different unified selves under very different narratives at different moments of our lives. These different unified selves are so many characters in different dramas. In them, we make sense of ourselves in just the same way that we do the "characters" of the fictional stories we encounter and tell. Both in the "stories" of our lives that we tell ourselves and are told, and those we tell and are told as "stories," we are always linked with others and their stories. Our individual identities are always already group identities.

This follows, in part, from the fact, long recognized, that the self is also and always already another. This recognition forms a central part of Aristotle's analysis of the subject as substance. In *Metaphysics* Theta, while analyzing the dynamic of act and potency which he understands to be the central feature of all being, he talks of the self being always in relation to itself as another to itself. Its potency and activity are always a relation, one element as actor and another as acted upon, one as potency, one as realization of potentiality. In the same way, consciousness is a relation to itself as both other and public, something observed, and therefore part of appearance as well as subjectivity. This ontological status underpins the shift of self from interior and private to spectacle that we will discuss in a later chapter.

That this communal story- and self-telling is at least in large part a natural and comfortable operation for us is amply evidenced by the explosion of social media, as noted above, a central dynamic of which is the presentation of the self to oneself and others. The now familiar categories of self-representation on social media are reflections of pre-existing genres (or "decorum" as Bruner puts it) about what matters, about how to represent oneself to oneself in the proper ways, by means of categories such as family, school, likes, values, beliefs, activities, but also, importantly and increasingly, image, material consumption, and tribal groupings. In other words, it is not just our "selves" that must account for expectations in their making, but also our self-representations, our "telling" of ourselves to ourselves and to others. As Bruner says, self-making and self-telling are about as public an activity as such a "private" act can be.[48] Such activity goes beyond intersubjectivity and inhabits the realm of *nomos*—cultural standards and customs.

Nelson, from whom we borrowed our definition of narrative ethics, argues that identities are narratively constructed by means of loosely connected first-person and third-person stories we weave together around the things about us that matter most to us and others, the acts, experiences and characteristics we care about the most, and the roles, relationships, and values to which we are drawn. We are what we care about.[49] She does not fully explore the way in which "what we care about" is narratively and socially constructed; but she does refer to "master narratives" (a term she borrows from MacIntyre) as sources and agents of group and individual identity formation. These master narratives, different at different times and in different cultures, are always ineluctably moral because they are about what "matters," and must, therefore, narratively frame why they matter.

THE MORAL OF THE STORY

I have been arguing that self-making and world-making are narrative arts, informed and perhaps constrained by memory and perception, and by experience (which I have argued is itself narrative by virtue of being interpretive), and by cultural models, both spoken and unspoken, explicit and implicit, about what the self and the world should be or shouldn't be, what they might be. As Bruner points out, the activity of telling ourselves and others about ourselves involves thinking about what they think of us, of what we want them to think, of what we and they think we ought to be like, what people in general ought to be like.[50] Self-narration accounts for and draws from expectations. It is our principle means of establishing ourselves as uniquely ourselves, while always in relation to others. Therefore, I argue, self-making is thoroughly and inherently moral, because it cannot escape the registers of goal and expectation, or the register of "ought."

Ricoeur argues that storytelling always carries ethical implications. Stories are about world practice, about actions and their contexts, whose agents, the characters of the narrative, are or become the persons they are by virtue of the fact that their actions reveal them as praiseworthy or blameworthy. The evaluative opportunity presented by every "story" is inseparable from its meaning or sense. Our stories are not just about what we are, but what we might be, and that potency is teleological and deontological. As Benjamin notes in his well-known essay, the art of storytelling is originally and primarily the art of exchanging experiences, not observations or theoretical positions, but the popular and possible exercise of practical wisdom about what might best or ought to be.[51]

Our stories also "shift our views," as Appiah argues.[52] We constantly measure and compare acts and feelings in the stories we tell about each other, and in the stories we are told, including the many stories we take to be "fictional." Stories give us a way of seeing things, the world and its possibilities, and such a presentation is inherently value laden. Our language is frequently evaluative even when we are not deciding what to do. Appiah argues that evaluative language is "first a tool we use to talk to one another, not an instrument for talking to ourselves," and such language maps an expansive field of norms and values, where even little words can entail complex beliefs, values, and attitudes. We use that language not primarily to think about ourselves, but in an effort to guide or direct one another. As he argues, "our *language* of values—not just the concepts but our actual mobilization of them in speech—is one of the central ways we coordinate our lives. We appeal to values when we are trying to get things done *together*. And we talk value-talk all the time."[53]

Stories also naturally perform an ethical critique upon each other, as Wayne Booth has cogently argued.[54] Each narrative world we "inhabit" is an alternative life, alternative to all other narrative worlds, including what we usually think of as the "real" world. Even the simplest narratives, such as those we encounter in a 30-second television commercial, imply whole worlds, and in these alternative worlds, different relations obtain different structures. It is inevitably the case that since each narrative presents only one of many possible worlds, those worlds compete, in a sense, and may or even must be evaluated relatively. Each world is, in an important sense, a *criticism* of other worlds, presenting how things are and should be in comparison. Everyone knows this, even if not consciously, because we recognize that each story is, at best, a partial description of what is possible, and offers a description about what might be.

From our earliest experiences of narrative, beginning with the stories our parents tell us when we do something of which they particularly approve or disapprove, we know, without needing complex interpretive theories, that stories have a moral, a lesson we are supposed to learn and integrate. Indeed, many of the stories we are told are carefully selected to present particular pictures of the world rather than others for precisely this reason. When young, it is our parents who practice the selection, but as we get older, other institutions, including commercial interests, also vie to present particular lessons rather than others by means of narratives about the world. As Bruner argues, our educational systems are narrative forces of precisely this sort, using language that is carefully selected and anything but neutral to propound a particular view of the world in order to socialize us.[55]

Such lessons are more cogent and more readily assimilated when they take narrative rather than argumentative or deontological form. There are plenty of rules propagated by our parents, our social institutions, and our own heuristic activity. But we seem to recognize, without much thought, that lessons in the form of rules have significant shortcomings. Plato teaches, most explicitly in the *Gorgias*, that general rules always suffer from the flaw that they are general, whereas our decisions and actions are particular, concretely enacted in concrete circumstances. One of the key features of narrative is that, in it, the general is concretized.

In each narrative we encounter as story, we are not usually told what *must* be done, at least not directly. We are told what was done, what happened in some particular situation, and are allowed to try that possible way of being on for size in our own projected or concrete circumstances. Indeed, we are invited, as Booth explains, to inhabit the narrative world as our own, to compare the narrative world to our own narratively constructed lived world, and discover the points of relation and conflict, agreement and departure. Such activity is necessarily, as he says, an ethical critique. By means of that activity, we try on and try out what might be done, allowed not merely to accept or reject, as we must any proposition articulating objective necessity, but to weigh and valuate, to measure and fit, what *could* be done until we derive what *should* be done, at least by us in the given circumstances, which is what we always need to decide. A rule pretends to be about all circumstances, much as a mathematical formula pretends to be about all and any entities that can be counted or treated as a function. But as with the math formula, the gain in clarity and universality is paid for by complete abstraction. We are not really talking about things anymore. The formulas are self-, not really world-referential. They describe closed systems. Their propositions are univocal, but in an important sense, empty. Moral rules are the same. Stories, usually, are not.

Stories *can* be told in such a way as to produce universal absolutes, with some significant degree of abstraction, if we are so inclined. Such stories are told in practically every culture. What *was* done and turned out well, in any particular story, *can* be transformed into what *must be done*. It is worth looking closely at those kinds of stories to assess the motivations and needs that are addressed by that "elevation" of status from contextual and contingent to absolute, the transformation of what was chosen into what is right and obligatory. Such stories, like the "noble lie," seek to lay out the conditions and grounds for a particular formulation of the good by means of narrative "argument." That is the point of the "noble lie." We must be provided with the story that shows why, that explains how the world is and how it relates such that this choice or act or value is good or right and necessary. Indeed, every maxim or command implies and requires a grounding narrative. Unlike math formulas, moral rules can't be proved to be sound and valid by means of definitions and recursive rules. They must be unpacked in world or empirical terms, that is, in narrative terms.

My point is that stories come to us in moralized form, just as much as any maxim or command, something we already know in lived experience. The story, however, unlike the command, provides us with the process whereby the moral is derived. The maxim presents the conclusion, without any account of the production. The story gives us the whole picture, the way the world is and how it relates such that a given or possible choice or behavior or character is right and good. Plato thought the "good" was a name for the order of things, since what is good flows out of how things are and how they relate.[56] Stories depict an order of things. Commands are just shorthand formulations of conclusions that can be derived from those stories. In this way maxims or rules are, for Plato, inadequate, not primarily because they are universal in a particular world, but because they leave out how one gets to where one arrives, making it difficult, if not impossible, to find our way on our own.[57] Any moral rule is grounded in a particular view of the "good" which must, itself, derive from some particular story.

MASS MEDIATED SELVES

Charles Taylor insists that selfhood, also, is bound up together with ideas of the good. "To know who you are is to be oriented in moral space, a space in which questions arise about what is good or bad, what is worth doing and what not."[58] He argues that we are selves only insofar as we seek and find an orientation to the good, within a narrative framework that defines the shape of the good and locates us in relation to it. This "moral space" is now largely occupied and maintained, I will argue, by marketing narratives, which are always both about who we might be and about achieving our best self by means of acquiring goods. For Taylor, this space is inextricably teleological. It is not primarily about where we *are*, but where we *are going*. Again, this dynamic is central to marketing discourse, which is always about who we *might* become by participating in the marketplace of goods. Since ethics and morality are about identity and our obligations to those to whom we are related in some important way (family, group, tribe) and to whom we owe some kind of duty, then marketing is thoroughly moralized before and without the need to explicitly reference "good" or "right" or any specific "moral" value. Marketing narratives, like all self-narratives, are grounded in the choice of what kind of person to be and to what group we may "belong."

Who we *might be*, thoroughly teleological, is also inherently comparative. Comparison inevitably operates within the register of better and worse. Each option, presented either as desirable or undesirable, comes with theoretical or ideological commitments, which help to perform and cement identity construction. One is who one is by being part of something larger, and by choosing well from the realm of possible goods. Each choice aligns us with one or another possible "kind" to be. Within the comparative and evaluative register, other options are therefore never merely different, but relative: either superior or inferior. These theoretical and ideological commitments generate internal and external expectations. These expectations serve not only to shape behavior, but entrench the identities, not least because we do not think of these expectations as being conventional, but as flowing out of the structure of things, as reflecting the way things simply *are*.

As Kwame Appiah has noted, these expectations shape our decisions about how to conduct our lives, the decisions of ethics in other words. And while his arguments focus upon the kinds of social group identities much written about in recent decades—race, gender, sexuality—they apply equally well to the sort of social group identities that marketers and mass media journalism focus upon—identities built in part out of socio-economic categories, certainly, but, more influentially, also spiritual, psychological, and intellectual categories. In other words, mass media stories enmesh us in what are perhaps new kinds of class categories, such as "successful" or "loser," "conformist" or "individual," and, of course, "liberal" or "conservative," or more complex amalgams of these more simple elements, such as "mainstream, blue-collar, family values oriented, plain-spoken, well-meaning, sports-fan" as opposed to "metrosexual, retro-hip, artist/creative type, slick, clever, devious, 20-something."

Indeed, in marketing media, and to a growing extent, other mass media deeply influenced by marketing discourse and conceptual categories, "types" are often simultaneously superficial and complex. They group a number of simplistic sub-categories together, providing the illusion of original and tailor-made identities. The ability, the impetus, to mix-and-match a set of prepackaged simple categories of "types" fits extremely well into the growing boutique shopping-mall market dynamic, in which consumer convenience is paired with the discourse of specialization, both in terms of product and consumer-target. I will argue that it is these market-driven, market oriented categories that play an increasingly greater role in shaping both our expectations of ourselves and others, and our ethical choices and actions.

That these categories are more fluid, arguably, than the more traditional demographic and political categories is a boon to their popular efficacy and influence. In one sense, we are attracted to this way of thinking because, in it, we are figured as powerful and free to do what in important ways we recognize we do not really have the power to do, i.e., control our identities, choose who to be and how to be whatever "kinds" we desire, as if the social and role dynamics we have been discussing do not constrain us, and all that is necessary to change identity is consumer action. This is a powerfully seductive story, a deeply appealing "noble lie," which offers the opposite of Socrates' version: each of us is not only completely free to pursue our own interests and inclinations, unbound by society or duty, but "right" to do so, since the point of living is the accumulation of things, by means of which our happiness, the only thing that matters, is secured. Such configurations of the self, ironically and paradoxically, both abandon the idea that there is a fixed self and appeal to it by reconfiguring the fixed self as the market agent, a kind of empty subject free to predicate itself in any way it chooses.

These categories also need to be fluid, as far as marketing purposes go, so as to be readily attached to each new campaign and ostensible "product;" but not so fluid as to lose meaning. This is the conundrum of market categories, and not all of them succeed in resolving it. These new categories are also fluid in the sense that they are uniquely migratory. Consumers of these identity "packages" are free to slip in and out of them, by choice and self-declaration, marked only by the material culture and discourse sets associated with them. In popular culture, one is encouraged to migrate across identity possibilities both by means of material exchange, and in order to maximize material accumulation. We are allowed (and encouraged) to exchange identities by exchanging material culture. One is not queen 100 yards from the carriage.

It is this nebulous and migratory character, moreover, that lends these new categories a unique moral force. We are no longer talking about "kinds of people" marked by their bodies (race, gender) or their consistent life-practices (sexuality, religion), but "kinds of people" as self-marked, and thus generating and shaping practices as one chooses: identity as consumer choice, the result of consumer freedom, grounded in the nature of these categories as transient and malleable, able to fit any number of bodies and life-practices. Further, these identities are also explicitly and firmly connected to less-tangible, less-material aspects of our sense of the world and our "selves:" spirit, style, personality, values, worldviews. Indeed, and this is crucially important to the marketplace, these identities foster a kind of identity brand loyalty merely by virtue of the fact that without spending the energy to maintain them, they dissipate. This feature simultaneously allows for almost instantaneous change of heart. That one is a certain kind of consumer identity is always largely open to a different consumer choice. One may "become" another radically different "kind of person" by simply shifting one's identity *accoutrement*.

In the marketplace of identities, it is this particular kind of fluidity that has come to shape our attitudes about many of the more classic "identities." We each may be labeled according to more traditional categories, such as race or gender, but, we are told, falling under one or another of those categories isn't what is important, because it is what we "make of ourselves" that matters. We are "tolerated" for being what we do not choose to be because we "can't help it." However, our consumer and ideological identity choices are held for or against us with some passion. Further, the material and behavioral trappings of the old identity categories are fair game for commoditization and consumption, resulting, among many possible examples, in such phenomena as "gangsta" culture.

The importance of the idea of identity freedom, and therefore moral culpability, is echoed in the heated discourse around the question of the "causes" of homosexuality, in which the question of whether sexuality is freely chosen directly impacts the degree of condemnation, for instance. We see it operating again in the growing mega-church movement, in which traditional religious categories, once inherited through the family, are adjured as regressive, perhaps even blasphemous, and replaced by a consumer model of spiritual practice in which God's primary concern is with our success and happiness, and the divine message needs *and wants* to be tailored to the consumer impulses and tastes of the religious marketplace.[59]

In other words, "who we are" as configured by our social and personal narratives, has always been understood in relation to many aspects of our lives, some under our control, but many not. Now, I am arguing, "who we are" is largely presented, in popular discourse deeply influenced by marketing, as a matter of choice, and as a choice with clearly consumerist overtones, but retaining the inevitable moral register. There is also a kind of consumer intolerance encouraged. Just as what kind of car we drive or clothes we wear or music we listen to or even the things we say marks us as one "kind of person" or another in ways that are not value-neutral, who we "choose to be" is morally valuated, often harshly, by those who "choose to be" something else. For those who use Macs, PC people are not just making a different computing choice, they are being stupid, and stupidity is a moral deficiency. Those not in our "tribe" are not merely different kinds of people. They are worse kinds of people. The marketplace (and mass media journalism) enthusiastically encourages this judgment. They live on it. Of course, we have perhaps always viewed difference relatively, the other as superior or (much more commonly) inferior; but where difference that isn't chosen might be forgiven, difference we actively seek out and acquire, difference for which only our own free choice can be held responsible, is difference thereby more vehemently condemned.

I would not argue against the idea that there are myriad factors at work in our environments and in our own physiology that have strong impact on our choices as well as on how we story, on how we see the world. I also would not argue against the idea that we often respond or react from impulses of which we have little or no awareness, triggered by external or internal factors completely out of our cognizance. Ample social science research appears to have established this likelihood quite well. But whatever else we may discount about classical theories of moral action, it seems unassailable that under any determination that is to make sense, to count an act as moral requires choice. Moral judgment is utterly misplaced, substantively impossible, in the case of automatic or conditioned behavior. Understanding the moral dynamic of our lives means examining what happens when it at least feels to us that we have choices, what it is that influences those choices, and why we make the ones we do when we do.

Perhaps a great deal of our behavior is triggered by mechanisms of which we are not conscious agents; but it is those behaviors resulting from what at least feels to us to be through our own agency that is the domain of moral inquiry. Even if what causes us to choose some particular option or behavior isn't what we think it is and tell ourselves it is after the fact, it is that telling, those stories about why we do and *should* do what we do that constitutes our sense of morality. Telling ourselves such stories builds particular kinds of worlds rather than others; and it is certainly my argument that the world we think we inhabit does indeed set limits on what we will believe possible and desirable. I don't know that we will ever determine with precision the complex set of interactions between our conscious narratives about the world and those stimuli and triggers that also guide, if not even perhaps sometimes direct, our behaviors. The question of morality, though, the question of what kind of person to be and how to treat others doesn't mean anything at all unless we take it seriously as a choice we consciously make. And so it is those stories about how we make those choices, and more importantly, about how the world is such that certain choices are presented as appropriate rather than others, that matters for understanding morality as a human concern.

Marketing is in the business of telling stories that quite intentionally seek to create particular situations from which we will act because of their emotional significance and particular appeals to authority. Indeed, I believe it is very important that we recognize that marketing appeals directly to our classic notions of human nature—that we are the most important things, that happiness is the most important goal, that there are absolute values—but it uses modern notions of human nature derived from social psychology about the motivational force of the emotions and the situationalist dynamics of our behavior to get us to do what it is they want us to do, to see ourselves primarily as consumers and the world primarily as commodity.

NOTES

1. Paul de Man, "Autobiography as De-facement" *MLN* 94 (1979): 920.
2. Paul Smith, *Discerning the Subject* (Minneapolis: University of Minnesota Press, 1988), 6.
3. Paul John Eakin, *How Our Lives Become Stories: Making Selves* (Ithaca, NY: Cornell University Press, 1999), xi.
4. Robert Sokolowski, "The Method of Philosophy: Making Distinctions," *The Review of Metaphysics* 51 (1998): 515–32.
5. For a very interesting examination of the moral register of literature, see Wayne Booth, *The Company We Keep: An Ethics of Fiction* (Berkeley: University of California Press, 1982).
6. It is also interesting to note that although the ad claims to offer a "true story," the picture is rather obviously not in any way "true." First, the sandwich in the picture appears to be made with meat. Secondly, there are multiple versions of this ad, with different sandwiches (some of which appear to actually contain peanut butter) and different settings. From these pictures, the "cafeteria" of what is presumably American Century Corporate headquarters in Kansas City in which the founder's office is located (if it is to be believed, perhaps the only investment firm offices in America with a cafeteria) has a surprising variety of furniture and wall surfaces. My point is that it is hard to credit the marketing team with the intention to make us believe that they took a picture of the actual founder's lunch in any actual corporate "cafeteria." So, despite their emphasis on the narrative's truth, both they and we recognize the usual marketing fictions to be at work. I will discuss the significance of this strange mixture of "truth-telling" and clear falsity in the next chapter.
7. See Roland Barthes, "The Rhetoric of the Image," in *Image, Music, Text*, translated by Stephen Heath (New York: Hill and Wang, 1977); and Pierre Bourdieu, *On Television* (New York: New Press, 1998), particularly pp. 19–20.
8. Hilde Lindemann Nelson, *Damaged Identities, Narrative Repair* (Ithaca, NY: Cornell University Press, 2001), 36. In this work, Nelson offers a helpful summary of the narrative approach to ethics (ch. 2) and the narrative construction of personal identities (ch. 3) in her overall project of forming "counter-stories" to repair the damage caused to persons and groups by external narratives.
9. In addition to Nelson, see, e.g., Carlos Sluzki, "Transformations: A Blueprint for Narrative Changes in Therapy," *Family Process* 31 (1992); Jill Freedman, *Narrative Therapy: The Social Construction of Preferred Realities* (New York: W. W. Norton, 1996); Tina Besley, "Foucault and the Turn to Narrative Therapy," *British Journal of Guidance & Counseling* 30 (2002); Adam Hill, "Ethical Analysis in Counseling: A Case for Narrative Ethics, Moral Visions, and Virtue Ethics," *Counseling and Values* 48 (2004); Clive Baldwin, "Narrative, Ethics and People with Severe Mental Illness," *Australian & New Zealand Journal of Psychiatry* 39 (2005); and Tom Wilks, "Social Work and Narrative Ethics," *British Journal of Social Work* 35 (2005).
10. I owe some of the formulation of the ideas of this paragraph to Chris Elford, an exceptional student in my History of Western Philosophy: Ancient class in the fall of 2007.
11. Booth, 303.
12. A helpful source for thinking through questions about modern identity is Charles Taylor, *Sources of the Self: The Making of the Modern Identity* (Cambridge, MA: Harvard University Press, 1992). Taylor offers a history of the concept of the "self," arguing that our contemporary notion of self-hood, common both in popular culture and across theoretical disciplines in the west, is both modern and by no means shared by all cultures.
13. Paul Ricoeur, *Oneself as Another* (Chicago: University of Chicago, 1992), 116.

14. For a survey of the development of the concept of the self in modern social psychology, see James Holstein and Jaber Gubrium, *The Self We Live By: Narrative Identity in a Post-Modern World* (Oxford: Oxford University Press, 2000).

15. Ian Hacking, "Making Up People," *London Review of Books* 28 (2006).

16. His article examines in some detail the relation between new diagnostic labels, such as multiple personality disorder, or autism, and the frequency of occurrence in the population. A classic social psychology experiment, Muzafer Sherif, O. J. Harvey, Jack White, William Hood, and Carolyn Sherif, *The Robber's Cave Experiment: Intergroup Conflict and Cooperation* (Middletown, CT: Wesleyan University Press, 1988), shows how quickly and thoroughly group discourse shapes individual identity, and how loyal to those identities we tend to be. A significant dynamic displayed in this experiment and in numerous other findings is that such shaping can be quite arbitrary or accidental to begin with, but once formed, influences all other perspectives and choices.

17. Heidegger has a great deal to say in this vein about language; but the idea that language works to call features of the world to light, to generate or cement concept categories, and to "identify" objects, both in the sense of naming and in the sense of adducing them as distinct identities, is common in the philosophical tradition from the Greeks through the moderns and into the twenty-first century.

18. Plato's notion of *idea*, or what are usually called the "forms," are the "look" (a literal translation of his term) or pattern of things by which we may recognize them.

19. G. E. M. Anscombe, *Intention* (Oxford: Basil Blackwell, 1957).

20. Milan Kundera, "The Hitchhiking Game," in *Laughable Loves* (New York: Alfred A. Knopf, 1974): 77–106.

21. Michel Foucault, *Discipline and Punish: The Birth of the Prison* (New York: Vintage, 1977).

22. George Herbert Mead, *Mind, Self, and Society* (Chicago: University of Chicago Press, 1934), 138–140.

23. Michel de Certeau, *The Practice of Everyday Life* (Berkeley: University of California Press, 1984), xi and 78.

24. Paul John Eakin, *Fictions in Autobiography: Studies in the Art of Self-Invention* (Princeton, NJ: Princeton University Press, 1985), 277.

25. See also Holstein and Gubrium, 31.

26. Erving Goffman, *The Presentation of Self in Everyday Life* (New York: Doubleday, 1959), 252.

27. Goffman, xi. Facebook, for instance, seems to me to be precisely oriented around this kind of framing and controlling of presentation. In this regard, its ubiquitous third-person narrative form seems quite appropriate and even natural.

28. Jerome Bruner, *Acts of Meaning* (Cambridge, MA: Harvard University Press, 1990), 34.

29. Bruner, 35.

30. Nelson Goodman, *Of Mind and Other Matters* (Cambridge: Harvard University Press, 1984).

31. Oliver Sacks, *The Man Who Mistook His Wife for a Hat* (New York: Simon & Schuster, 1970), 110. For philosophical perspectives on the relation of narrative and the "self," in addition to Taylor and Ricoeur, see Alasdair MacIntyre, *After Virtue* (Notre Dame, IN: University of Notre Dame Press, 1981); David Carr, *Time, Narrative, and History* (Bloomington: Indiana University Press, 1986); Anthony Paul Kerby, *Narrative and the Self* (Bloomington: Indiana University Press, 1991); Marya Schechtman, *The Constitution of Selves* (Ithaca, NY: Cornell University Press, 1996); and Kim Atkins, *Narrative Identity and Moral Identity* (London: Routledge, 2008). There is a vast range of literature from many disciplines on narrative in general, and, more specifically, the relation of narrative and self. From among these, two that have informed my thinking on this specific relation are W. J. T. Mitchell, ed., *On Narrative* (Chicago: University of Chicago Press, 1980) and George Rosenwald and Richard Ochberg, *Storied Lives* (New Haven, CT: Yale University Press, 1992).

32. Anthony Rudd, *Self, Value, and Narrative* (Oxford: Oxford University Press, 2012), 1.

33. Rudd, 175.

34. Holstein and Gubrium, 107.

35. Eakin, *How Our Lives Become Stories*, 99.

36. Galen Strawson, "Against Narrativity," *Ratio* XVII (2004): 428–452.

37. For instance, a colleague of mine, Eric Selbin, has written a widely regarded book on the relation of story and revolution, *Revolution, Rebellion, Resistance: The Power of Story* (London: Zed Books, 2010). In it, he discusses the power of story in social organization and social change; but the term story signifies, for him, mostly those narratives we take to be narratives, rather than, as for me and many of the authors listed above, the more general interpretive activity of our daily lives which share, feature for feature, almost all the qualities of storytelling.

38. For example, see Mikhail Bakhtin, *Problems of Dostoevsky's Poetics* (Minneapolis: University of Minnesota Press, 1984), 43: "Artistic form, correctly understood, does not shape already prepared and found content, but rather permits content to be found and seen for the first time."

39. Parmenides, one of the earliest Greek philosophers, seemed both to make this distinction and call it radically into question. He several times claims that being and thinking are the same, and, in Fragment 8, that in "being" there is always already "expression."

40. Friedrich Nietzsche, *On the Genealogy of Morals*, Section 13.

41. Eakin, *How Our Lives Become Stories*, 124.

42. Eakin, 101.

43. Eakin, 100.

44. Eakin, x.

45. Paul Ricoeur, "Narrative Time," in W. J. T. Mitchell, 165–186.

46. Ricoeur, *Oneself as Another*, 158ff.

47. Ricoeur, 147–148.

48. Jerome Bruner, *Making Stories* (Cambridge, MA: Harvard University Press, 2003), 70.

49. Nelson, 71–72.

50. Bruner, *Making Stories*, 66.

51. Walter Benjamin, "The Storyteller," in *Illuminations* (New York: Schocken Books, 1969), 83–109.

52. Kwame Anthony Appiah, *Experiments in Ethics* (Cambridge, MA: Harvard University Press, 2008), 159.

53. Appiah, 157.

54. Booth, 338–342.

55. Jerome Bruner, *Actual Minds, Possible Worlds* (Cambridge: Harvard University Press, 1986), chapter 9. We will have more to say about this in the next and final chapters.

56. See, in particular, the *Gorgias*, 506ff, and the *Republic*, Book VI.

57. Plato's *Ion* offers an interesting formulation of this insight.

58. Taylor, *Sources of the Self*, 28.

59. On this latter example, see Ron Fournier, Douglas B. Sosnik, and Matthew Dowd, *Applebee's America: How Successful Political, Business and Religious Leaders Connect with the New American Community* (New York: Simon & Schuster, 2006), chapter 3.

Chapter Two

Truth-Telling Narratives

"It is a curious thing that the more the world shrinks because of electronic communications, the more limitless becomes the power of story-telling." [1]

"What makes it news is its dissemination, not its objective reality." [2]

The analysis of marketing narratives to come will be grounded in the argument that our identities, our morality, and in an important sense, our communities are shaped, if not also constructed, by and in narratives which are inherently social, in both process and content. I have argued that the stories we tell set the parameters for what it is possible for us to be(come), what we owe to each other, and what is good. I point out that all stories perform an ethical critique upon each other and upon the narratives we fashion around our own lived experiences. I have also noted that marketing narratives, grounded fundamentally in stories and images about who we might be and to what tribes we might belong, are already inherently moral even when not explicitly moralistic. Before we turn to examine marketing narratives in western consumer culture, though, I need to make a further important distinction.

The power of stories to shape our worlds varies, naturally, according to our modes of reception. There are myriad mass-mediated stories in our world, and many more stories we tell or encounter outside mass media, although the latter are deeply influenced by the former. The focus of my analysis is on marketing narratives that largely inhabit a particular narrative convention that sets them apart and gives them a great deal of power to influence how we see ourselves and the world. They are what I will call "truth-telling" narratives. That label may strike the reader as odd, given the fact that marketing talk is almost by definition taken to be at least hyperbole, if not outright mendacity. Marketing presents itself, however, as being about something real in the world, a tangible product or service, and, further, it purports to tell us the "truth" about that product, within accepted parameters of exaggeration. We have consumer protection laws precisely because of the fundamental expectations for this form of narrative.[3] There is a lot a marketer can say about any product (that it is "better," "brighter," "newer," "bigger"), and a marketer can avoid saying anything at all about a product, as happens more frequently than otherwise in contemporary marketing; but if a marketer makes a particular claim for a particular product, he is legally liable should the product fail to meet the normal expectations such a claim would create.

Marketing once primarily made claims about the qualities of the products or services it sought to sell. Such claims were, at least nominally, proffered as truth value propositions. By that I mean that regardless of the degree of license for exaggeration or bias we were willing to grant to the marketer, we inhabited a genre expectation that the claims made were grounded in our normal truth conventions. They were either true or false. They told us the truth about the product and its relation to other products, or they lied. This is a very different genre expectation than the one we inhabit when the media message we are consuming is understood to be strictly for entertainment. In other narrative conventions, suspension of disbelief is allowed or encouraged. We don't ask whether the lyric of a song is true or a lie. We do not engage a sit-com narrative, for instance, with anything like the same truth expectations, nor do we expect other forms of narrative to argue for claims. Even when we treat a song or a story we encounter as fictive as able to teach us something true, to enlighten us, we do not approach it with the same expectations as we do when we engage what we take to be a straightforward, if biased or exaggerated, claim about the world.

Marketing has traditionally purported to be making claims about the world, not to be entertaining us. They hope to entertain us, of course. The carnival barker or pitchman knows that he will be more persuasive if he can capture our fuller attention, and facts are poor honey compared to the novel, humorous, or pleasurable. The balance has shifted in recent decades. Many, perhaps most, marketing now seeks first to entertain, to arrest our attention by amusing us or inspiring us or titillating us before it offers any propositions about its product or service. Often, no claim is made. The product or service, or more precisely, its brand, is simply connected to the images or narratives that entertain.

But we carry forward the genre expectations built by long practice. Even now, when many marketing messages make no claims, we engage them as a kind of proposition. Marketers count on that. We still take marketing to be about the world, even if we scoff at the idea that its claims are truthful. Indeed, marketers benefit from the conflation between propositional discourse and fiction that their new practices foster. We are encouraged to both suspend disbelief, as we do when we encounter messages and stories we explicitly recognize to be fictive, and to inhabit a truth value decision, as we do when we encounter a claim we believe to be offered about the world. Since we still engage the marketing narrative on the level of truth value, then the images and narratives that entertain us are grounded to that degree in what we take to be reality, no matter how fanciful or improbable. We engage them both as spectacle, not quite to be taken seriously, and as saying something possible to accept or reject (a possibility we almost never inhabit when responding to what we take to be fiction).

In our world, marketing is perhaps the dominant source and medium of argument, and its particular forms of argument are the argument forms with which we are most familiar. Outside of law courts, or a few other very specialized and formal practices of arguing in our culture, no other practice is as fully engaged in "argument" as marketing in the classic sense of that term: a discourse that aims to produce conviction or provide persuasive conclusions by means of linked evidence in the form of grounds for belief and authoritative backing. Marketing arguments purport to tell us what we should believe about ourselves and the world; they are, quite simply, our primary cultural form of persuasion.[4]

Marketing achieves this status if for no other reason than its saturation levels. As Louise Story wrote in the *New York Times*, there is very little space that isn't occupied by marketing.[5] There was perhaps a time when marketing was primarily a kind of hawking of products, not unlike a mass mediated version of the carnival barker, whose clear job it was to arrest attention and induce consumption. In such cases, the public distinguished the activity of the hawker from the normal activity of the majority of their lives. Such activity was a break from the norm, an entertainment, perhaps, but a novelty at least. Now, not only is it difficult to find any space that isn't carnival space, as it were, that isn't crowded with mass media barkers, but, if we take into account the way marketing has integrated with most other mass media, such messages are the stuff of daily life, the primary interpreters and narrators of experience for most of us. Moreover, marketing has colonized many other narrative forms, inhabiting them as market space. Not only are the tropes and images of journalism or entertainment narratives used by marketing in their own narratives, but entertainment and journalism narratives have themselves integrated with marketing, and utilize marketing tropes and images. This adoption and adaptation has allowed marketing to fold itself "seamlessly" into other narratives, including much entertainment media, and, increasingly, even education.[6]

For these reasons, it is important for us to examine the conventions of the dominant mass-mediated truth-telling narratives in the contemporary world, in order to see more clearly the structures, practices, and boundaries within which marketing narratives are expected to operate. If marketing presents its narratives as "truth-telling," then our expectations for such narratives will be shaped by (and, of course, shape in turn) the other common truth-telling narratives we encounter. There are a number of important and common narratives in our world that are "truth-telling": news and education, the sciences, certainly, but also religion and politics. Religion is simply too large a field to plow for our purposes. The claim that politics is a truth-telling narrative may strike the reader as even more incredulous than that made for marketing, and it is true that there are no equivalent "truth in electioneering" laws on the books; but like marketing, and given the expectation of even extreme exaggeration and a surprising tolerance for outright deception, political talk at least purports to inform us about what we are supposed to take to be the case. We may suspect it is not honest in its accounts, but that is the pretense in which those accounts are offered.

In this chapter, I will focus on the narratives of journalism and education, both because I believe they are interestingly linked, and because I believe they shape our expectations of truth-telling narratives in significant ways. I would also argue that we have very little access to the other truth-telling narratives (setting aside religion, although it is both increasingly mass-mediated and market-oriented) outside of these two primary venues. The reception channels for the narratives of the sciences, for the vast majority of us not practicing in a particular scientific field, and even for those few with respect to other sciences, are news and education; for the narratives of politics, primarily news and marketing. Further, journalism and even education are increasingly integrated with marketing, and both have become increasingly political. These three truth-telling narrative forms—marketing, journalism (particularly television journalism, whose structures and techniques have come to set the standard for all journalism), and education—have experienced a series of developments in the last century that, not intentionally linked at their outset, have produced a new set of mutually reinforcing narrative expectations.

It is worth noting that both journalism and education are remarkably reflexive discourse practices. They spend a lot of time thinking and talking about themselves, and their roles in society, without, perhaps, a great deal of clarity. Among developed countries there is a universal emphasis placed upon the duty of educating the young. Very few people, however, even if pressed rather hard, could articulate clear and *detailed* reasons for that emphasis above almost all other duties to the young. Even fewer would likely be able to articulate a coherent curriculum along with a clear list of its goals (and I do not exclude educators themselves from this claim). We are rather befuddled when it comes to articulating exactly *what* the educational process is supposed to accomplish, usually falling back upon such conventional platitudes as "equipping the young to be full citizens," "delivering the skills necessary for success and happiness," "providing the basic essentials of knowledge," or "expanding our horizons to cure us of parochialism." Such formulations are unobjectionable, but also far from illuminating.

I believe we similarly lack clarity about the purposes and best practices of journalism. We usually acknowledge the Jeffersonian ideal of an informed citizenry able to participate fully and wisely in democratic processes, but, as with education, I am not sure we have very clear ideas of what exactly comprises being "informed," much less what we mean by full and wise "participation" in governance. Clearly, since education has become a central element of our governmental bureaucracies and also a recurring political platform plank, there must be some political utility from universal education. Journalism has also developed variously strong ties to political powers and machinery in most societies. The relationships are vexed, to say the least, however, and discourse between and about each rarely rises above conventional formulations. In the face of this ambiguity of process and goal, however, both education and journalism talk endlessly about themselves, primarily in vague terms of the value they offer society and their centrality to the good.

Both mass media journalism and education are also unusually pervasive elements of our society. Almost from cradle to grave, one or both are familiar elements of our experience. In modern western societies, almost every home has a television, computer, tablet, or several instances of all of these, which frequently operate, with or without our attention, a great deal of the time, always accessible. In our societies, such devices precede literacy (if not, increasingly, pre-empt it), and offer our first "reports" about the world. Add to that technological window into the "larger world" the phenomenon of universal education and we have created an unprecedented system of "information," in which larger and more varied "publics," from the nursery to the nursing home, from one pole on the socio-economic spectrum to the other, share an increasingly homogeneous cultural system of messages and images, along with the assumptions embedded within them. Together, they offer a universal curriculum.

Into these dominant truth-telling narratives, which have always exhibited a moral impulse, we have recently transferred a great deal of moral authority. We live in a media age of image and carefully tailored, exquisitely focused, and breathtakingly numerous messages broadcast to audiences of staggering proportions at unimaginable frequencies and saturation levels, all saying largely the same few things. During the last few decades, a fascinating shift has occurred in which many of those messages have become even more overtly moralistic at the same time that they have grown vastly more numerous. If we are essentially storytellers and story consumers, and if our ethical possibilities are fashioned and consumed as narrative, if our morality is a matter of narrative models and essentially narrative choices, and such narratives have come increasingly from consumer culture, then we have handed over the role of primary and central moral teachers to a loosely but increasingly synergistically related set of mass media "truth-telling" voices.

SHOW AND TELL

In the following analysis, I will examine the structural dynamics of journalism and education and unpack a number of their central conventions, showing them to be closely related in practice and impact. To begin, I call to mind the elementary school practice of "show and tell," as I believe this analogue illuminates key features of these particular truth-telling narratives and our reception modes for them. In that quaint early school practice, an appointed authority is placed in front of a passive and receptive audience to present an account, frequently using images or other "visual aids," which purports to inform us about some part of the world, almost always a part of which we are expected to be ignorant. "Show and tell" is not supposed to be about what we all already know. The key dynamic is, of course, "educational." The audience is to be taught, the goal to learn something new.

The authority of the presenter is a particularly interesting dynamic. It flows from the role and its surrounding larger structures, often bestowed by some higher authority for the moment at least, in the supposition that some special expertise is in play. Although a "question and answer" opportunity may be tagged onto such presentations, the presentation is what matters, and the credentials of expertise assumed by the presenter are never put to genuine question. The presenter may be invited to expand on their presentation, offering additional anecdotes or details, but we do not, nor are we equipped, to ask about the "evidence" that would ground whatever claims, including claims of expertise, that are made. In many ways, "show and tell" occasions in our early schooling are understood to be a kind of theater in which new learners can try on the role of "teacher" for a moment, and so explicitly mirror larger educational structures and expectations.

Television journalism has, I would argue, become an elaborate (and expensive) version of the same dynamic. Jon Stewart, of *The Daily Show*, once commented while presenting his usual collage of recent clips from the major news networks, that television journalism has become a kind of *Mystery Science Theater 3000*; meaning that images are presented on a big screen while talking heads sit in front and comment, seemingly off the top of their heads, unfortunately with less wit and intelligence than the original. This dynamic is not that recent. Over a decade ago, the 2004 edition of Pew Research Center's Journalism Project report, "The State of the News Media," introduced its analysis of cable TV news with the following words: "The most notable finding here is that cable news has all but abandoned what was once the primary element of television news, the written and edited story. In doing so, it has de-emphasized . . . the chance to verify, edit, and carefully choose words and pictures. The stress in cable news is on immediacy and cost efficiency of the live interview and unedited reporter stand-up."[7]

In television journalism, "show and tell" conventions dominate. The authority of the presenter is remarkably similar in structure and effect, bestowed by simply inhabiting the role within well-established larger structures, and with assumed or unquestioned credentials. The presentation is largely the same, with an emphasis on attention-grabbing visual aids while offering superficial summaries that always seek to maximize entertainment value. The response of the audience is structured, both because of the physical realities of presentation and the specific narrative practices, so as to allow very little beyond the passive reception expected of the "show and tell" audience, and we are similarly configured as ignorant but eager for enlightenment about whatever trivial matter is selected for presentation.

In his cogent analysis of television journalism, Pierre Bourdieu presents a range of structural dynamics that shape the presentation of "news" in what I would argue reflects "show and tell" conventions.[8] Among the many dynamics he adduces, there are several that are particularly relevant to our analysis and that I will argue, going beyond what Bourdieu intended (or may sanction), are equally at work in our educational systems. These include practices of censorship and selection, which result in a kind of reality effect in which only what gets presented counts as what has happened. What is selected and presented is sensationalized, and, moreover, dramatized, in ways that usually trivialize or decontextualize. Stories are crafted and presented in which conflict is key, but controlled, and commentary offered that hinges upon conventional or received wisdom and the ability to think fast and "fast-talk." The role of expertise is crucial, and, again, is marked by a significant degree of insularity, with the same few fast-talking "experts" available to serve across networks. All of these, I would suggest, are mirrored in our educational systems and practices.

Bourdieu argues that one of the key structural dynamics in journalism is the selection/censorship process where what counts as "news" is selected. He notes that there is a high degree of insularity at work in this process in which news outlets listen primarily to each other, and conventions set expectations. Because of this insularity and the expectations it fosters, journalism only knows how to tell a limited range of "stories," and each outlet vies to tell largely the same stories—about crime, waste, fraud, natural disaster, and social danger, etc.—in the most entertaining or ostensibly timely fashion. There are a limited number and kind of "events" in our world that count as news, and both we and the networks know what those are.[9] As Kathleen Hall Jamieson has noted, a "newsworthy event" exhibits a fixed set of qualities: "it is (1) personalized—it happen[s] to specific individuals; (2) dramatic, conflict-filled, controversial, violent; (3) actual and concrete, not theoretical or abstract; (4) novel or deviant; and (5) linked to issues of ongoing concern to the news media."[10] To count as news, what is presented must exhibit these qualities, or be made to.

Educational dynamics are quite similar. There is a tremendous degree of insularity and dominant, largely unquestioned conventions set expectations, which are a primary reason almost all curricula resemble each other from earliest schooling through graduate programs. There is a limited amount and kind of information that counts as important to learn. The "three R's" dominate early education, to be followed by an only slightly expanded range of "disciplines" at the secondary level. In both education and journalism, there is an almost studied inattentiveness to concrete informational or educational needs of individuals and local groups, with mere token acknowledgement of "special needs" or "interests." In both education and journalism, that "one size fits all" formulation of content and presentation is driven by marketplace forces, by monetary and political economies. In both cases, the result is a kind of reality effect, in which what gets presented, simply by virtue of that presentation, counts as worth presenting, as important, as what happened. If it's not covered by the network news or the curriculum, it must not be worth knowing.

What gets covered, in both journalism and education, what comes to count as important and "real," is often just what strikes us as sensational, what stands apart from the ordinary, what can be presented as discrete events or ideas couched in terms of novelty and significance. Neither journalism nor education as it is currently practiced is well equipped to examine structural and long-term processes that lead to the "events" and "discoveries" that are presented as the newsworthy or important features of our world. Neither is able to offer or encourage penetrating analysis, given the time and attention constraints of current conventions. Therefore, in both, what is important to "know" is presented as self-contained and complete. In that presentation, care is taken to further sensationalize, so as to highlight the significance and, by no means least important, maintain attention. Television news and textbooks both offer graphical and, in the case of interactive educational programs and news, auditory enhancements ostensibly for the purpose of highlighting significance, but clearly aimed at entertainment and arresting attention. "Show and tell," after all, is supposed to be captivating, a departure from the dreariness of complex and lengthy lessons and worksheet drudgery.

Such practice leads to a kind of trivializing and decontextualizing of both the news and educational content, in which "events" and "discoveries" appear to result from mysterious and ultimately iconoclastic forces at work in individual agents. They come out of nowhere, and lead we know not where. In news, as Bourdieu pointedly notes, a natural disaster is followed by a soccer score, which is followed by a human interest story, thus presenting the world as a series of disconnected and ultimately un-connectable events without context or reason, "which can be neither understood nor influenced," inciting curiosity, but not analysis.[11] In education, the school day is carved into "classes," each of which is discrete and disconnected from what precedes or follows, thus presenting the world of knowledge, if not the world itself, as carved into separate "disciplines" each of which occurs in a kind of epistemological vacuum. As in the practice of "show and tell," in both journalism and education, what we encounter, what gets presented as what matters, is both unpredictable and largely ungrounded in any related presentation or in any ongoing analysis of larger structures and practices, and so can only have sensational or entertainment value. Its ontological character is thematic and episodic, rather than developmental and ongoing.

In both education and journalism, the narratives that are crafted and presented are highly dramatized. Since they are ungrounded in larger analysis or narratives, each must tell a discrete story, with an immediately accessible and self-contained plot and characters. In both, character takes precedence, and usually drives the unfolding action, privileging individual agents as the sources of and explanation for events. In politics, it is not the legislative process or policy itself that matters, but politicians (and their "values"). In crime, it is not the social dynamics or structures within which any given criminal behavior occurs, but individual criminals and their activity. In science classes, it is not often not the slow development of ideas and theories through interlinked research programs, but individual "discoveries" and their "discoverers" that figure prominently. In history and literature, it is the same; we are presented with genius and pivotal characters shaping the world and leaving their mark. News and education are very much alike in this respect, that what we are offered from them are stories about a world removed in time and space. In both, we are invited to learn about what we have not ourselves experienced through narratives that use the clear and familiar structures of drama to formulate and communicate what "happened."

These dramas, as presented in both venues, highlight conflict, where the tensions between elements of society or individuals concerning both events and ideas are presented as what ultimately matters, either driving "progress" or creating "problems."[12] Moreover, a kind of controlled conflict is modeled as a central element of informational or educational practice. In journalism, the pretense of impartiality is maintained primarily by means of the practice of presenting binary opposition on every topic, in which "both sides" are allotted equal time and voice. In education, the dynamic is a bit more complex, but the result is similar, in that the epistemic world is carved into two exclusive camps, the true and the false, and the student's role is largely reduced to distinguishing the former from the latter, usually by means of multiple choice or True/False tests.

In both, commentary almost exclusively calls for and exhibits conventional or received wisdom. Real or thorough analysis is eschewed, and priority is placed on the commentator who can, as Bourdieu puts it, "fast-talk," offering ready, often pre-packaged responses, to any query or problem. The status of "expert" in both education and journalism is primarily granted to the one who can provide the "correct answers" the most quickly. As in "show and tell," one is expected to take up the role of presenter primarily through the adoption of established presentation conventions, which include assumed expertise and the ability to respond to or answer any question with a ready and "correct" formula. In education, our textbooks adopt remarkably similar expertise conventions, in which assumed authorities "highlight" what matters, usually by means of various graphical techniques that are meant to encapsulate and summarize what is important. In textbooks and television journalism, these take quite similar form, including bold headings and sub-headings, graphs, charts, helpful summaries, informational tables and text objects.

I believe these structural dynamics have important relations with narrative expectations in marketing. Marketing clearly inhabits "show and tell" dynamics in many of the same ways, including the assumption of expertise, the dramatization of its arguments, the focus on spectacle, and the utilization of and reliance upon conventional wisdom. Marketing practices an extreme form of selection and censorship, grounded in a fundamental insularity, creating its own highly skewed "reality effect." I believe the structures and practices of journalism and education significantly enhance the storytelling authority and force of marketing in ways that have not been fully explored or analyzed, and which, unfortunately, we do not have the time and space to do here. In the remainder of the chapter, however, I want to unpack some of these elements, those I believe most influence our reception of marketing narratives as truth-telling, in fuller detail. I want to look at the ways that both journalism and education inhabit and express various kinds of authority and, finally, the way they orient themselves in these dynamics to moral registers.

ANONYMOUS AND IMPARTIAL

Near the end of its relatively short run, the cable news network, Newsworld International (NWI) aired a promo in which a collage of "news" images faded into the following screen-filling graphics, each line growing and fading into the next:

> Every one has a story
> Every story has two sides
> Every side has a voice[13]

Henry Jenkins notes: "The conventions of news reassure us that it has provided all we need to know to make sense of the world and that it has presented this information in a "fair and balanced" manner."[14] This phrase has clearly become a term of art in journalism—Fox News Network uses it as a brand label—and it means, essentially, that "both sides" of a binary are presented, under the conceit that "every story has two sides." Journalism pretends to be disinterested, and maintains this pretense primarily by means of a studious dedication to presenting "both sides" of every story, no matter how hard they may have to work to find spokespeople for one of the "sides." Television news, and journalism more broadly, claim authority on the basis of impartiality.

Part of what is at work here involves interesting elements of political, jurisprudence, and scientific history. In both journalism and education, there is an assumption of impartiality bestowed through the office inhabited. Just as a judge, upon donning her robes, both acts and speaks as if she is no longer a complete individual in her own right, with inevitable biases and a range of prejudices, but rather an impersonal force of law, of social structure and interest, and just as a laboratory scientist, upon donning the lab coat, acts and speaks as if he is a mere instrument in an objective epistemic process, rather than biased and deeply interested in the hypotheses he generates and tests, the reporter or anchor and the teacher are assumed to be something less or other than full emotional and interested human beings, but, instead, dispassionate instruments of information and knowledge. [15]

In education, this pretense is furthered and fully embodied in textbooks, the compendiums of knowledge in a given field produced by the major curriculum publishers whose real authors are various editors and writers at the publishing house. These textbooks frequently list "authors" in the front matter, all of whom can make some claim to expertise in the field; but the convention of the textbook is that the knowledge presented within is "authorless" in an important sense. What the textbook tells us is simply the truth, attested to primarily by virtue of the authority of the textbook as textbook, i.e., as a vehicle for the impartial synopsis and transmission of the facts. The authority of textbooks derives, in part, from that anonymity. If one were told, in them, that such and such a conclusion was the finding of some particular investigator, drawing from the evidence gained from some specific research program, we would then be invited, at least implicitly, to examine that finding and its process to assess its cogency and validity. Instead, information is selected and articulated in universal and absolute terms approaching disembodied direct revelation. It is given to us as simply what is the case, and, not inconsequentially, what we need to know to pass the test.

Testing is a similar instance of authority with deeply suppressed authorship. Even if we recognize that a particular test was created by a particular teacher, the conceit is that the teacher, as expert, simply knows the facts themselves, which are important to test, and how it is appropriate to test them. Such a conceit reaches its height in the high-stakes entrance exams such as the ACT, SAT, GRE, MCAT, and LSAT. These pretend to measure aptitude and chance for success, even though the measures themselves change significantly with some frequency; there is a profitable associated industry of "prepping" test-takers to do better on tests touted as impartial measures of objective academic preparedness or intellectual skill sets.[16] The now ubiquitous and equally high-stakes "standardized tests" created by political pressures and for political motives, which pretend to measure whether our institutions are accomplishing some idealized and abstract notion of the bare minimum of "education," also inhabit this ideal of anonymous and unbiased authority, despite repeated research findings that show clear bias in all such tests both in construction and results.

The primary form of testing in elementary and secondary education, at least, and common still at the college and national test level, follows a multiple choice format. This form has significant epistemic entailments. It structures knowledge as truth-exclusive and absolute (like much religious knowledge) rather than as constructed and defended. An answer is right, or it is wrong; there is rarely any in between. It privileges certain kinds of questions (those which can be presented as having determinate answers), and structures them as a kind of puzzle, in which there is usually only one correct, and usually four incorrect, and often "tricky" alternatives, even when one is allowed an "all of the above" or "none of the above" option. Active use of context knowledge, analytic skill, or even explanatory argument is structurally discouraged. Formulating the question oneself, or altering it to provide a more productive inquiry, and, most importantly, drawing from a range of possible answers to generate a more complete response is simply impossible, and therefore configured as completely irrelevant to the process of learning and knowing.

In all of these educational structures—textbooks, content tests, entrance exams, and standardized tests—knowledge is configured as discrete, decontextual, and most importantly, impersonal. Knowledge is not something individual persons construct and defend through personal research and argument, but something already and always universal and complete that individual persons can "have" (and, upon demand, regurgitate), by accepting its revelation from anonymous authorities.

EXPERTS

In both journalism and education, knowledge is the property of experts, whose status as experts are never or at least rarely questioned, and certainly structurally difficult to question, and grounded in the same universal and anonymous dynamics. In extended conversations with my students, many of them are bothered by what they perceive as an inability to become well-enough informed to determine who is "right" or "wrong" on issues. In other words, they despair of becoming experts, even as they repeatedly inhabit the "theater of expertise" demanded by their regular scholastic activities—giving class presentations, writing papers, taking tests. They are not apathetic, they are frustrated. The attitude, as I usually encounter it, is that there are experts out there, who study issues all their lives, and who must have access to both kinds and amounts of information far surpassing what can be obtained by the average person, so that they, the uninformed and confused, are in no place to judge. They cannot tell you what basis they have for assuming such experts and expertise other than the proclamations of authority made by those asserting that status, and a complete ignorance about how one might achieve it.

I believe that such attitudes have been formed and reinforced by educational practices in which we train students to passively accept whatever information their teachers or textbooks present to them as accurate and truthful accounts without ever admitting the tentative nature of such information, much less inviting them to investigate its development or critique it. Indeed, students are often actively discouraged, if not even punished, from questioning the authority of the textbooks or teachers. Information is the point, and it is to be accepted, memorized, and regurgitated. We make that abundantly clear through the obviously central element of the educational process, testing. We train them to believe that information, of a rather sterile, context-free sort, is the thing to have, to accept that some information is correct and the rest false, and that only authorities can tell the difference so one must trust the authority at hand (teacher or textbook). This training leads to frustration whenever one encounters competing claims to accuracy or truth and no (accepted or trustworthy) authority is at hand to distinguish the true from the false. Certainly, the students cannot be expected to make such determinations themselves. They have no training in doing so.

In our educational systems, students are rarely offered opportunity to become practiced in the normal intellectual skills of analysis and critique, and so it is no wonder that they are never expected to exercise them when consuming journalism, or, for that matter, marketing. An information-based education privileges passive absorption of data, not active engagement and processing.[17] Students aren't encouraged or allowed, for the most part, to formulate problems and questions for themselves in a process of sifting through and organizing relevant information. They are not practiced at *making sense*, only in memorizing. Thus, when confronted with a range of alternative accounts, each making conflicting claims on the same data, their response is to throw up their arms and trust the "experts" to work it all out. I have found that such attitudes are so deeply entrenched that even when students practice analysis and critique, which they all necessarily do in some form in their daily lives, they fail to see the process at work and discount its results. They all admit that they understand things much more deeply whenever they can connect information to their lived experiences, that, on issues that matter to them and impact their lives, they do indeed filter through competing perspectives and form one of their own; but they usually and simultaneously discount whatever insight they have gained as mere subjective "opinion," since they arrived at it themselves without the imprimatur of "expert" authority.

Education, structured in this way, is a kind of initiation, whose authority is subtended, in part, by its regulative structure. One is supposed to follow the (seemingly arcane and illogical) rituals to be shown the mysteries, and so, in the end, claim novice expert status oneself. As Leon Botstein has noted, our disciplinary structure and folk psychology about education as training for expertise in a particular field (and, almost always, also vocation) results in viewing all "other" areas of knowledge as the exclusive domains of their particular practitioners.[18] I, as do, I presume, most teachers, repeatedly experience students who dismiss whatever fields of knowledge lie outside their own "major" as irrelevant, and view the selection of one's own field as a function of interest and aptitude. The general idea is that each of us is good at one particular discipline, can't expect to be interested beyond that, and probably shouldn't "dabble" in fields in which we cannot be expert. What lies in some other field of knowledge can only be viewed as quaint or mysterious to the non-practitioner. We have systematically dismantled the idea of broad, even if amateur, participation in ideas and their critique. Each of us is to locate and inhabit, as soon as possible, our distinct fields, and whatever isn't circumscribed by those fields is taken to be beyond our capacity for analysis, and, appropriately beyond our interest.

I see this attitude in a quite interesting way on those occasions on campus when student "research" is presented to a public audience. The public is apparently expected to simply view the display of expertise passively, since my usual efforts to initiate some discussion about the matters on display are just as usually met with surprise or a kind of disdain. Surely I'm not being audacious enough to actually attempt to talk with them, the experts, about this highly technical matter. Even when my questioning reveals some degree of knowledge, the usual response seems to be a kind of skepticism about my actual ability to fully understand, since, after all, I haven't taken whatever course was the genesis for the particular "research" project on display, and am not even a member of that discipline! In short, I am clearly recognized not to be an initiate, and so unable to really judge the matters at hand. This is an interesting obverse of the phenomenon noted earlier: if those lacking expertise despair of understanding matters beyond their ken, then those possessing (or pretending to possess) expertise despair of explaining their subjects to those who lack it. Both sides shy away from engaging each other.

These same dynamics are exhibited by television journalism. In journalism there is a similar configuration of expertise and the authority deriving from it, as well as a similar institutional pretense of impartiality and anonymity. The "news report" however sourced in individual accounts, eye-witness reports, or expert testimony, is presented, as a whole, as an impartial account of "what happened." Like the authoritative truth of our textbooks, the news report is accepted as a distillation and summary of the important facts, a presentation of the true story, equally influenced and colored by the structures and practices of journalism.

While the most watched television news network shows, such as NBC Nightly News, still spend some of their budgets producing and airing traditional news segments, segments that involve journalists investigating a story, writing and editing it, and then reporting it on air, the 24-hour news networks have changed drastically how much of such reporting happens. These networks simply cannot afford to produce news in such a manner. So to cut costs and to fill air time, even more traditional programs such as the various NPR news segments rely heavily on interviews. These interviews take two primary forms. The most common is to invite an "expert" to comment on what may happen.[19] Ironically, much of our "news" is of this sort, about events or actions yet to come. The second form, only slightly more valuable, is when experts are asked to report from their knowledge about what has actually already transpired, and, often, about what motives were at play in the shaping of events. The second half of this task, fraught as it is with speculation, appears to be the most popular, and "reporters," who almost never "report" anymore, but rather ask interview questions seemingly off the top of their heads, without any idea of what the person about to speak is about to say, typically emphasize these "making sense of it all" questions where the guests are invited to boil it all down and explain.

"ARGUMENT"

In both journalism and education, the natural authority carried by argument is short-circuited and applied to what, in practice, is largely the absence of argument wearing a thin veneer of its outward form. A sharp emphasis on brevity and concision, usually grounded in a fear of boring the audience, frequently forces those presenting their ideas to merely tick off their claims. An expert, voicing his or her conclusion about the advisability of one policy or another, is almost always required to do no more than briefly list the harms or benefits. Almost never are experts asked or allowed to offer evidence to support their claims. We are expected to accept or reject the claims largely upon the authority of the expert and some vague sense of potential data which might support them. Television journalism almost always presents two parties arguing for two opposing points of view or paths of action, who, if they refer to reasons or evidence to persuade, do so only in the abstract, such that all that seems important for their claims is the mere "having" of evidence, rather than its presentation and examination.

A result of this dynamic, both in education and journalism, is that it is easy, absent our own expertise, and trained in conceptions of disciplinary specialization, for us to view such opportunities to accept and reject mere exercises in opinion, as indeed they are, using Booth's definition of opinion as a way of seeing things wrenched from the context of its development and divorced from the living thought processes that produced it.[20] Indeed, both education and journalism are structured so that we have no alternative, since we are not able to or are discouraged from asking for evidence or to have the process of thought connecting the evidence to the conclusions explicated for us. We are led to believe, by these practices and structures, to suspect that any such explication would of course be compelling, as would any explication of the connections between counter-evidence and the opposing conclusions, so we might as well skip to the chase, present directly the opposing conclusions, and decide the matter according to our interests (or lack thereof) and our loyalties.

There are occasions when an analyst will be prodded to defend or explain a conclusion. Often these occur when the analyst offers a conclusion that conflicts with the perspective presented by the interviewer, such as when an interviewer has built toward a particular interpretation of the matter in question over the course of an interview or story presentation which an analyst rebuts. Most often, however, in recent journalistic practice, such challenges are directed to the expert representing the "other side." Rather than ask one of (almost always only) two experts to defend or explain his or her claims, the interviewer merely turns to the other expert and asks, in a general way, for reaction to the claims just offered. Of course, the response is most often that the first expert is mistaken, muddled, or, worse, mendacious. The second expert then proceeds to repeat the process, offering his or her own conclusions with, at best, vague gestures toward evidence that might support them. There is no natural end to this exchange, only the arbitrary announcement that "time has run out." There is no possibility of any real understanding or, at least, some clarity of examination through exploring the evidence for what it may show or seeking to determine the limits of reasonable interpretations available from it.

Such practices portray the very process of judgment as arbitrary and even mystical. There is no obvious structure to it other than that of superficial and cartoonish opposition and the mere form of reasonableness empty of substance. Such a process has no inherent "goal" or "end." Argument is presented as interminable and pointless, or, at best, as a kind of empty entertainment hopeless of deeper or more balanced understanding. It echoes, if not even largely produces, our more general attitude toward argument: that it is fine for those so inclined and who find it enjoyable, but ultimately only hinders productive action. In short, pragmatically speaking, there is rarely any time for it. When it is time to act, we must rely upon the pre-formed judgments of those who have had time and opportunity and expertise to examine the issues and determine, from their fonts of mystical evidence, what is the appropriate or correct course of action. Arguing about what to do when something must be done only delays action and needlessly and hopelessly repeats a process already accomplished by those supposedly better equipped to perform it. And if it is not time to act, why waste time arguing?

Of course, there are particular economic and structural forces at work in mass-media journalism that are not at work in general discourse, such as the need to maximize audience share, which leads to briefer and briefer news stories, a significant if not complete homogenization of news presented, and the effort to "scoop"—to maximize miniscule and largely unnoticed differences in coverage—or the economic forces that privilege improvised interviews and analysis over researched and prepared "investigations." In public discourse more generally, there is no similar felt need to maximize audience "share" or to reduce the "costs" of discourse. I believe that even with such differences, however, media and public discourse mirror each other to a significant degree. We may not be forced to calculate the bottom line of various discourse strategies in selecting how we talk to each other the way broadcast journalism does when selecting its news formats, but we have grown increasingly impatient with discourse that takes significant time to develop its analysis and unfold the complexities of the matters it engages. Further, we broadly apply a kind of "efficiency" measure to our discourse with each other, such that we more and more demand that whatever discourse seems necessary (and we seem more and more to view discourse as a necessary evil to be dispensed with as quickly as possible so that we may proceed to action, which is, of course, what really matters) should confine itself to the most salient elements, as if Sgt. Friday is always over our shoulders urging us to limit ourselves to "just the facts," which we would prefer as quantitative data when at all possible.

The market forces at work in mass media journalism also conspire to privilege a small set of regular commentators and analysts who have demonstrated the required and desired characteristics: they are inoffensive to corporate sponsors and audience alike, have an ability to speak fluidly, if not necessarily cogently, to off-the-cuff questions, are telegenic, and primarily exhibit the ability to represent entirely conventional polarities so that the media outlet can make a justified claim to be balanced and unbiased. Either the audience or the producers attempting to divine audience preference seem to desire that these figures be at odds in congenial ways. Most of these analysts know each other well, have had frequent professional opportunity to repeatedly engage each other and could, for the most part, fill in for the other should the need arise.

My point is the degree to which our larger public social discourse has come to reflect this model. We more and more insist, in our own discourse, upon engaging in the same or very similar sorts of congenial but largely conventional "positions" which are understood from the outset to be mutually exclusive and primarily a matter of alignment. We do not so much argue with each other over ways of seeing and reasons for such perspectives, as we inhabit such ways as pre-packaged alternatives according to our tastes or set of beliefs and then oppose those to each other in a kind of self-identification process, when we do not shy away from the exercise altogether out of a suspicion that the practice has little to offer outside of such identification. Increasingly, we either remain silent except in those situations where we can identify our interlocutors as like-thinkers, or, when forced, put forward claims in conventional ways always with a tone, either of grace or partisanship, that seeks to reassure our interlocutors that we understand that such debate doesn't really accomplish anything. In other words, we debate perfunctorily, but for the most part congenially, or we yell at each other from the fortresses of our exclusive ideologies. Certainly, in private, or in small conversations, we engage in other practices, more productive and hopeful discourse strategies; but in public, in almost all venues, we seem to be able to reproduce only those narrow models offered for and through mass media consumption.

We inhabit these polarities so deeply that we have come to see anything else, anything like a subtle or nuanced engagement that tries to synthesize or, worse, to find the value in different perspectives, as a kind of moral weakness, an intellectual infirmity. Those who refuse to take sides are cowards. This can easily been seen in the frequent political charge of "flip-flopping." Change of mind can only mean weak-mindedness, or, worse, lack of conviction or perhaps mere political calculation. We have been trained to view all statements of position as identity politics, as professions of ideological loyalties, because every issue has two sides and only two sides and any other alternative must be mere wistfulness, a refusal to face hard facts and make hard choices. To change our minds reveals ourselves to have been wrong or stupid to begin with, having chosen badly the wrong "side"; or to be a Pollyanna now, hoping for a world other than what is; or to be morally deficient, lacking the strength of our convictions. The one possibility we do not seem ready to countenance is that a change of mind can reveal ourselves to be what all of us should be, constant analysts, thinking carefully without premature convictions in the effort to always more richly understand ourselves and our world and allow that understanding to guide and modify our beliefs and behaviors.

THE AUTHORITY OF THE WITNESS

Another source of authority in journalism and in education flows from the fact that "reporting" or "informing" is a kind of witnessing. What is reported, in a news story or a textbook, is not happening with and to you directly. You are not there, at the scene of the crime or historical event, or in the lab at the moment of discovery. The journalist or the textbook is the witness that brings "what happened" before you, by means of a distillation of the "facts" and highlighting what is "important," thereby rendering you a different and mediated witness. In this secondary witnessing, you come to see the world differently, to know it indirectly. We easily become persuaded that, upon having "witnessed" these events ourselves, via mediation, we now know something, perhaps everything we "need" to, about world events or structures. The natural authority of the witness is the authority of direct experience, which comes, usually, from engagement with and in the world in a fuller sense. The transference of that authority to the "report," journalistic or educational, elides the selection process at work in the latter. The true witness is merely present in and to the world; the "reporter" or textbook "author" selects what will be witnessed. Whatever forces are at work in that selection, the result is the unarguable elevation of whatever gets "covered" to the status of "important happening." News and education are, *de facto*, about what is important, because the act of selecting and reporting whatever gets "covered" gives it that importance.

By means of our collaborative witnessing, not only has something in the world become real where it didn't before exist for us, in an important sense, but what has been created and made real in our witnessing need not, and for the most part can't possibly, bear much relation to the fuller and complex dynamics actually at work in the world. Any selection is always an attenuation, which, given the constraints of our journalistic and educational structures discussed above, wrenches what we "witness" from its rich contexts and lays it before us a cartoon version of its real complexities. What we are offered to "witness" as mediated by journalism and education, since it is beyond our own normal experience, is thereby ripe for further cartooning and manipulation. In other words, our collaborative witnessing often accomplishes nothing but the creation of a kind of pseudo-event, bearing little or no relation to reality, which we elevate to significance and then largely forget, unless we need to recall it at some future point to illustrate or symbolize some equally cartoonish instance of other events and structures.

From this process is distilled a kind of vocabulary, by means of which we largely determine our worlds and to which we far too frequently surrender our critical faculties. Pierre Bourdieu has noted that certain words take on symbolic and synoptic meaning, such that their capacity for determining the dimensions of experience are vastly exaggerated.[21] These words are given serious significance or tragic character out of all proportion to their ability to label or serve as an element in saying something. Terrorist, liberal, conservative, freedom, and even tragedy or scandal are examples of such terms in journalism; the list is far too long to intelligently sample in education.[22] Both news and textbooks are full of such "key terms," carving the world into tidy categories, clearly demarcated and offered as central to the ability to "make sense" of ourselves and our world. The words themselves come to stand as witness, entraining larger ways of seeing, authoritative interpreters which provide shorthand formulas for understanding.

Journalism and education both present themselves and are largely taken as authoritative because of their pretended anonymity and impartiality, because of the way they present information and argue (or at least make claims under the guise of argument), because of the reality effect generated by their methods and selection processes, and, ultimately, because they straightforwardly claim authority on the basis of "expertise" and their role as "witness."

Marketing adopts and benefits from each of these vectors of authority as well, as we shall see. The habits of mind, inculcated from long exposure, generated by these practices and conventions of authority in both journalism and education, have conditioned us to either unquestioning acceptance with respect to all truth-telling narratives, or a kind of apathy generated by expectations of ignorance, or, sometimes, both. Truth-telling narratives are not to be analyzed, merely accepted or rejected, or dismissed as irrelevant to one's own interests and expertise. A habit of passivity, a dismissal of the need for or importance of analysis, keeps us not only from exploring the claims and grounds for those claims in the persuasive narratives we encounter, but, more importantly, keeps us from noticing the ways in which those persuasive claims do indeed act upon us regardless of whether we believe we attend to them or not. We will examine this particular dynamic in our consumption of marketing in later chapters.

HEROES AND VILLAINS

Bourdieu comments that what counts as "news" is formed by an "emphasis on that which is most obvious in the social world, meaning individuals, what they do, and especially what they do wrong; and, finally, a readiness to denounce or indict."[23] In the broadcast media that has the most to do with moral questions, with political and social "problems" and situations, we are almost never presented with any models of deliberation. We are, instead, presented with what we may suppose (safely or not) are the products of deliberation: set attitudes and beliefs, opinions and perspectives. We are shown these pitched either in battle against others or at us for ideological consumption. By means of these practices, as Bourdieu notes, "our news anchors, our talk show hosts, and our sports announcers have turned into two-bit spiritual guides, representatives of middle-class morality. They are always telling us what we 'should think' about what they call 'social problems'."[24] He recalls Gide's dictum that worthy sentiments make bad literature, but notes that they seem to make for good audience ratings.

Kathleen Hall Jamieson offers five main topoi inhabited by almost every news segment: These are:

1. *Appearance versus reality.* This reflects an emphasis on conflict and the "objective" role of skeptical newsgatherers who uncover hypocrisy. On the positive side this theme holds public officials to high standards; on the negative, it invites the cynical assumption that those who aspire to lead are all corrupt.

2. *Little guys versus big guys.* This theme reflects an emphasis on the personal and individual by taking a particular interest in the underdog or outsider or exposing corrupt and self-interested actions by the powerful against the powerless.

3. *Good against evil.* The essence of drama, this theme is related to crime as a news model and to investigative journalism as a norm for reporting and the reporter's role.

4. *Efficiency versus inefficiency.* This is usually an attempt to uncover waste and mismanagement, illustrating the emphasis on politics and government in the news.

5. *The unique versus the routine.* Reflecting a stress on novelty, this theme is illustrated by the human interest stories appearing at the end of most newscasts or in syndicated newspaper columns.[25]

Jamieson does not specifically note nor develop the fact that all of these themes are explicitly moralistic. For the most part, that claim doesn't require much explanation, since it is evident in both the labels and the descriptions. Even the final theme, however, which might not strike the reader as moralistic on its face, is most frequently exercised in the presentation of stories about "heroes" and "villains." Even the common natural disaster news story, for instance, almost always includes vignettes featuring individuals affected by the event, and who, without exception in my experience, are presented as maintaining hope in the face of tragic loss and a commitment to rebuild. When the news ties an event to individuals, as it almost always does in order to personalize and dramatize the story, it does so in a way that offers moral paradigms, caricatures of either admirable or problematic sentiments, behaviors and attitudes.

Television news, at least, traffics in such caricatures almost exclusively. It focuses on individuals and their activity, primarily in binary and cartoonish terms. Each individual is an instance of a type, morally good or bad, and the stories are really about those larger paradigms. A person presented as involved in scandal, or waste, or corruption, or criminal activity, or some other transgression which warrants his or her newsworthiness is interchangeable with any other person so involved, except for the concrete details, which are presented only to distinguish the particular instance from the larger type. Those presented as exemplary in some way, models for our admiration or emulation, are equally avatars. In both cases, popular middle-class and middle-of-the-road mores are idealized and reinforced.

The morality on display and invited by these topoi is what Appiah calls "quandary" ethics, in which "moral discourse has effectively been relegated to instances of conflict, to 'problems.'"[26] In news coverage, particular problems, both those categorized as moral quandaries, such as stem cell research or euthanasia or abortion, and those not explicitly configured as moral, but rather as larger social problems, are presented as calling for something like a moral "intervention" or a moral "dispensary for the afflicted," as Appiah characterizes it. Morality is a problem to be solved, usually by the experts, or at least those who rise to the challenge and stand apart and above the normal run of person in so doing; or morality is presented as something to trouble us, as a spectacle of failure and disappointment, inviting moral judgment and dismay.

Earlier, I remarked that such moralizing primarily practices, and prompts us to practice ourselves, an exercise in external evaluation. Such a practice is not primarily reflective, an evaluation of our own moral character, but other-oriented. We are invited to view and judge the moral failures or successes of distant and practically unknown others. Because of this, television journalism can only offer moral caricatures, two-dimensional at best, fitting pre-determined moral ideals and models. Each particular story merely instances one of a limited number of such models, never providing us with enough context and detail to see the agent as unique, acting in a unique concrete situation.

One of the more interesting tensions within marketing is the need to simultaneously create dissatisfaction in the auditor with her life and lifestyle, while also validating, even valorizing popular culture and its associated lifestyles in general. The goal is not to make the consumer dissatisfied with the world, just her place in it. Contemporary television and print journalism feeds this overall impression by having the moral order glorified in the breech, as it were, telling us stories of one moral failure after another which, paradoxically, may serve both to cast into doubt the moral system in which these acts count as failures, but also to more firmly entrench it. Marketers play off this dynamic by suggesting that we are failing to live up to our personal or cultural possibilities, to be as sexy and successful and happy, not as we might *desire*, but as we *ought* to be. Our failure to realize our more perfect potential in the material universe is a moral failure.

In the news, as Bourdieu argues, moral rules and values are presented as serving to perpetuate and consolidate a moral and social order, and the moral paradigms offered always aim at "promoting social conformity and market values."[27] Presentations of "problems," moral lapses in which, as is bound to happen, one's behavior fails to fully realize established norms and values, configures morality as a goal to be realized through individual achievement and conformity. The primary theme of news reports is scandal, which, in the original Greek, *skandalon*, means quite literally the elevation of a "stumbling block" or "obstacle" to the status of moral lesson. Lull and Hinerman define scandal, as "covered" by journalism, as the presentation of "private acts that disgrace or offend the idealized, dominant morality of a social community . . . made public and narrativized."[28] As John Tomlinson argues in the same work, "scandals perform a specific role of 'regulating' the tacit moral order of a community. They provide contexts for communal moral reflection and debate."[29]

"Scandal" is the very model of morality as spectacle, the opportunity to judge (and, ostensibly, "learn" from) the examples of others, creating an inevitable moral relativism that invites self-righteousness, whether formulated as a kind of superiority to those offered as "lessons" or derived from the supposed ability to benefit from their example. As already noted, contemporary journalism focuses upon the individual actor because it can film him or her. It cannot present video footage of social or political structure, unfolding dynamics of change, multiple vectors of power and influence. It can only present footage of events isolated from their historical and larger material structures, which it almost always reduces to individual actors and the consequences of their acts. It shows us people, individual people, as paradigms, models for moral types, or symbols for narrative motifs and characters. This structural dynamic, by itself, has significant consequences for how we think about morality. Most actual moral issues are social issues, community issues. The fact that our primary moralistic narratives frame the world as composed of individuals and their individual needs, desires, and acts effectively obliterates the social, or reduces it to some arbitrary and abstract aggregate of individuals and their individual desires and activities, framed as conforming or failing to conform to established and expected standards.

Education, as well, is replete with heroes and villains. Universal education, shaped, as it is, by national curricula and national standards, is an ideal place to inculcate cultural ideas and moral lessons, as we will discuss further in the final chapter. Indeed, there is a great deal of talk, both within and outside the academic community, about how education falls short of fully serving this central and crucial purpose. The primary realm for this idealized moral teaching seems to be the discipline of history, a cornerstone of lower education curriculum, but it is present in the sciences as well. As Stephen Jay Gould notes in an essay about how we teach the sciences, scientific developments, like news stories, are usually configured to present heroes and, if not villains, then at least "fools."[30] As we narrate the development of scientific ideas, we carefully juxtapose those who later gained the acceptance of the larger community as heroes working against the corruption of scientific ideals due to ignorance, interest, or obstinate deviance by those whose ideas were ultimately rejected. The classical metaphor of science as the building of an edifice of knowledge, one stone at a time, is often presented as a struggle against those forces at work trying to delay or destroy that building process. Those who succeed, scientifically, are often portrayed as doing so through greater moral character and a dedication to the truth.

As James Loewen wonderfully argues in his book, *Lies My Teacher Told Me*, history textbooks "portray the past as a simpleminded morality play." He notes that the very titles of American history textbooks illustrate the moralism they contain: *The Great Republic, The American Pageant, Land of Promise, Triumph of the American Nation*.[31] As he examines most of the key "episodes" and "figures" taught in these textbooks, he notes, over and again, a process he calls "heroification," in which the textbooks "turn flesh-and-blood individuals into pious, perfect creatures without conflicts, pain, credibility, or human interest."[32] In each case, narratives are carefully constructed to reinforce particular ideas about who we are and should be in the world and conventional values, urging both a moral and social conformity above anything remotely resembling a careful and full analysis of the complex dynamics and pluralistic motivations of persons and events. As Bruner remarks, "the medium of exchange in which education is conducted—language—can never be neutral . . . it imposes a point of view not only about the world to which it refers but toward the use of mind in respect of this world."[33]

Such stories are couched within larger reflexive narratives about authority and impartiality which ironically, even paradoxically, lends them a persuasive capacity and air of truth far beyond what we usually credit. We *buy* these narratives *and* their meta-claims, both as teachers and as learners (consumers). Our picture of our world, and of ourselves, is importantly shaped by them, in ways I find hard to imagine if such narratives were offered through any other convention than those understood and accepted as "truth-telling." Together, they shape the world we inhabit in significant ways, and combine to constrain and channel our sense of our possibilities, as we will explore in more detail in the next chapter.

NOTES

1. Walt Disney, *The Listener*, February 16, 1984.
2. Jacques Ellul, *Propaganda: The Formation of Men's Attitudes* (New York: Alfred A. Knopf, 1965), 48.
3. In the US, the Federal Trade Commission regulates advertising, and on their website, has this to say about truth in advertising: "When consumers see or hear an advertisement,

whether it's on the Internet, radio or television, or anywhere else, federal law says that ad must be truthful, not misleading, and, when appropriate, backed by scientific evidence." "Truth in Advertising," *Federal Trade Commission*, accessed March 20, 2014, ftc.gov/news-events/me dia-resources/truth-advertising.

4. See, e.g., Douglas Walton, *Media Argumentation: Dialectic, Persuasion and Rhetoric* (Cambridge: Cambridge University Press, 2007).

5. Story, Louise. "Anywhere the Eye Can See, It's Likely to See an Ad." *New York Times*, January 15, 2007.

6. "Seamless integration" is a popular marketing catch-phrase indicating efforts by the industry to place branding and products in all forms of popular entertainment, and, to the extent possible, all social institutions, including education. A primary journal of the marketing industry, *Advertising Age,* created a separate division, *Madison and Vine*, to monitor and report on this new marketing strategy.

7. "The State of the News Media," Pew Research Center's Journalism Project, accessed February 13, 2008, stateofthemedia.org/2004/cable-tv-intro/content-analysis. Out of 240 hours of cable news programming on CNN, Fox, and MSNBC, viewed by ADT Research for the study between May and October 2003, only 11% of the on-air time and 8% of the stories were written and edited. The vast majority of cable news occured in "live mode," primarily by means of impromptu interviews with "newsmakers" or "expert" guests.

8. Pierre Bourdieu, *On Television* (New York: New Press, 1998).

9. For a powerful, and still timely, analysis of what comes to count as "news" and how that process is manipulated by political forces, in particular, see Daniel Boorstin, *The Image: A Guide to Pseudo-Events in America* (New York: Vintage, 1961).

10. Kathleen Hall Jamieson and Karlyn Kohrs Campbell, *The Interplay of Influence: News, Advertising, Politics and the Internet*, 6 ed. (Belmont, CA: Thomson Wadsworth, 2006), 41–42.

11. Bourdieu, 51 and 8.

12. For instance, In E. D. Hirsch's controversial book, *Cultural Literacy* (Boston: Houghton Mifflin, 1987), 146–215, he offers an appendix that lists what every well-educated person is supposed to recognize (not know anything about, in his argument, just recognize as significant in some ambiguous sense). The list includes only six dates. Of these, five are dates for wars, and the remaining date is that of the supposed "discovery" of the "new world," all of which privilege conflict as what signifies importance.

13. This promo aired on a number of other cable channels in the summer of 2004. NWI was originally produced by the Canadian Broadcasting Company (CBC) and largely repeated CBC broadcast coverage. In typical fashion for television networks in the past several decades, it was sold to USA Network in 2000, which was then bought by a company that then became part of Vivendi Universal. In 2004, the channel was purchased by former vice president Al Gore and Joel Hyatt. It was re-launched as Current TV in 2005 which aired until 2013, when the channel was sold to Al Jazeera Media Network, which re-launched the channel again as Al Jazeera America, returning it to an "international" news format.

14. Henry Jenkins, *Convergence Culture: Where Old and New Media Collide* (New York: New York University Press, 2008), 227.

15. On this pretense in law, see Patricia Williams, *The Alchemy of Race and Rights* (Cambridge, MA: Harvard University Press, 1992), 8–11. On the pretense in science, see Friedrich Nietzsche, *Beyond Good and Evil*, §207. Since the TV news coverage of Hurricane Katrina anchors and reporters have felt freer to express personal emotions, if not also judgments, in the course of reporting the news. In Alessandra Stanley's April 19, 2007 edition of TV Watch in the *New York Times*, "Amid Chaos, One Notably Restrained Voice," she remarks: "Hurricane Katrina, even more than 9/11, emboldened television newscasters to fold themselves and their feelings into the story, and that has led to the Anderson Cooperization of the evening news. Network anchors often behave as if they are the nation's grief counselors."

16. See Nicholas Lemann, *The Big Test: The Secret History of the American Meritocracy* (New York: Farrar, Straus and Giroux, 1999).

17. Perhaps the most widely read exploration of this dynamic remains Paulo Friere, *Pedagogy of the Oppressed* (New York: Continuum, 2000), particularly chapter 2.

18. Leon Botstein, *Jefferson's Children: Education and the Promise of American Culture* (New York: Doubleday, 1997), 202–211.

19. For illuminating analysis of how "experts" are configured by the public relations industry and used in journalism, marketing, and even education, see Sheldon Rampton and John Stauber, *Trust Us, We're Experts: How Industry Manipulates Science and Gambles with Your Future* (New York: Penguin, 2002).

20. Wayne Booth, "Knowledge and Opinion," in *Now Don't Try to Reason With Me* (Chicago: University of Chicago Press, 1970), 82–84.

21. Bourdieu, 18ff.

22. Again, I note that the "list" of cultural capital terms in Hirsch's book, presented by him, if not exclusively or comprehensively, as just such a vocabulary, runs 64 pages in double columns per page.

23. Bourdieu, 2–4.

24. Bourdieu, 46. McLuhan also argues that under the ubiquitous influence of mass media, those who count as our teachers, our moral guides, our mentors, have exponentially expanded. As he puts it: "Character no longer is shaped by only two earnest, fumbling experts [one's parents]. Now all the world's a sage." Marshall McLuhan, *Understanding Media: The Extensions of Man* (London: Routledge and Kegan Paul, 1964), 14.

25. Jamieson, 51–53.

26. Appiah, *Experiments in Ethics*, 197–198.

27. Bourdieu. 46.

28. James Lull and Stephen Hinerman, *Media Scandals* (New York: Columbia University Press, 1998), 3.

29. John Tomlinson, "'And Besides, the Wench is Dead': Media Scandals and the Globalization of Communication," in Lull and Hinerman, 68.

30. Stephen Jay Gould, "On Heroes and Fools in Science," in *Ever Since Darwin* (New York: Norton, 1977).

31. James Loewen, *Lies My Teacher Told Me: Everything Your American History Textbook Got Wrong* (New York: Simon & Schuster, 1995), 6.

32. Loewen, 11.

33. Bruner, *Actual Minds*, 121.

Chapter Three

Spectacle

The Ontology of the Image

"Publicity adds up to a kind of philosophical system. It explains everything in its own terms. It interprets the world."[1]

"We are getting closer and closer to the point where the social world is primarily described—and in a sense prescribed—by television."[2]

"A democratic civilization will save itself only if it makes the language of the image into a stimulus for critical reflection—not an invitation for hypnosis."[3]

In order to look at marketing narratives as moralistic discourses, we need to spend some time thinking about the nature and dynamics of image. Most marketing works through images. There is language attached, usually, and sometimes the language takes center stage, making explicit arguments or claims; but more and more often language takes an auxiliary role, near the end of the television commercial or as a few carefully selected words on the advertising image. It is important, still, but serves most often to augment and cement the message of the image rather than the reverse. It is not the case that images are powerful and words are not, as is often debated in media analysis after McLuhan. It is that images create what Bourdieu notes many literary critics call a "reality effect."

There is a distinctive authority in images. It is the authority of the "real," borrowed, ontologically, from the lived world. The image is "life-like." As Barthes explains, in every image, at least every marketing image, the coded iconic message, the message the image maker intends to convey, the argument that seeks to persuade us to buy in the case of the ad image, is grounded in the authority of the non-coded iconic "message" of the image, the "fact" of

67

the "objects" present in it that represent an actual world.[4] Such a message carries tremendous authority because it appears to us to be a message without a code, to be, simply, a direct representation of what is.

When the "reality" depicted through image and word are not part of our normal life experiences, or, as in the case of marketing, often represent an idealized life, then both the image and the words which interpret it achieve extraordinary power to shape the way we see the world, and even, by extension and over time, ourselves. Image technologies, over the course of the last half-century, have increased their fidelity to "life" and extended that power, shifting our views of ourselves such that we increasingly understand ourselves in terms of image, and inviting us to "read" the world along an increasingly attenuated set of narrative motifs, referencing and altering both our actual lives and our fantasies.

THE STEREOSCOPE AND THE STEREOGRAPH

At the end of an essay published in 1859, Oliver Wendell Holmes expressed a series of fears prompted in him by a new technology, the photograph.[5] This was a technology that could, as he put it, divorce form from matter, taking the skin of the world and leaving behind the flesh and bones as of little worth. Inured, as we are today, to the image as a ubiquitous element of our world environments, it is worth thinking, with Holmes, about what a radical change this new technology has wrought. Until that time, all images were clearly representational, obviously material in ways that were determinative of their character as images, and obviously produced by someone as an interpretation of something clearly and utterly distinct: material reality. The production of images was labor intensive, usually resulting in a single, unique product, which was, for the most part, not intended to "capture" reality, but rather to glorify it, to flatter it, to manipulate others, or to offer a "message." Even the often aesthetically striking anatomical and naturalist drawings of the modern scientific era were more than strictly representational, providing more than information. The image was not a mirror, and the map was understood to be something utterly different than the territory.[6]

The camera changed that, in the blink of a shutter. The image produced by the camera was not the result of the same kind of intention and interpretation, or of the same kind of material manipulated in similar ways by an image maker. It introduced a radically different method for producing images, including the ability to produce as many as desired. It offered, as Holmes puts it, the skin of reality, stripped from its substance, and rendered apart and whole. Holmes feared that form, divorced from matter in this new way, would come to exert tremendous influence over our sense of ourselves and the world, usurping the authority of lived reality; that we would come to prefer the image over the thing. Matter is, after all, "fixed and dear," as Holmes puts it; whereas form, as images, is cheap, transportable, and as numerous as desired. There is only one Coliseum, as Holmes remarks, but potentially millions of "faithful" representations. He feared a kind of "poaching" of the "skins" of all actual objects wherein the image of them would not primarily serve to call to mind the original, but rather that the original would come to stand as equally an instance of what might be called the Platonic "form" of the thing itself, captured and available in every image of it.

The shift Holmes feared is an ontological shift, a change in our way of being in the world, since exacerbated by refinements in the fidelity of representational technologies. We have come far beyond the "stereograph." New forms of mechanical reproduction, to use Benjamin's famous formulation, transform what transpires into what is transmitted and displayed. What happens in the world of our activity, our lives as lived, is not consumable as spectacle in its own right. That world is a world of engagement and interaction, goal-driven activity; it unfolds toward something in the making. Filming that world, re-presenting that world, changes its ontological status. From a world in which, as Heidegger would put it, we are *already-alongside* as *ready-to-hand* (equipment) *together-with* involved in some project, we are transformed into "objects," *present-at-hand*, now able to be examined, questioned, appropriated. The world shifts from a *world-we-are-in* engaged in activity into a *world-over-against-at-a-distance* to be observed and "possessed," even, perhaps, bought.[7]

Less clumsily (with apologies to Heidegger), the world of our activity, familiar and intimate, the context as it were of our being and doing, becomes an image world, the world of seeing and being seen, a little strange and distant no matter how familiar. It becomes spectacle. This transformation is not, or not much, an epistemological transformation, not a matter of *seeing* the world differently. It is an ontological transformation, a different way of *being* the world and being in it. One is a world in which our behavior is the substance of what happens, the other a world in which our behavior is the content of a completely other happening: the representation of "happening."

This ontological shift is not new, of course, and not created by mass media. To take some part of the world with which we are engaged in activity toward some goal and begin to ask after its nature is to perform something like this same ontological shift. Such inquiries are as old as philosophy and science. Indeed, I would argue, in some ways, modern science has helped make modern advertising possible, in that it helped *create* interchangeable objects and, more importantly, interchangeable subjects.[8] We have been trained by the metaphysical assumptions of the sciences, filtered into the popular mind, to treat ourselves as objects, explainable in universal terms, so that we need not look for or consider individual narrative histories, the specific impact of the past on each thing, except in the stylized and generalized form of cause and effect. We have come to believe that all, or at least almost all, aspects of ourselves, perhaps even our ideas, our convictions, and our perspectives, are the same sorts of things that we can find in the Petri dish, and thus on the page in a magazine ad: an instance of a universal, an interchangeable, even fungible, example of a type. We *create* these idealized *objects*, as we think about ourselves in these ways, and then treat them, as both the scientist treats them and the ad exec desires them to be treated: as unquestioned and unquestionable brute fact, to be examined and manipulated, to be adopted, bought, sold, possessed, but not brought into critical conversation, not engaged so as to unfold their narratives, in short, not as *concrete and individual*.

What Holmes feared was that new image technologies would naturalize and normalize this ontological shift, because they magnify the interchangeability as they multiply the outward form, taken as the thing. Since a given image is interchangeable, at the level of representation at least, with all other images of the same object, the sheer weight of that interchangeability, in part because of its variety, transfers to the object itself the ontological character of mere instance of the form. Further, the camera image, still or video, is different from other modes of visual representation because, we believe, it is an objective instrument, capturing, within its mechanical limitations, what is "there" in front of it. The resultant image may be manipulated after the fact, through CGI for video images, or various forms of "photo-shopping" still images; but that process is largely invisible to us in the final image, whereas the "fact" of its reproduction through mechanical means is vividly present. The mechanical image carries the authority of reality because we take it to be the product of an impartial, unimaginative, straightforward reproduction of what is "there."

This shift matters for our analysis because different ontological status entails different commitments and different potentialities. Both worlds are not habitable in the same ways with the same purposes. To vote, for instance, and to view voting broadcast as part of some election event have almost nothing in common as activities, in a strict sense, but operate by means of completely different dynamics, goals, consequences, and meanings taken on their own. Indeed, it could be argued that, in television coverage, the activity of voting is treated merely as an element, however essential, in a larger pseudo-event that exists primarily in and through media coverage: the "election." In much news coverage, various poll and analysis dynamics parse the activity of voting as a kind of play in a sporting event where what matters is who leads and who is coming from behind and what the odds are. The "race" is what is real and what matters, voting is merely how it is run, and voters are merely players on opposing teams.

The dynamics of mechanical reproduction confuses these ontological differences as it generates them, however. The broadcast of voting, for instance, is the broadcasting of some people actually voting. It is the representation of the substance of one activity, voting, as the content of another, the one we are actually engaging at the moment, the viewing of the news about the election. As McLuhan noted, the "living room has become a voting booth."[9] Participation by means of auditing televisual representations of citizenship has come to count as political activity and participation. Such conflation cannot but transform the character of what we take to be the world activity being represented. That is the defining character of spectacle, the presentation of whatever is presented *as* meaningful and valuable *because* it exists to be seen.

While certainly a controversial figure, Marshall McLuhan has influenced a number of cultural critics and media theorists, prompting them to take the ontological impact of technology seriously. However speculative his histories, or imaginative his analyses of the developments and influences of the various media, his work encourages us to look for the ways in which, as he puts it: "All media work us over completely." For him, media is "so pervasive in their personal, political, economic, aesthetic, psychological, moral, ethical and social consequences that they leave no part of us untouched, unaffected, unaltered;" such that "all understanding of social and cultural change is impossible without a knowledge of the way media work as environments."[10] For McLuhan, mass media are *primarily* technical models that influence our engagement with the world in ways that overshadow the influence their content has upon our opinions or concepts. As he says: "The effects of technology do not occur at the level of opinions or concepts, but alter sense ratios or patterns of perception steadily and without any resistance."[11] As Wayne Booth has said, "as viewer, I become *how* I view, more than *what* I view."[12]

Baudrillard was influenced by McLuhan, and developed his thinking about the ontological transformations wrought by and through technology specifically with respect to the consumerization of society. In "Mass Media Culture," he argues:

> Self-evidently, most of the time, the content conceals from us the real function of the medium. It presents itself as a message, whereas the real message, with regard to which the manifest discourse is perhaps mere connotation, is the deep structural change (of scale, of model, of habitus) wrought in human relations. Crudely put, the "message" of the railways is not the coal or the passengers it carries, but a vision of the world, the new status of urban areas, etc. The "message" of TV is not the images it transmits, but the new modes of relating and perceiving it imposes, the alterations to traditional family and group structures. And we may go even further and say that, in the case of TV and the modern mass media, what is received, assimilated and "consumed" is not so much a particular spectacle as the potentiality of all spectacles.
> This, then, is the truth of the mass media: it is their function to neutralize the lived, unique, eventual character of the world and substitute for it a multiple

universe of media which, as such, are homogeneous one with another, signifying each other reciprocally and referring back and forth to each other. In the
extreme case, they each become the content of the others—and that is *the*
totalitarian "message"of a consumer society.[13]

The argument is that both image, as a partial and reductive reproduction of
the world, and the technology by means of which the image is produced have
re-shaped our world, effacing some aspects and foregrounding others; and
both claim the kind of authority natural to the world as lived, transferring it to
both its "skin" or "face" and to those instruments capable of capturing and
presenting them.

THE CONFLATION OF WORLDS

In recent decades, images of life in action have achieved a fidelity to lived
experience such that they perhaps cannot help but effectively blur the ontological boundary just adduced. Recent generations have grown up entirely in
a world where life and image are fully conjoined and integrated, mutually
referential and reflective. Before the middle of the last century there was still
a distinction between the world as lived and even mechanical representations
of that world. There was life and there was image and the two were not only
clearly separate, but one was dominant and occupied the vast portion of our
experience, while the other was an occasional, perhaps novel, and largely
recreational encounter. This relation has been turned on its head.

There was a time when interpretations of the world offered by marketing
and the actual condition of the world as experienced were clearly distinct for
most auditors, even stark in their contrast. On those occasions when the
world presented by marketing found itself juxtaposed against the world presented by journalism in the morning paper or during the commercial breaks
of the cable news programs, or, in the case of those classes whose conditions
do not include consumer power, those occasions when marketing images
intruded into their decidedly different circumstances and environments, the
two worlds were not difficult to disentangle. But for many, those who enjoy a
sufficient level of socio-economic privilege, the actual conditions of the
world have come to resemble quite closely those they encounter in marketing, and when other, less familiar worlds impinge, they do so mostly in
images, offering a glimpse of a distant world, thus turning the dynamic
around, such that it is the marketing world that feels more present and faithful to our lived experiences. The now more distant, but still ostensibly "actual" world is mostly encountered in exactly the same way as the marketing
world has traditionally been encountered: as a series of images. Because of
that, we are at least implicitly and structurally invited to encounter both as
images in the same way, so that the image of the "actual" world, of the tragic

event, for instance, and the marketing image are subsumed under the same scheme: representations of the world as it is.

The news is still our primary access to that "actual" world beyond the boundaries of our lived experiences. It purports to inform us, to reveal the nature of events and people, and to illuminate the ways things work. Yet one of the most interesting aspects of media journalism is the ironic tension between the claim that the news informs us about the world, and the fact that what we watch is in some way removed from our lived lives. What we watch on TV or a tablet or computer screen, we watch knowing that what we view is something distant, something elsewhere, happening to others. As Baudrillard notes: "What the TV medium conveys by its technical organization is the idea (the ideology) of a world endlessly visualizable, endlessly segmentable and readable in images. It conveys the ideology of the *omnipotence of a system of reading over a world become a system of signs*. TV images present themselves as the metalanguage of an absent world."[14] The images we encounter, increasingly indistinguishable across genres, both report a world we are to take as actual, and therefore inclusive of our own lives and situations, and, necessarily, present a world as other, as spectacle.

Perhaps the primary factor in this tension is the simple fact that the news is, after all, a packaged media product, indistinguishable in many respects from other televisual and print media. The images are often the same, the graphics or soundtracks, the "sets." Both are broadcast through the same physical boxes and screens, which, of course, no matter how large and immersive their images, are still screens, separating what they show us from the lives being lived by those viewing them by a completely different way of being. What we watch is spectacle, constructed precisely to be watched, whether we are presented with images we are supposed to take as direct and faithful representations of real events, or images we acknowledge to be constructed and packaged with a specific purpose, such as marketing or entertainment. In reality, we only ever encounter the latter. News images are as edited, packaged, and presented to tell specific narratives as any image we encounter. The primary distinction between news and entertainment media, as noted in the previous chapter, are the truth conventions of each, which is a difference in expected reception rather than in presentation.

The line between "real" and image was further blurred when marketing began using images of the non-commercial world, of revolution or famine, of conflict or social crisis, in its own campaigns, as material for its own world constructions. Marketing is always looking to inhabit new representational territory, and so is always looking to transform elements of radically non-commercial ways of life into stock elements in its own constructions. It is aided in the process by the phenomenon I am calling attention to: the way that so many non-commercial ways of life have been "captured" and primarily experienced *as* images. The technological advances of mechanical reproduction, utilized equally in marketing and all other media, coupled with a swing in mass media journalism toward entertainment and marketing motifs have done much to blur this boundary between the actual and the image. The images we receive from journalism of an "actual" world of crisis and conflict, pain and need, are both in substance and in style, both in technical detail and narrative framing, no different from those images we encounter in marketing.

They are, increasingly, no different in content as well. Witness the Benetton campaign ads (figures 3.1–3) where images of war, or racial conflict and/or harmony, or death and illness are presented, without commentary, as commercial images harnessed to the purpose of exciting consumer interest in their brand.

In Benetton's press information about their campaign, they say:

> The photos of the AIDS patient, the soldier and the Albanian emigrants [not shown] were not taken for the ad campaign but were actual agency photos, in typical reportage style, used for conveying the news. These were photos that portrayed the "real" world, fell within the conventions of information, and introduced a new and intriguing question about the fate of advertising: can marketing and the enormous power of advertising budgets be used to establish

Figure 3.1. "Soldier," United Colors of Benetton.

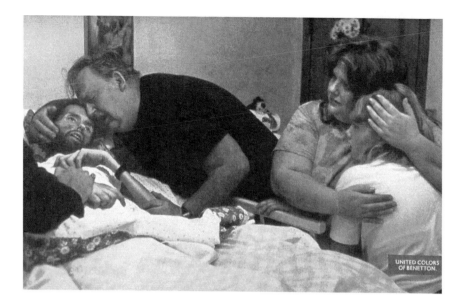

Figure 3.2. "AIDS patient," United Colors of Benetton.

a dialogue with consumers that focuses on something other than a company's products? Where was it written that advertising could only portray the absence of conflict and pain?[15]

In these ads, the images "borrowed" from journalism are selected and presented based upon their ability to arrest our attention, to strike our senses, and, even, as would seem obvious, with an eye to their aesthetic composition. I would not argue that such factors were not also at work in their selection as news photos. Indeed, it would be surprising if they were not. Their use as ad images, however, calls attention to the fact that the pretense of "informing," of initiating a "dialogue," of making one "think," present in them as news images, is already divorced from their contexts, and just as available to marketing purposes. They are usable in ads because there is almost nothing operating in them as news images that is lost, or that could serve to mark them as different and exclusive, other than the surprising nature of their subjects.

Another telling example is Kenneth Cole's longstanding marketing strategy of pairing typical and clearly recognizable marketing images with a plethora of "social" messages about abortion, violence, voting, AIDS, the death penalty, and other such "issues," all provided with campaign titles meant to elide the boundary between marketing and moralistic discourse, such as "Are You Putting Us On?" and "Where Do You Stand?".

Figure 3.3.   "Bosnian soldier clothes," United Colors of Benetton.

As is typical of these "activist" marketing campaigns, there are associated websites, such as that advertised in figure 3.6, "www.where doyoustand.com", which will redirect you to their equally pithily entitled website www.awearness.com, where you will be informed about the "issues they support" and invited to "get involved" yourself. We will look much more closely at this phenomenon in chapter 6. In these examples, it is the "social message" that can be seen to be already, in some senses, divorced from their contexts and amenable to market use. In both cases, image and message, market and "world," can be brought together with very little if any dissonance. What surprises us, if we are surprised, is the novelty, the unexpected juxtaposition, not any structural incompatibility. We may not like the co-option of social message or "real world" image; but that is merely an issue of personal preference, since the fact of their mingling clearly demonstrates an underlying consonance.

Whether it is images borrowed from the non-marketing world paired with a marketing message, however, or marketing images paired with ostensibly non-marketing messages of social consciousness, the blurring is intentional, and pervasive. There may have been a time when encountering, in some journal or newspaper, an image of starving children in Ethiopia while viewing on the facing page or under the fold some advertisement for perfume or a luxury automobile might have caused some cognitive dissonance, might have generated some at least momentary recognition that the world is not wholly

IN THE TIME IT TAKES TO READ THIS, ANOTHER PERSON WILL HAVE BEEN INFECTED WITH HIV. ARE YOU PUTTING US ON? -KENNETH COLE

KENNETH COLE new york

Figure 3.4.   Kenneth Cole Fall 2004 Campaign.

market, that not all events or choices confronting us are consumer opportunities. I deeply suspect that this is less and less the case. We have seen too many images of both sorts, and there has been too much crossover.

Even if some images of world conflict do not include in their frame familiar consumer symbols and signs, these are not necessary for the interpretive conflation to occur, since much marketing often no longer intends those symbols and signs to gesture toward particular consumer products but rather to evoke emotional and moral identities, to call up formulaic narratives of possible lives, to "seamlessly integrate" with images and narratives of the "actual" world. As Baudrillard argued, there is a reciprocity of image and motif across genres, a mutual referentiality, that makes of each media voice an extension of the same shorthand and simplistic set of possible perspectives, the same narrow set of interpretations as to how the world works. The result is that we often view "real" events in the world as examples of the limited sets of dynamics that marketing has worked hard to create. Such a tendency is perhaps a natural development of normal human heuristics, magnified by the increased general familiarity with a limited set of near-universal motifs that truly mass (global) media and marketing has propagated. But the categories are vastly more general now, and the authority for forming them has shifted from personal experience and local authorities to mass media.

Figure 3.5.   Kenneth Cole Fall 2004 Campaign.

Of course, as marketing infiltrates every possible space to break through the clutter, as it develops new techniques explicitly designed to suppress the outward markings of marketing, to appear to be journalism or advocacy or public discourse or simply the "real" world, then the fact that it utilizes the same media, the same vehicles of image and narrative as is used by all other forms of discourse just mentioned, increases the conflation of the message. It is, for all practical purposes, the *same voice* constantly speaking to us. Telling us about the world no longer occurs in clearly distinct categories with clearly distinct functions and mediators, such that we can recognize the authority and motivation of the truth tellers as different one from the other, teacher from reporter from salesman. I am not talking about the way in which one form of truth telling can be seen to be like another, as when we collapse any distinctions under a reductive recognition. I am talking about the very real way in which none of the territory of any one of these forms of truth telling has remained intact and discrete. There is no content or process of education that hasn't been appropriated by journalism or marketing, and vice versa. All these forms of world talk, of world presentation and representation, have both intentionally and unconsciously borrowed from each other, if only as a result of the perhaps innocent impulse to innovate, to use the latest technique/technology, to borrow and adopt the most appealing narrative frames.

Figure 3.6.   Kenneth Cole Fall 2011 Campaign.

SELF AS IMAGE

It is not only the world as lived and the world as re-presented to us that is increasingly conflated, however. We have also grown to see ourselves increasingly in terms of spectacle, as image, as captured or at least always ready and possible to be captured by the camera's eye in a world endlessly visualizable and readable as images, as Baudrillard puts it. A magazine ad for Skyy Vodka running in 1993 (part of a series with similar motifs) offers a clear illustration of this conflation, the idea that the primary mode of being is being seen and desired, and desired primarily as something to be seen.

The young woman in the image caresses the camera as she mugs for another and as she physically arrests the attention of the inevitable symbol of the male gaze.[16] Beyond the sexism present in this, and many ads, the larger

Figure 3.7. "Starlet," magazine ad for Skyy Vodka.

message here and in almost all advertising is that we and the world exist primarily to be seen; to be desired, to be envied, yes, but to be desirable and enviable *as* something to be seen, as spectacle. Everything in this image is arranged to be seen, has meaning only as spectacle, expressing nothing more than a flat, two-dimensional and, significantly, atemporal reality. Yet it presents itself as a slice of life, as a momentary capturing of some event unfolding, however ambiguous or decontextualized, or even ludicrous under critical examination, an event in which we can, in some unspecified (but always consumerist) way, participate. Most marketing images work in this way.[17]

Much of our social interactions have come to mirror these carefully staged "moments," including their gestures and stylized behaviors, however awkward they may be when not arbitrarily framed as image. A "Kodak moment" may have once been understood as those occasional, even rare times in our lives worth capturing and memorializing on film. I would suggest that, more and more, we live our lives in the effort to instantiate the images that surround us. We have come to think of our world of activity as a model or instance of the spectacle rather than the other way around.

There is a great deal of scholarship that explores this phenomenon, a significant portion of it developing out of Lacan's concept of the "gaze," the perspective of another before whom the subject imagines itself. Žižek has developed this concept in his numerous writings on "cyberspace" or "virtual reality." He argues that the subject understands itself in terms of this gaze; strives for its realization as an ego ideal, from which his or her actions can be seen as making sense, as having value; requires it to be able to act.[18] For Žižek, the subject always sees itself as being seen. It is, perhaps, the ubiquity of the representations, the degree to which we are flooded with our being in the world *as content* of mechanically representing the world as happening that has contributed most to the blurring of the boundaries between self and image. The world we inhabit as agents has been remapped as the world we observe as spectacle. I don't want to belabor this point, as many others have articulated this phenomenon with great care and insight. I simply wish to call attention to the way in which this conflation, this transformation, in which the reproduction subsumes the production, allows for our world of activity, for ourselves, to be seen by us as consumable after all, as product, as marketable good.

A clear example of this dynamic is the online dating phenomenon. Online dating services have exploded in the last decade, creating a market so saturated that services attempt to exploit niche demographics in order to carve out some market share from the crowded field, such as the heavily marketed ChristianMingle.com, whose slogan is "Find God's Match For You." Clearly, these services can only operate under the assumption that one is a product to be marketed, and that relationships are consumer goods, to be comparatively shopped. What is more interesting for our purposes, however, are the numerous auxiliary services that have sprung up focusing on helping those looking for love to present themselves with the best "packaging." Services such as Dating-Profile.com, ProfileHelper.com, E-Cyrano.com, or LookBetterOnline.com, offer to write your personal profile for you, to make it even more "personal," as e-Cyrano claims, or to help you generate the "most important element" of your online dating profile, your image, as LookBetter Online claims.

Such services buy into and perpetuate the idea that image is what matters, but suggest further that constructing the best image requires expert help. Not only are you a product, but you need an advertising firm in order to position yourself successfully in the market. They argue that to find a suitable romantic partner, which means, of course, being able to capture and retain the attention of consumers, one cannot afford to rely upon one's own sense of self. The presentation one is able to generate oneself must be, necessarily, amateurish and unexciting, we are told by these services. Ironically, services which are offered to everyone who can afford the sometimes steep rates, and which cannot take any real time to get to know a given individual, are presented as better able to capture and communicate what is unique about you than your own efforts. Nevertheless, the underlying assumption on the part of both service and consumer is that a uniform process producing largely homogeneously packaged, market-ready profiles will be received as unique and uniquely informative, as unpretentious and sincere.

That assumption appears to hold up. The services do very good business, claiming significantly increased rates of "interest" in their client's profiles (an important distinction from claiming increased interest in their clients). In a *New York Times* article about these services, one successful suitor remarked that he was particularly attracted to the professionally staged photograph and professionally polished personal essay of one potential mate in particular because he found her profile "to be authentic, sincere and honest."[19] The recipient of his attention remarked that she felt that the services she purchased were well worth the money, since the result was that she didn't feel like she had to subsequently "sell" herself to those who responded to her profile: "They were already sold." And should you worry that a professionally written profile or studio photograph might "oversell" you, might present you as something other or "more" than you can actually offer, do not be concerned: most of these sites offer dating coaching as well, presumably to help you maintain your professionally constructed persona, at least until the "sale" is finalized.

One of the more interesting aspects of these services is, of course, the focus on the photographic image. Most services offer to at least help you select and "polish" your photo. This usually involves image enhancements accomplished by means of photo editing programs, which, again ironically, alter, without acknowledgement, what was "there" in front of the camera. For a bit more money, however, you can front your online profile with images produced during an hour-long studio photo-shoot, producing results indistinguishable from the best advertising images. The services sell these packages through marketing that offers testimonial after testimonial of the vastly increased interest generated by such pictures. While these claims may indeed be true, they hardly seem necessary. We all already know that the visual representation of ourselves is what matters most, and that presenting ourselves in terms closely approaching the market ideal is desirable and best. This is but one example of the importance of image and the incursion of marketing into the most personal and intimate aspects of our social relations. The comfort we feel with such consumerist metaphors, e.g., online dating services as "marketplaces" in which people attempt to "sell" themselves to others as expressions of human romantic and sexual practices, says a great deal about the colonization of all aspects of our lives by the market. [20]

THE ABSTRACTION OF SELF: ONESELF AS AN OTHER

Marketing images flood our experiences of ourselves and our world, crossing many, if not quite yet all, genre boundaries, and blurring ontological boundaries, presenting the world and ourselves in it as market product, as consumable spectacle. The marketing image is structured to communicate a "message," of course, but it is only really a single message. As Baudrillard says:

> This technological process of mass communications delivers a certain kind of very imperative message: a *message-consumption message*, a message of segmentation and spectacularization, of misrecognition of the world and foregrounding of information as a commodity, of glorification of content as sign. In short, it performs a conditioning function (in the advertising sense of the term: in this sense, advertising is the 'mass' medium *par excellence*, and its schemata leave their stamp on all the other media) and a function of misrecognition." [21]

Berger explains that "every publicity image confirms and enhances every other," and that all such images intend to excite envy, of oneself for a possible future self, and of others for oneself as idealized. Marketing images are not about objects, they are about idealized social relations. [22]

More than a century and a half ago, Kierkegaard called attention to how the individual is in danger of being subsumed into the marketplace. In his little book, *The Present Age*, remarkably applicable to our own still, he claims that his age was "the age of advertising and publicity," in which "everything is transformed into representational ideas." [23] In that transformation, he argues, the "publicity" presentation of "events" took the place of anything actually ever happening, and "indications" were the only achievements of the age. In such an age of spectacle, he notes, "to be a subject has come to mean something different; it means to be a *third party,*" an observer.[24] The unifying principle of such an age, he claims, is envy, by which we are all bound together, unable to break free from "reflection," since we remain trapped by the reflections of those around us. Such reflection stifles and hinders action, he argues, because its primary dynamic is a kind of "leveling" by which everything is reduced to the same. To accomplish this leveling, "it is first necessary to procure a phantom, its spirit, a monstrous abstraction, an all-embracing something which is nothing, a mirage—and that phantom is *the public.*"[25]

For Kierkegaard, both the "public" and the "press" are abstractions. The "press" is not ever a particular entity speaking in its own name and for its own purposes, but an abstraction conjured by particular entities to speak to further abstractions that it participates in co-conjuring as well. Both the "press" and the "public" are nothing in themselves, less than any single individual, as Kierkegaard puts it, but pretend to be everything and all-inclusive, and to speak for and to everyone with a voice of authority from nowhere. That voice addresses us as both and neither an individual or a society, as the need arises. The publics it addresses are many and varied, although gathered under a single name, and are created at the moment of referring to them and by means of the ways in which its discourses configure and structure them.

Marketing, of course, does not need or want to address us as a mass in terms of its explicit communication, since societies don't buy their products or become brand loyalists, individuals do. Marketing always markets to individuals; but it does so, as we will see in the next chapter, by grouping us. One of the most interesting aspects of marketing dynamics is the way in which each marketing message needs to say to each individual auditor—while, of course, simultaneously speaking to millions of people—that the message is to him or her specifically, and about their individual lives, making each feel, ironically, the same, i.e., as if each were unique and uniquely addressed. One of the ways it does this, as we will see, is by offering us the opportunity to "belong" to individualized groups, to "tribes," by means of which we understand ourselves to be uniquely who we are.

As Bourdieu has noted, journalism focuses upon the individual actor because it can film him or her. It cannot present video footage of social or political structure, unfolding dynamics of change, multiple vectors of power and influence. It can only present footage of events isolated from their historical and larger material contexts, which it almost always reduces to individual agents and the consequences of their acts. It shows us people, individual people, but as paradigms, models for personality types, or symbols for narrative motifs and characters. When an abstraction like "the news" speaks to (and for) another abstraction like the "public," it can only speak of abstractions, which it calls "events." Such events, Kierkegaard argues, make no real

difference in any individual's life. Boorstin calls the events the media conjure for us to take the place of something actually happening "pseudo-events"
and argues, like Kierkegaard, that they are produced to be consumed as
spectacle rather than to accomplish anything. Both argue that we frequently
prefer the "event" to lived experience.[26]

In our own age, McLuhan says, the "public" has been subsumed by the
mass audience, but Kierkegaard would argue that there never was any real
difference.[27] We exist as a mass by means of and for the purpose of viewing
the spectacle. Things don't seem to us to be events unless they bear the marks
of having been processed to be seen. But such events, however much they
purport to tell a story, have no dynamic aspect, as Bourdieu has made clear.
They don't unfold. The illusion of video images is that we are seeing the
world unfold, but we do not see cause and effect, just effect, for which a
cause must be manufactured and reported, or increasingly, merely puzzled
over. We do not learn of the world in ways that show us the development of
the "events" we view. So the "events" have no real event dynamics. It is odd,
but the immediacy of video media have made their images the narrative
equivalent of still-frame photographs, capturing no more than a moment in
time, however long they play, an artificially truncated and objectified representation of life.

This atemporal aspect of "events" presented by televisual media has been
reinforced by the essentially eventless nature of marketing, which, as Berger
suggests, exists always in the *subjunctive* tense.[28] Events don't unfold in
marketing, no matter how a particular marketing narrative is structured to
project something happening. Instead, marketing images only promise an
unfolding for the consumer upon the condition of their participation in the
market. And it's always the same promise. Marketing images, for all their
often jittery, multiple frames per minute presentation, are narratively static.
The same goals beckon, the same procedures apply, the same mechanisms
obtain. The only variable is the material element: this car rather than that, or
rather than a particular airline or even clothing item, offers the same promise
of freedom or luxury.

For us, perhaps all events have become visual experiences, as Kierkegaard suggests and as Baudrillard or Boorstin argue.[29] A telling illustration
of this ontological conflation is the not insignificant number of people who
do not believe the US space program ever landed anyone on the moon;
believing, instead, that it was all filmed on a Hollywood soundstage. This is
the flip side of the reality effect. If events don't "happen" except in the form
of images that "witness" to their happening, then happening is equivalent to
visual experience and reducible to it, and the experience is indistinguishable
in terms of "actual" or "constructed." These people may speak in terms of
fraud or hoax, but their deeply salient point is that the image industry has
achieved a technical proficiency such that it can be difficult or even impos-

sible to tell the hoax from the faithful witness at least in terms of final visual product.

It is but a small further step to recognize that the conflation that matters here is not technological, but, again, ontological. A world which has the possibility to represent itself in ways that are indistinguishable from the images of lived experience is a world in which the authority of lived experience extends to all images; but, because of this conflation, all images, even those provided by the perceptual field of lived experience, have come to feel constructed in some sense. It is not that we believe that the mirror has distorted, either itself or the world, producing a fun-house experience of off-kilter representations, stretched or contorted to fit the character of the mirror or the design of the image maker; but that the world itself is, newly or perennially, malleable, able to be stretched and contorted to fit our needs and desires, and captured faithfully by the mirror. There is an "actual" world, but it is not fixed in its dimensions and character. There is a "real;" it is simply hyperreal. This is not to say that the map engenders the territory, as Baudrillard puts it, or that the mirror engenders the mirrored image. I am arguing, instead, as does Baudrillard ultimately, that the mirror and the mirrored have become utterly conflated, such that the authority of "reality" has been transferred to the image, and the representationality of the image has been transferred to the world, and the distinction between map and territory collapses in the face of their twinned character.

We, ourselves, are twinned in like manner. We are both ourselves and the image of ourselves offered by marketing and journalism, indeed, all mass media. We are both the observer and some distant other: either some frequently anonymous distant other as offered by journalism, or some other and future possible self as offered by marketing. If our moral sensibilities are excited, and both marketing and journalism have come to depend upon exciting our moral sensibilities as a primary attention strategy, they are excited by and projected upon both that other, and ourselves as that other, never, really, as we are, now, here. Experience is deferred and projected. Everything that happens in these worlds happens to someone else somewhere else, even if we are to imagine that someone as us. We are invited to and can merely observe, envy, judge.

In this conflation of image and self, a person's qualities are never presented as their own, recognized as such, detached from how others view them, ungrounded in anyone's desire to emulate them. In marketing, a person's qualities are presented as potential, grounded in a social dynamic, requiring a social system of validation. In journalism, as we have discussed, character is presented as fixed and ideal, paradigms, if not caricatures. In both cases, however, the moral import is remarkably similar. The paradigm of particular and independent moral character as presented in journalism serves as a model, usually in the negative sense, of the sort of person that the consumer who fails or succeeds at actualizing the promise of advertising can become. In both cases, one is addressed in abstraction, as mass, however projected upon the individual. The exemplars in journalism and advertising are avatars, exhibiting moral possibilities that require the correct (consumer) actions of the auditor to realize. Both are framed within the same social sphere with the same moral norms.

Intercalating advertising with entertainment and journalism media has the effect of effacing the boundaries of those separate messages and their goals, such that the "drama of world history" alternates with the tragic-comic drama of sit-coms or reality TV which alternates with the manufactured and often at least equally if not more emotionally charged drama of consumer culture. It is difficult to decipher which is the background or context for which, as Berger has eloquently noted. Baudrillard feared that the ultimate result of this conflation is the systematic *"equivalence* of history and the minor news item, of the event and the spectacle, of information and advertising *at the level of the sign."*[30] Such a conflation has made for easy migrations of content and message from one media platform to another, from marketing to journalism to entertainment. In a way, I need not argue that moralizing has become a commonplace motif rehearsed across disparate media occasions and structures; I might merely show how odd it would be, given the analysis above, for it not to.

In an age of spectacle, we subsume ourselves and our individual experiences under these abstractions, becoming third-parties to ourselves and each other. Everything we do is done to give others and ourselves as third-parties something to observe, something about which we may gossip, something, almost always the same thing, to envy. In such cases, according to Kierkegaard, even our principles and our values become abstractions, something purely external and for show, primarily serving to identify us according to abstract categories, for the sake of which one does one thing as willingly as another. It is important to note that this feature, by itself, has significant consequences for how we think about morality. Most moral issues, as I have said before, are social issues, community issues. The fact that mass media narratives frame the world as composed of abstract individuals and their abstracted individual needs and desires, that they reconfigure social obligation as consumer tribal affiliation, has the potential to radically alter our moral sensibilities, as we will see in the ensuing chapters.

NOTES

1. John Berger, *Ways of Seeing* (London: Penguin Books Ltd, 1972), 149.
2. Bourdieu, 22.
3. Umberto Eco, "Can Television Teach?" *Screen Education* 31 (1979), 12.
4. Roland Barthes, "The Rhetoric of the Image," *Image, Music, Text,* trans. Stephen Heath (New York: Hill and Wang, 1977), 32–51.

5. Oliver Wendell Holmes, "The Stereoscope and the Stereograph," *The Atlantic Monthly* 3 (1859): 738–48.

6. For seminal examinations of the power of representation and the changes wrought by new technologies, see Walter Benjamin's "The Work of Art in the Age of Mechanical Reproduction" and John Berger's development of Benjamin's ideas in chapter 1 of *Ways of Saving*.

7. For Heidegger's analysis of this fundamental ontological shift as a feature of human being, see the early sections of *Being and Time*.

8. On the interchangeability of object and subject, or what is sometimes called the "intra-being" between subject and object, generated by the metaphysical assumptions of modern science, see, in particular, Bruno Latour, *Pandora's Hope: Essays on the Reality of Science Studies* (Cambridge, MA: Harvard University Press, 1999), and Isabelle Stengers, *Power and Invention: Situating Science* (Minneapolis: University of Minnesota Press, 1997) or *Invention of Modern Science* (Minneapolis: University of Minnesota Press, 2000).

9. McLuhan, 22.

10. McLuhan, 26.

11. McLuhan, 27.

12. Wayne Booth, "The Company We Keep: Self-Making as Imaginative Art," *Daedalus* III (1982): 56–7.

13. Jean Baudrillard, *The Consumer Society: Myths and Structures*, (London: Sage Publications, 1998), 123

14. Baudrillard, 123.

15. Press release retrieved from benettongroup.com/media-press on March 15, 2011.

16. In this she is no different from almost any female figure in any advertisement, such as David Yurman's series of ads featuring celebrities like Naomi Watts or Kate Moss, in which the women merely pose in more or less provocative positions, in exotic settings and often in lingerie, for three or so minutes, with only some jewelry and the company name at the end of the commercial to provide any relevance: naomi-watts.org/2013/09/05/old-david-yurman-advert-video/. Such ads only make explicit what is at work in most: the conception of the female figure as almost exclusively for viewing, that females are desirable not for what they think, or what they can do (beyond the more or less veiled reference to sexuality), but for how they look, cashed out almost always in terms of sexuality.

17. See chapter 7 of Berger's *Ways of Seeing* for a cogent analysis that more fully unpacks these dynamics of what he calls "publicity" images.

18. Slavoj Žižek, Ernesto Laclau, and Judith Butler, *Contingency, Hegemony, Universality: Contemporary Dialogues on the Left* (London: Verso, 2000).

19. Jennifer Alsever, "In the Computer Dating Game, Room for a Coach," *New York Times*, March 11, 2007.

20. Michel Callon and Koray Caliskan write about the "marketization" of many non-market aspects of our lives. They lay out their program of research into this dynamic in Koray Caliskan and Michel Callon, "Economization, Part 1: Shifting Attention from the Economy Towards Processes of Economization." *Economy and Society* 38, (2009): 369–98.

21. Baudrillard, 123.

22. Berger, 131–132.

23. Søren Kierkegaard, *The Present Age*, trans. Alexander Dru (New York: Harper & Row, 1962), 35, 40.

24. Kierkegaard, 44.

25. Kierkegaard, 59.

26. Boorstin notes a study by a team of University of Chicago sociologists who monitored participation and publicity surrounding a "MacArthur Day" parade in Chicago on April, 26, 1951, one of the first such "events" to be televised live. The sociologists found that those who actually attended the parade were almost uniformly envious of those who were able to watch the "pseudo-event" on television at home, believing them to have had a much more exciting experience, while also finding their greatest excitement from being present themselves to be the opportunity to appear on television (26–28).

27. McLuhan, *Understanding Media*, 22.

28. Berger. 153.

29. See Jean Baudrillard, *The Gulf War Did Not Take Place* (Bloomington: Indiana University Press, 1995) and Jean Baudrillard, *Simulations* (New York: Semiotext(e), 1983).

30. Baudrillard, *The Consumer Society*, 122.

Chapter Four

Tribes

Hyperrealized and Mythical Belonging

"The act of acquiring has taken the place of all other actions, the sense of having has obliterated all other senses."[1]

As we saw in the last chapter, Holmes worried that new technology would create images so faithful in their reproduction of the world that we would come ultimately to prefer them to reality, or, worse, he feared, that we would come to see them *as* reality, or to experience reality primarily in terms of image and representation. The latter ontological conflation, in which two modes of being become interchanged or interchangeable, is not unique to images, however. Indeed, to say this about images is to say that images can be symbols. The broader phenomenon of the relation of object and reproduction, or, more specifically and powerfully, of objects (reproduced or original) and their symbolic functions, has perhaps always been present in human experience. It is, of course, impossible to know what functions were served by prehistoric cave paintings, but the desire to re-present the world and to invest at least some of the resulting imaginative fabrications with symbolic power has a very long history. In religion, in politics, in most social institutions, there have always been objects which serve as symbols, which, as Paul Tillich (drawing from Jung) explains, are different than signs in that the symbol does not merely signify, but participates in some way in the meaning and power of what is symbolized.[2] A traffic or commercial sign, a period, an animal track, words (at one level) are signs; a national flag, a personal name, a rose (or any object taken in a particular way) can be and often are symbols.

THE PROCREATIVE POWER OF SYMBOLS

From the scepter, the crown, the cross, the crescent moon, or sacred scripture, to the ruler, the apple, or the chair with arms at the head of the table, all such objects do more than merely signify something else in the world—political power and rule, the divine, the teacher, or the father—they in some sense embody those things. The symbol, participating in the ontological status of what it symbolizes necessarily stands with, if not also in place of the thing itself, especially when the thing itself is abstract or transcendental or inaccessible to direct perception, as Jung argues. As Tillich also explains, signs are invented or constructed, but symbols are largely organic—they are born, grow, live for a time, and sometimes die. This makes symbols ineluctably social phenomena. It is possible for a single individual or group to attempt to invest symbolic power in a given object, but it is always a matter of social agreement (whether conscious or not) that determines the character, power, and life-span of the symbol.

The marketing world is a world of symbols, in which all consumer goods symbolize something abstract, transcendental, and inaccessible except by means of the procurement and consumption of the market good as symbol. Such a world is beautifully illustrated in a story by Jorge Luis Borges, "Tlön, Uqbar, Orbis Tertius." The fantastic events of the story are set in motion by the recollection of a pithy observation in a fictional entry in a counterfeit encyclopedia about an imaginary country's mythical literature: "For one of those gnostics, the visible universe was an illusion or (more precisely) a sophism. Mirrors and fatherhood are abominable because they multiply and disseminate that universe."[3] The story introduces the delightful notion of secondary (or even more tertiary) objects called *hrönir*, that are produced by the desires of those who search for something, "the accidental children of absent-mindedness or forgetfulness."[4] These *hrönir* have become targeted in that world for methodical reproduction. The story offers the playful observation that "the *hrönir* of the second and third degree—that is, the *hrönir* derived from another *hrön*, and the *hrönir* derived from the *hrön* of a *hrön*—exaggerate the flaws of the original; those of the fifth degree are almost uniform; those of the ninth can be confused with those of the second; and those of the eleventh degree have a purity of form which the originals do not possess."[5] By the end of the story, in an ominous "postscript," the world of the imaginary country from the counterfeit encyclopedia has penetrated into and begun to efface our own.

Borges is speaking, in part, about symbols, in terms that are very illuminating for thinking about the symbolic world of marketing. *Orbis Tertius* means, in Latin, a world at third remove, not the reproduction of reality, but the reproduction of the reproduction. It is the poetic name for the Roman underworld, signifying a shadowy realm in which objects and people are mere shades of their more real selves. Symbols are "mirrors" that multiply and disseminate the universe, and the marketing world is a world of symbols not once removed, offering a reproduction of reality, but often at least twice removed, offering a self-referential reproduction of its own reproductions, which, as is the case with some images, promises or presents a world that is "purer" and more desirable. We all recognize such a world to be a world of illusion, if not also sophistry; but, as with Tlön, that world increasingly impinges upon our own, threatening to replace it.

An individual, in purchasing and consuming market goods, places him- or herself within a system of symbols, not created, but certainly manipulated and in some sense maintained by the market and marketing activity. Therefore, consumer objects always "say something" about their users, understood within the system of symbols of any particular market group, and derive their meaning and power primarily in terms of that ability to "speak." As symbols, consumer objects also participate in the meaning and power of their users. This in some sense natural dynamic (natural because simply part of the symbolic potential in human experience generally), when conjoined with the ontological power of the mechanically produced image as faithful reproduction of reality, expands the reproductive and supplementary power of marketing in which the consumer object comes to stand for, and in some sense, stand in place of the self, or at least the self as desired, the dream self.

Let us examine this dynamic at work. Almost all ads work in this way, but a clear example is the Volkswagen marketing campaign "Drivers Wanted," created by Arnold Worldwide in 1995 and running for a decade. By 1995, sales of Volkswagen cars in the US had dropped to their lowest point, and Volkswagen was thinking of dropping the brand from the US market.[6] Instead, they created a new marketing campaign proclaiming that "On the road of life there are passengers and there are drivers: Drivers wanted." The campaign worked. The slogan became the most recognized automotive marketing slogan at the turn of the century.[7] Subsequent Volkswagen sales and market recognition far exceeded projections and its continuing place in the US market was secured, at least so far.

The cars, of course, were the same boxy, unattractive (according to consumers' reports) designs, sporting largely the same features (not only as before the campaign, but as almost every other car in the marketplace). The ads were mostly like any other car ad, featuring cars in various tones of silver (or sometimes black) wandering along twisting back-country roads, or sitting still on white backgrounds, or in idealized urban or rural landscapes. Ads for most automotive brands mostly show almost indistinguishable silver boxes on wheels in largely the same settings. The difference in the Volkswagen ad (as, again, with almost all such ads) is the symbolic message, in which the consumer object is transfigured as an idealized identity package. Through the Volkswagen "brand," one *becomes*, or at the very least identifies oneself as, a "driver" rather than passenger on the road of life, as someone in control of one's own destiny.

One such ad featured the Jetta model poised in front of an iconic plains landscape (see figure 4.1), usually on a two-page spread (in which the second page, not shown, was simply an extension of the landscape), and captioned:

Figure 4.1.   "Drivers Wanted," magazine ad for Volkswagen Jetta.

"Free. Like wild horses, like geese bound for Canada. Leave food for the cat." Through the image and caption, the consumer is configured as needing, or at least desiring, to escape (a central theme of much marketing, but particularly automobile marketing), and enabled to do so by a particular market good. The argument is that by the power somehow vested in this consumer product, one can be freed from the mundane responsibilities of life and empowered to head off into an absolutely ambiguous unknown. In such a message, it does not really matter that horses are incredibly territorial herd animals, or that migrating geese are almost the opposite of free, instead rigidly following quite definite paths to quite definite destinations in large groups, over and over again (images that, not coincidentally, invoke herd behavior congenial to marketing needs). What matters is what is invoked by the conceptual ideal of wild horses or geese winging across the vast expanse of sky: freedom and power. The car, here and in much automotive marketing, is a symbol of freedom, a freedom that is utterly abstract and intangible, perhaps even incomprehensible. There is no destination signified in the ad. We are just going to "go." This ambiguity is not a problem, however; indeed, it is absolutely essential in order for the object to possess the kind of symbolic power it expresses.

Market symbols are like all symbols in this respect, whose dynamic is best illustrated, perhaps, by the religious symbol. As Tillich explains, our relation to the religious symbol (a relation he uses the term "faith" to label) is a relation of "ultimate concern," in which the subject is required to orient themselves to the symbol as a centering feature of their personality or psyche in order to actualize its promise of ultimate fulfillment.[8] It is the promise that draws us, and in both the religious and the marketing symbol, it is always necessary for such a promise to be formulated in ambiguous terms. Its power derives, in part, from that ambiguity, a kind of emptiness ready to be filled by the needs, desires, or available elements in the meeting of consumer and consumer object. It can be figured in concrete terms, but only if the concrete is understood symbolically. One cannot really desire a particular car or beer or athletic shoe *as* a centering and meaning orienting power in one's life unless one understands those products to promise something ultimate, which must be necessarily abstract and vague: personal "salvation," the means for achieving a more fully idealized self, or, in equally idealized terms, achieving "true happiness."

THE SELF AS BRAND

There is a reason that car ads aren't very different from one another, and the same is true of much marketing. The reason is that what is being "sold" is not directly the product on display, although that product (whether or not on display) is certainly the thing the marketing wants you to buy. Since the advent of brand marketing, at least, what is sold is an emotional attachment to symbols. Branding continues to be a dominant concept and practice in marketing.[9] The term itself derives from the practice of burning symbols onto cattle to mark particular ownership. The American Marketing Association offers the following definition: "A brand is a *customer experience represented* by a collection of images and ideas; often, it refers to a symbol such as a name, logo, slogan, and design scheme. Brand recognition and other reactions *are created by the accumulation of experiences* with the specific product or service, both directly relating to its use, and through the influence of advertising, design, and media commentary." The definition also notes, most significantly, that brands often include explicit symbols that are "developed to represent implicit *values, ideas, and even personality.*"[10]

Douglas Atkins, a brand marketer and author of *The Culting of Brands*, explains the recent development of branding in marketing in an episode of *Frontline* written and produced by the media theorist Douglas Rushkoff, entitled *The Persuaders*:

> There was a time when brands and brand symbols were marks of identification for the producer to say: "This is my product. You can rely on its consistency, the same quality time and time again." Nowadays, producers of brands realize that the consumer needs to say: "No, this is my product, I identify with it. The Apple computer is my computer because it stands for creativity and nonconformism, just like I do," or, "The VW Beetle is my kind of car because it stands for antimaterialism, just like I do." So the ownership of the brand has switched from the producer saying, "This is my product," to the consumer saying, "This is my brand."[11]

The fundamental location of the brand is no longer in the logo or symbol on the hide of the object, as it were, but in the "hearts and minds" of consumers who view the external marks of a product or corporation as representing ideas or values or qualities they understand themselves *to be*.

Speaking as an industry executive responsible for brand management, he explains the changes in his responsibilities and in the industry as a whole in these terms:

> When I was a brand manager at Procter & Gamble, my job was basically to make sure the product was good, develop new advertising copy, [and] design the packaging. Now a brand manager has an entirely different kind of responsibility. In fact, they have more responsibility. Their job now is to create and maintain a whole meaning system for people through which they get identity and understanding of the world. Their job now is to be a community leader. Their job now is to create a whole system of symbols in their brand for every single touch point for the brand that reflects back that meaning that kind of engenders that community.[12]

Atkins might be forgiven some degree of hyperbole in describing the significance of his own role and that of brand managers in general, but I would
argue that his description is rather precisely on the mark. The "brand" has
become the primary and usually most valuable "intangible" asset of corporations and products precisely because it is intangible and located primarily
within the consumer as member of a symbolic community. By means of it,
marketers co-opt, *attempt* to manage, and benefit from "whole meaning systems" that serve as the real content of consumer and market discourses. The
brand is a combination of narrative and image into a powerful, even mythical, frame of reference for locating and understanding ourselves.

The point of the brand is to provide the consumer with a symbolic object
around which they can orient their identity, i.e., to be a symbolic object
connected to more concrete symbolic objects within a play of symbols which
includes the consumer as symbol. This symbolic transference of identity is
sharply exemplified in ads from yet another car company. In a television ad
for Jeep, entitled "Reality," produced by GlobalHue, we are shown a series
of images of images, beginning with a close-up of a television remote, and
proceeding through shots of various locations in the home, office, and gym in
which some form of television is present displaying images the marketer
clearly wants us to find both trivial and paradigmatically representative. The
narration accompanying these images tells us, in a somewhat chiding tone:
"Jeep . . . 'Going' reality isn't captured by a hidden camera. It doesn't come
in episodes either. You see, I don't live to live through anyone, ever. So
while everyone waits to see the next best 'this,' or an unbelievable 'that,'
here's the reality: there's no 're-run' when you're living in the now. So,
while you tune in, I'll be somewhere, getting out." The final image is a white
screen onto which fades a Jeep Liberty (again, in silver, and the first time we
see any image of the product being marketed) and the words: "i live. i ride. i
am. Jeep."[13]

Setting aside the obvious but no less interesting irony of fussing at spectators in a spectacle designed to embody the dynamic it is critiquing (not least
by showing us at the end an image of what it hopes we will consider the
"next big this"), the main argument of the ad is that something it calls "life"
is not available through images, can only be trivialized and diminished by
trying to capture it on video, and needs to be "lived," in this particular
instance by driving a car. The promise is the same as that in the Jetta ad, that
driving a Jeep, particularly the not so subtly named Liberty, will free us, in
this case from the demoralizing and diminishing consequences of our age of
spectacle, to be our truer and more real selves, "going" we know not quite
where (except, instrumentally at least, to a nearby Jeep dealership). Indeed,
in the Jeep ad, the magical word "ride," rather than "drive" or some other
more mundane expression of transportation, invokes again the myth of horse-
culture (riding into the sunset) and the magical "freedom" Jeep offers.

A further example should drive the point home, and marketing is mostly comprised of such examples, only slightly differentiated, according to product and the associated product image conventions, such as logos, colors, market slogans, etc. Dr Pepper's "One of a Kind" campaign launched in 2012, following an earlier campaign with the slogan "Be You," which itself followed the culturally resonant "Be a Pepper" campaign of the 1970s featuring the iconic jingle "Wouldn't you like to be a Pepper too?" The evolution in Dr Pepper marketing, mirroring a similar evolution in much brand marketing, transits from an invitation to identify oneself *as* the brand, sublimating oneself to the brand, in a sense, to needing the brand to uniquely identify oneself, becoming who one truly is by means of the brand. The company press release for the new campaign explains that the original commercial ad "is a cheerful celebration of people who are confidently and proudly revealing interesting traits that make them one of a kind."[14]

The first commercial in the campaign opens with a scene in an urban commuter rail station filmed in shades of gray with the camera focusing on one of the anonymous commuters, pausing and standing as if unsure how to proceed, and holding a Dr Pepper can (the only object with color in the scene). A modified version of the iconic Sammy Davis, Jr. song, "I Gotta Be Me," begins playing, and the Dr Pepper commuter significantly takes a sip from the can and begins to tear off his shirt and tie, invoking the common superhero motif, revealing a red T-shirt underneath with the slogan "I'm One of a Kind" (see figure 4.2).[15]

The "hero" of our ad then begins to move through the crowd with new urgency and purposive air, again, with no clear destination signified, and an

Figure 4.2.   "Always One of a Kind," Dr Pepper commercial.

unfocused gaze which may be an attempt to communicate introspection, but just as well communicates the abstract nature of all symbolic "goals." As he passes others, they are inspired to tear off their own outer clothing to reveal different versions of the same red "I am . . ." T-shirts, sporting slogans that identify them by means of stereotypical categories: e.g., "Dreamer" worn by a street musician, "Cougar" worn by a somewhat older woman in tight skirt and high heels, "Fighter" worn by Paralympics athlete John McFall, "Rockstar" worn by a scruffy individual with no other clear identity markings except his willingness to jump out a window and "surf" the crowd, and, with perhaps playful and intentional irony, a red letter on white T-shirt worn by a girl with a knowing smirk walking the opposite way through the growing crowd with the slogan "I am a Rebel," and two T-shirts with the slogan "I am a One and Only" worn by identical twins jumping rope.

The larger irony, of course, is that the "individuals" in the ad are desperately asserting their uniqueness through identifying themselves by means of cartoonish stereotypes, each of which represents a clear and pop-cultural "type" rather than a unique quality or trait. The conceit is that they were hiding these "identities" under a gray conformist mask or shell, and that Dr Pepper somehow inspires them to break free to become who they are (to borrow a phrase from Nietzsche). As the commercial progresses and the original "hero" winds his way through town with somewhat diminished urgency (revealing that a primary goal of consumer symbols is sparking the admiration of others who want to be like you), the crowd through which he moves falls into place behind him. They become a flood of red T-shirts moving like a school of fish or flock of sheep together through the city, celebrating, all together as one, their "uniqueness" while the scene grows more and more homogeneous and monochromatic, the earlier grays now replaced by the branded Dr Pepper red (see figure 4.3).

The commercial comes to a close when the "destination" is finally revealed to be an attractive "heroine," who appears to have been awaiting the arrival, and who is handed the original can of Dr Pepper which presumably started this whole revolution of individuality in that gray, dismal train station left far behind. She takes a quick sip, and then unzips her own jacket, somewhat provocatively, to reveal the final T-shirt with the slogan "I'm a Pepper," nostalgically referencing the original advertising campaign the marketers hope will still emotionally resonate with consumers. The argument of the ad is that we should all allow Dr Pepper to free us to be our true selves, and we are given to understand that Dr Pepper is both instrument and goal within the symbolic framing of self as "Pepper."

As the press release trumpets: "Nearly a thousand Dr Pepper fans take to the streets in the new commercial proudly showing off their own original expressions on T-shirts describing what makes them unique and different from the rest of the crowd"; a crowd, which by the end, of course, is indistin-

Figure 4.3. "Always One of a Kind," Dr Pepper commercial.

guishable in its individual members, except for the slogans on their identical red T-shirts. It is difficult to take such proclamations with a straight face; but the marketing argument is, at an important (and uncritical) level, genuine and serious, and we often participate in its conceits willingly. Spelling out that argument in words, as in the press release, will always fail to do justice to the emotional and symbolic power it actually intends (and appears) to generate. Analyzing the ad, as I have done, shows its argument to be ludicrous and self-contradictory at the rational or logical level, but the ad doesn't seek to work at those levels. It works at a level that connects to and draws from already established symbolic and emotional sign systems, systems we already feel to be important and seductive, to be essential to our being in the world.

"Fans" of Dr Pepper can (and do) visit their website still today and order a custom made red T-shirt with their own slogan, credentialing them, in a sense, as true individuals by purchasing and wearing clothing designed to identify them as merely an interchangeable instance of the mass entity understood to be "Peppers."[16] It is virtually impossible, of course, to think of a slogan to put on such a T-shirt that would actually serve to uniquely identify one. Not only does the consistent and brand identified red of the T-shirt, or the Dr Pepper logo that comes on it, serve to group the wearer, but any slogan one can think of, including the many offered as examples on the webpage, must necessarily speak in terms of category and stereotype. Every "I am . . ." must be followed by some version of ". . . an instance of a type." It is the ideal of individuality, the emotional and symbolic resonance of the abstract promise of uniqueness that draws us and in which we participate as symbol and consumer; but it does so by inviting us to see ourselves as belonging to a group. We are invited to be "one of a kind" by being merely one of a "kind," in Hacking's sense, a general and generic category.

A magazine ad for Curve Perfume makes this structural dynamic and larger marketing meme into the point (see figures 4.4–4.7). The ad, which ran in a number of youth oriented magazines, presents a four page spread in which the first page is blank except for the slogan, "Curve lets you choose your own personal fragrance. Now Curve lets you personalize your own

Figure 4.4. "Make your own ad," Curve perfume.

Figure 4.5. "Make your own ad," Curve perfume.

fragrance ad!" On the following two pages are a series of stickers that the consumer can choose between to create their own individual ad on that blank first page. These stickers include slogans, images of personality types, and bottles of perfumes. The types are extremely (and one supposes intentionally) cartoonish, including such options as "improbably hot nerd girl," "culturally ambiguous girl," and "unrealistically diverse posse." The final page features the "unrealistically diverse posse" saying "yo!" and making gestures which would seem to indicate approval of whatever selection the consumer has made.

Figure 4.6. **"Make your own ad," Curve perfume.**

In many ways, this ad epitomizes the dynamic we have been analyzing, offering the pretense of unique personalization through an extremely limited and cartoonish set of identity options. In the marketplace in general, individual consumers are constantly invited and "allowed" to "choose" how to best and uniquely represent themselves by means of the symbolic objects known as brands, but the options are always pre-packaged and idealized and designed for mass consumption and mass identities, even when they are not so cartoonish. In the Dr Pepper ad, even the "rebel" was only allowed to rebel in the most limited of ways: inverting the colors of the self-same identifying t-shirt, and walking against the tide, but nonetheless within the crowd. She was

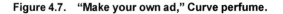

Figure 4.7. "Make your own ad," Curve perfume.

not, most significantly, allowed to altogether opt out of the market choice presented by the ad. The promise these ads offer is of a kind of consumer freedom that unleashes our possibilities and enables our "true selves" to emerge; but the reality is that an extremely attenuated set of market-oriented identity options masked as "choice." We are "free" to choose among them, in a sense, in the same way we are free to choose our elected leaders, by selecting from a very limited set of options pre-determined by market and/or political structures; and in a similar way, we are surrounded by and enmeshed in these political and market dynamics whether we participate directly, by "choosing," or not.

The brand managers recognize and capitalize on this symbolic power. As Simon Pont, author and "brand-builder," says in speaking of social media and "digital" brands in particular: "We cannot get enough of our digital brands *because* they are truly *ours*, because they can make life easier and allow us to be who we are and live the way we prefer. We wear our physical brands like badges, to help define us—but we use our digital brands to help express who we are. They allow us to be, to hold a mirror up to ourselves, and it is clear. We like what we see."[17] This is what such marketing would have us believe—that we need the brand symbols to express, if not also *be*, who we are. Such symbolic being is not a new possibility for us, of course, but depends upon and builds from the larger nature and power of symbols. It is, however, a newly focused effort, drawing upon newly developed technologies, hoping, as Pont also says, to work upon us with refined efficacy: "As ever, [brands] look to seduce and captivate and intoxicate us, to draw us in, draw us close, never let us go."[18]

HYPERREALITY AND MYTH

Such a world of branded identity packages can only be seductive and compelling if we already inhabit a kind of hyperreality in which such options make sense because they are of a symbolic or emotional piece with their larger contexts. "Hyperreality" is a term coined to explain contemporary western cultural conditions in which, as with Holmes' "stereograph" or the *hrönir* of Tlön, simulated reality increasingly takes the place of actual reality. In *Symbolic Exchange and Death*, Baudrillard, borrowing from Borges, introduced the notion of a procession of "simulacra" in western societies which have progressed from the original, to the counterfeit, to the mass-produced mechanical copy, to a simulated, "third order" of simulacrum, a copy that has replaced the original, resulting in a system of references with no referents.[19]

Baudrillard gave the name "hyperreality" to this system, and Umberto Eco, in particular, has developed the notion; but others have thought and written about this phenomenon under different names. In essence, it is similar to Kierkegaard's idea of a complete system of abstractions which takes the place of reality. In his 1929 Gifford Lecture, John Dewey spoke about a growing psychological need for certainty in the western world and how it is often and increasingly achieved by settling for a "feeling" of certainty rather than any actual resolution to a real problem. He asserts that such a feeling is best and usually achieved by withdrawing from the real world and resorting to fantasies.[20] A "feeling of certainty" is, of course, precisely the kind of certainty that is constantly on offer in the various ideologies of our public discourses. For these thinkers, the essential sign exchange value of consumerism, in which brands indicate or embody what kind of person one is, is a contributing factor to the development of the hyperreal condition of our culture.

That hyperreality is marked by what Barthes describes as the emptying out of the interiority of things to the benefit of its exterior signs, the exhaustion of the content by the form.[21] We see this "emptying," a secular or consumerist *kenosis*, in the many consumer products trumpeted as offering the essence (or merely appearance) of a given thing without the substance, as Žižek frequently talks about: from decaffeinated coffee, sugar-free candy, sugar substitutes, non-alcoholic beer, fat-free cream, tobacco-free electronic cigarettes, all the way to phone sex (sex without the sex), the Colin Powell doctrine of war (war without the war), or contemporary multiculturalism (the idealized Other deprived of its Otherness).[22] Žižek uses the term "virtual reality" to label this phenomenon in which we are offered a reality that is *better* for not being real. In this hyperreal virtual reality, the very objects of our world, and we ourselves, are like the images in Holmes' early photographs, skins without the flesh and blood, appearance without substance, and preferable for that very reason, because less "complicated," without problems or potential harms, and because idealized.

We prefer these emptied realities, we prefer *to be* ourselves, if possible, the image, the skin, the hyperreal, in order, in part, to be *more* real than real. Hyperreality is a system not only of reality emptied of its substance, but reality *improved* by being less substantial. I am not speaking merely of such obvious examples as drinks consisting of flavors with no real counterparts (such as Gatorade's top selling "Glacier Freeze" or Powerade's "Green Squall"), "Reality TV," or retouched advertising photos. We are bombarded with hyperrealities that are offered as *better* than real, such as plastic Christmas trees that are touted as looking better and more festive than real trees ever could, national parks of carefully managed "wilderness," flower gardens, zoos, or even the typical suburban lawn (all examples of hyperreal "nature"); museums or "historical" parks (hyperreal "history" or "art"); many professional sports, and not only such obvious examples such as wrestling (hyperreal athletics); and the various hyperreal "destinations" in the western world—such as Las Vegas, Santa Fe, the many "Old West" towns, the various Disneylands, -worlds, -villages, if not also and increasingly actual cities and towns which are busy transforming into idealized "attraction" versions of themselves.

Even the retail store practice of "facing" offers an example, in which the ordering of consumer objects into a kind of endless, identical and idealized version of consumer possibility presents the world of products as hyperrealized choice, a cornucopia of material consumer wealth. Further, there is the hyperreality embodied by product packaging itself, where the outward form of the product *package*, and not the product itself, is intended to be the main attraction. Any search on YouTube for any particular consumer product will likely turn up multiple examples of "unboxing" videos in which the vicarious spectacle of the un-packaging of a given consumer item is presented as the quintessential consumer experience, as if all consumption is really and primarily about the thrill of opening one's presents at Christmas, rather than in the use of whatever the packages contain.

Umberto Eco, in *Travels in Hyperreality*, recounts visiting US museums of various sorts, theme parks and other attractions. His experiences lead him to speak of an "Absolute Fake Industry" in which what is sign aspires to seem reality and what is reality aspires to appear sign. The "authenticity" offered by these hyperrealities is not historical or veridical or rational, but visual. Everything in them *"looks* real, and therefore it is real; in any case the fact that it *seems* real is real," and the thing that seems real is real, even if it represents something that never existed.[23] This, of course, describes advertising. Like the wax museum or Disneyland, what advertising presents is almost always a representation of something we do not have access to in our daily lives, something removed and distant not only in space or time, but ontologically. Like the wax museum tableau of the "Last Supper," advertising offers us idealized versions of things we actually have in the world, like cars or shoes or soft drinks; but the version offered by the "Absolute Fake Industry" claims to be *better* than the original because the original is deficient in some way, is *merely* material, and so corrupted by time or neglect, as in the case of da Vinci's masterpiece in Milan, or impoverished because concrete rather than symbolic. The "Absolute Fake Industry" offers to give us something the merely material instance can never provide, a kind of emotional richness impossible except in hyperrealized form, which is in that sense therefore *more* real, and there is more of it.

As Eco also notes about the theme park or theme restaurant, once you are inside the advertising world, nothing must lead you to suspect that anything outside that world is possible. This is so even if the world constructed is admittedly fantastic. Advertising, like Disneyland, "not only produces illusion, but—in confessing it—stimulates the desire for it."[24] Further, advertising, like Disneyland, "blends the reality of trade with the play of fiction."[25] In advertising, the sets and characters may be "fake," the equivalent of the fake nineteenth-century dry-goods store clerked by a shop girl dressed like a John Ford heroine at Disneyland, as Eco puts it; but the actual stuff present in and referenced by the ads, is quite real at the material level, and the customer participates in the fantasy because of and by means of his own authenticity as a consumer of the material good.

In this sense, brands actively participate in what they, themselves, call a "myth-making" process.[26] The advertising image is supported by what Barthes calls "wholly mythical economics," in that such images present their idealized objects and subjects as at once near and inaccessible, whose consumption is almost, but not quite, fully accomplished simply by looking at them, and this even before we factor in the universal pretense that there are no real economic limits to consumption as depicted by most advertising. A 2008 television ad for Discover Card, called "Brighter" perfectly exemplifies this pretense, presenting a series of images of the idealized consumer world where there is lots of stuff to buy and arguing:

> We are a nation of consumers; and there's nothing wrong with that. The trouble is there's so much cool stuff it's easy to get a little carried away. But what if more credit card companies were like Discover Card? What if they actually helped us spend smarter [voiced over images of the Discover Card website with typical and almost universal budget analysis tools]? Maybe then we could have a better quality of life, *and* be in a better financial position while we are living it [highlighted by an image of a father holding his son up against the sky raising his arms above his head in triumphant gesture]. [27]

A central motif here is the "what if?" invitation to dream a more idealized world offered by most marketing. The primary "what if?" offered here, of course, is not what if more credit card companies could be like Discover Card, since they already are largely indistinguishable in product and service, as is the case with most consumer products. It is "what if?" we could spend without limit and without real consequences, could enjoy a "quality of life" grounded in and requiring material consumer goods and yet remain endlessly able to continue acquiring those goods. This is the primary myth of consumer culture: that there are no real limits, because the "reality" that would impose limits has been effaced by a hyperreality free of them.

For Barthes, myth is a particular kind of speech, which is defined not by the content of its message but the form of its utterance. It is "second-order" speech, in which something which means something on its own is taken as meaning something "more," something which unifies its usual referent with a larger concept or symbolic system. Language, images, even objects can be mythical, since, for Barthes, and as we have already argued, even objects can "say something." Myth is any communication in which the form "outdistances" the meaning. Ads are myths, and the consumer objects in ads are mythical, in this precise sense. Barthes argues: "Myth hides nothing and flaunts nothing: it distorts; myth is neither a lie nor a confession: it is an inflexion." [28] In relation to "first order" speech, myth negotiates the delicate balance between meaning and concept by naturalizing the concept, transforming activity, even consumer activity, into nature, into what we are, what the world is. Myth, in this sense, is metaphysics, and therefore, integrally connected to morality.

The ad is perfectly explicit at one level in terms of its motivations and desires: it wants us to buy things. Myth obscures that level, naturalizes it, transforming motives into reasons. The ad which shows an emotionally charged scene in a brief but mythic narrative about self-actualization is, at one level, clearly intending to "sell us something." But when we consume the ad *as myth*, when we take up and inhabit its mythic narrative, placing ourselves within it, then the elements of the ad marshaled in the service of commercial persuasion are read as personal motivations for participating in the myth by means of the material product. We "know" they just show us these things to sell us a car, or whatever, but we *buy* the car in order to participate in the mythic meaning system so constructed, in order to achieve the fantasy life signified. The ad doesn't "lie" to us, at the level of myth, nor can we take it straightforwardly to tell us something true, at least if we mean by that something like reporting the facts, either about the product or the world. At the level of myth, it *reveals us*, through a mythic world we desire to inhabit.

MYTHIC AND HYPERREAL COMMUNITIES

These mythic narratives are precisely ethical by virtue of being about identity and identity choices. Marketing offers prepackaged identities as consumable products, but it does more than this in the process: it tribalizes.[29] The construction of group identities is the way marketing negotiates the tension between presenting a message that purports to be about each individual consumer to mass anonymous audiences. The invitation to "*be* Jeep" or to be a Pepper is the invitation to realize one's self as a member of a group; and such groups are formed around brand identities or consumer products, not the traditional registers of genealogy or history or embodied identity markers. Brand marketing always works as an at least implicit, and often quite explicit, invitation to join a tribe, if not a cult, to find our primary meaning in the world as members of tribes. It addresses us in mass, but configures that mass as unique and uniquely procreative communities in which we may freely enroll as a means for becoming what we desire and what is desirable. It offers us the possibility to be who we are not as the inevitable result of who we have been, how we have lived, and how we are materially and physically located in the world, but as the result of market choices grounded in consumer objects as symbols embedded in symbolic communities.

In other words, not only does Dr Pepper invite us to be a Pepper too, suggest quite strongly that we naturally really want to be a Pepper too, and imply that not to choose to be a Pepper too is at least odd, perhaps wrong; but such marketing presupposes and constructs a new tribal identity in the process of applying the age-old marketing formula: buy our product and become the special person you always wanted to be and knew you deserved to be, *by identifying* yourself as a member of a particular group. Being a Pepper is a richer possibility for us, matters much more than just a simple choice of beverage preference, *because* we can be a Pepper *too*. These groups are hyperreal and mythic in just the ways analyzed above. They offer themselves as "emptier" versions of the same traditional ways of identifying ourselves into and as communities, yet better, because idealized, and because they are available through "free" choice by means of material consumption.

As silly as it may seem on the surface, the invitation to tribal affiliation is almost always genuine. We may scoff at being Peppers, but there are many, many more tribes from which to choose. We have been invited to be Marlboro men, or Virginia Slims women. We are told constantly that we simply are either PC people or Mac people. In an earlier age in my life, one was Ford or Chevy, Coke or Pepsi, Levi's or Wrangler. Inner city youth have located their group (and sometimes gang) identities through particular brands of shoes or clothing. Even when the choice is not explicitly configured as binary, however, it often amounts to the same. Harley-Davidson, for instance, would like us to believe that there are no real alternatives to their motorcycle/lifestyle brand, or, at least, that all other choices must be lumped together as "other." The choice may not be Harley-Davidson or brand-X, or even H-D or all "foreign" brands taken together, but even if it is H-D or nothing, the choice is presented as exclusive and consuming. Still, such choices are endlessly repeated, and our tribal affiliations are not limited as a whole, just within each prescribed set of competing brand identities.

Often, however, the invitation to a tribe is an invitation to join a more richly configured world of values and possibilities than simple binary brand loyalty. Even the choice between Mac and PC, for instance, as noted by Atkins, is the choice between what those things "stand for" far beyond their relative efficacy in computing power or differing operating structures. The car company Saturn heavily marketed its brand as something more and other than a choice in what car to buy, but rather as a community we may join, complete with nostalgic values and a better way of life. Starbucks would like us to believe that they offer more than coffee, that they offer a "third place" that is not home and not work, and where we can ourselves be something new and other than our normal or usual selves, or like the promise of Dr Pepper, break free from the conventions binding us and become our truer selves.[30]

Almost every ad offers us the chance to join such tribes, to *be* Jeep, or a Pepper, and the opportunity for tribal affiliation has exploded in our culture spreading to even the most ambiguously configured market objects. My own university, for instance, invites everyone to construct together what it means to be a member of "our" tribe through a social media public relations campaign it has run for several years in which everyone is invited to #beSouthwestern.[31] These tribal identities offer themselves as largely shallow but still more or less coherent sets of social, political and moral values, that is, as ideologies. Of course, these are nothing other than the largely shallow but still roughly coherent ideologies we find in our cultures. Being a Pepper is not really being anything new or different; but these new symbolic tribes cut across biological and social realities of all sorts, across historical and physical dynamics. They offer belonging as choice, as free and freeing, while simultaneously binding and grounding. The market inflected choice of belonging is always presented as double: not just who to be as an individual, but *with whom* and to what larger community we may belong.

Who we decide to be, what kind of person, is the central ethical question we entertain, and what we owe each other, both in and out of our "communities," is the central moral question. Marketing restructures both questions, and joins them into a more coherent unit than 2,500 years of moral philosophizing has been able to accomplish. In marketing, the decision of who to be is at the same time the decision of to what group we will choose to belong and with whom, and both are framed as consumer decisions, not social or political, much less historical, decisions. Marketing relies upon the fiction that we are completely free to make such moral/ethical choices *as consumers*. Therefore, in a strange conceptual twist, systems of values and responsibilities, codes of behavior and duty, may be shopped, not as the corollary of market choices—if we want to be a Pepper then we necessarily join all Peppers in community and take on the duties of that community, however minimal or nebulous—but as the point: we want to be a Pepper *because* a Pepper is articulated *as* a set of values and relations to others and the world that we desire or desire to perfect.

The self purchased, the self acquired through market decisions is not one who consumes and feels pleasure through brands, but is constituted *as consuming*, as identified with and through brands. Such a self *is* a Pepper, not another kind of thing that happens to like Dr Peppers. That's the primary significance of Dr Pepper's slogan. It doesn't invite us to purchase cans of corn syrup and feel pleasure in drinking them, or even in attaching ourselves to their brand. It doesn't invite us to take on new loyalties. It invites us to *be* that brand. That is the point of brands. They are not understood by marketers to be lifestyle symbols or commodity loyalties. They are understood to be pre-packaged meaning systems we can choose not so much to inhabit as to become. They are tribes.

We have become so used to this tribal character of marketing, the possibility of locating ourselves along identity spectrums by means of tribal labels of many and various sorts, that when we cannot fully do so (and we almost always cannot fully do so at some point or another), we seem not to know fully who we are, both within and outside (if there is an outside) the marketplace. For instance, I frequently hear people self-label, identifying themselves as conservative or Christian or some other major tribe, but then immediately offering a caveat as to how they don't belong in one particular sector of the tribal ideological spectrum, such as having a "position" on some issue or another that places them outside their understanding of the identity profile of that particular tribe. They might identify as conservative, but have a different view on gay marriage, for instance. This seems to cause some identity dissonance, so much so that labels to account for these identity schisms proliferate. It's as if we cannot entertain the possibility that one might be conservative on some issues but not others. One belongs or doesn't. One either *is* a conservative, or not at all, depending on one's willingness to toe the tribal ideological line on all issues. Therefore we have to come up with a new label, new tribes, to capture these different identities, such as Rhino, or Yellow Dog Democrat, or any one of the many labels we invent to accommodate each degree of difference.

What is particularly remarkable about all of this is that not so long ago, we wouldn't have expected anything other than that people would have a range of attitudes and ideas and questions about each and all of the social or political or economic, or, in short, life issues that they encounter. These things were not so neatly or comprehensively packaged. There have always been tribes, of course, and not all of them grounded in cultural, ethnic, physiological, genealogical or geographical dynamics; but we didn't expect to "belong" to so many all at once. We might have understood ourselves in terms of several groupings, such as nationality, race, profession, or class, but those usually overlapped. We understood ourselves to "belong" to whatever identity groups, grounded in one or more concrete associations, that, for the most part, others or our concrete circumstances decided for and about us, but to hold a range of attitudes and perspectives we did not expect to share with all others in our tribe. There have always been tribal worldviews, habits, and ritual pathways. It is a relatively recent phenomenon, I would suggest, that we encounter every worldview, habit or pathway as a tribe, and that we expect or allow for such pluralistic tribal belonging, each prescribing and conscribing attitudes and perspectives as a set, in the sense that each could be simultaneous yet exclusive identity entities we inhabit. We are newly "legion." And we are newly presented with tribal identity as "choice," particularly consumer choice.

This development highlights the power not so much of marketing in our world, of the symbolic systems of hyperreality and myth, of brand and brand identity, at least at the level of intentional marketing campaign, but of our own needs to understand ourselves, particularly our moral selves, our personal possibilities and communal ties and obligations, *by means of* the material at hand, and in terms of identity and belonging. I am not arguing that marketing has colluded to take over the role of moral teacher, constructing new tribal identities for unpacking and co-opting our moral possibilities; but that our own impulses to socialization, our own need for belonging, in moral terms, to some group, offering and securing some kind of mutual duty, will always inhabit the primary myth and material pathways available to us. In our age of spectacle, those pathways are increasingly and dominantly consumerist, and exhibit the ontology of the mirror, multiplying and disseminating hyperrealities.

As Berger has argued: "Publicity [by which he largely means marketing or advertising] needs to turn to its own advantage the traditional education of the average spectator-buyer."[32] What we have learned, from school and from our cultures more broadly, of history, mythology, science, and poetry can all be used by marketing for the manufacturing of spectacle in its own constructions of the self-same identity dynamics we already inhabit. Therefore necessarily vague historical, poetic, or moral references will always be present in marketing, as Berger argues they were in oil painting. The fact that such references will be imprecise, nebulous, perhaps even ultimately meaningless, is no disadvantage. They need merely recall for us in whatever inchoate way those earlier and larger cultural-lessons, however "half-learnt," as Berger puts it. Doing so mythologizes them, makes history and poetry and morality itself, mythical; but the larger cultural lessons themselves, the traditional education about how the world is and how it works, are present already, often enough already as myth. Increasingly, marketing forms part of that cultural foundation as it also at the same time seeks to colonize it.

Michel de Certeau argues that it is not the makers of the representations, nor whatever their intentions might be, that is decisive, but the users that determine the shape of the symbolic worlds constructed by means of them. What do the users make of the images and ideas they consume? What do they do with them? How do they act with them? Or take them up and interpret them?[33] Henry Jenkins argues against traditional notions of passive media spectatorship, and suggests a growing participatory media culture, in which (not only) content migrates across media platforms, but does so primarily through the agency of media consumers as much as media producers. He argues that producer and consumer are no longer really separate roles, or at least not always inhabited by separate entities. Not all "participants" are equal, of course, with some entities and forces exercising greater power over media content than most consumers, perhaps than any aggregate of consumers. In this collaborative process, however, "each of us constructs our own personal mythology from bits and fragments of information extracted from the media flow and transformed into resources through which we make sense of our everyday lives."[34]

As is the case with brands themselves, which, as we noted above, are fundamentally located in the consumer and constructed by means of the web of experiences, symbols, and myths at work in both consumer and, to the extent any is left, non-consumer discourses and both material and non-material culture, our moral ideas, parsed as questions of what kind of person to be and what obligations and duties we owe to whatever groups to which we belong, are now primarily located within the interchange of symbols and myths in which we willingly participate in consumer culture. They may or may not be much distorted by their mythic formulations in marketing, but they are certainly inflected by them. A primary inflection is accomplished by means of this invitation to see ourselves as brand, as a member of a tribe or tribes that we freely choose, but which, in choosing, allows us to become our true (moral) selves.

In the next part of this book, we will look at how marketing frames and expresses our cultural moral ideas and possibilities, both as market options for personal identity, and as explicit moral lessons utilized to maintain or cement the "meaning systems" attached to market goods as a primary means of selling us things. We will ask the obvious question of what it does to our moral ideas for them to be so co-opted and mirrored back at us by consumer culture; but we will also ask the more interesting question (to me at least) of what our moral ideas must already be, to what symbolic systems must they already belong, such that they *can be so used* by marketing.

NOTES

1. Berger, 153.
2. Paul Tillich, *The Dynamics of Faith* (New York: Harper Collins, 1957), 48.
3. Jorge Luis Borges, *Ficciones* (New York: Grove Press, 1962), 18.
4. Borges, 29.
5. Borges, 30.
6. "Resourcescasestudy: Volkswagen Strikes Back" *Business Strategy Review* 14 (2003): 83.
7. Francis Kelly and Barry Silverstein, *The Breakaway Brand: How Great Brands Stand Out* (New York: McGraw-Hill, 2005), 109.
8. Tillich, chapter 1. For Tillich, the object of faith (and faith is always faith *in something*) is experienced as an ultimate concern that demands ultimate surrender, i.e., subordination of all other concerns to it, and offers ultimate fulfillment as a consequence and reward for that surrender.
9. It is virtually impossible to read anything written by, about, or for marketers that doesn't emphasize the role, centrality or value of the brand. There is vast literature, both within the industry and in critical scholarship about it, that discusses the phenomenon of "branding." A good place to start reading would be the industry journal, *Advertising Age*, or its companion website, *Adage.com*. For critical analysis, a classic text is Naomi Klein's *No Logo* (New York: Picador, 2000). An illuminating "insider" examination of the relation of branding to the phenomenon of cults is provided by Douglas Atkins, *The Culting of Brands: When Customers Become True Believers* (New York: Portfolio, 2004).
10. "Brand and Branding," *AMA Dictionary*, accessed January 4, 2014, ama.org/resources/Pages/Dictionary.aspx?dLetter=B&dLetter=B. Emphasis added.
11. "Interview: Douglas Atkins," *Frontline: The Persuaders*, accessed August 13, 2009, pbs.org/wgbh/pages/frontline/shows/persuaders/interviews/atkin.html.
12. Atkins, "Interview."
13. "Reality," produced by GlobalHue for Jeep, accessed on January, 9, 2010, youtube.com/watch?v=MbcVr1nRDms.
14. "Dr Pepper Celebrates Its Legacy of Originality with the Launch of the New 'Always One of a Kind' Advertising," Dr Pepper—Snapple Group press release, accessed April 18, 2014, news.drpeppersnapplegroup.com/press-release/product-news/dr-pepper-celebrates-its-legacy-originality-launch-new-always-one-kind-ad. As with much marketing currently, social media tie-ins were designed to spawn consumer participation in brand identity, such as a competition, in conjunction with *The Walking Dead* television series, in which consumers submitted their own commercials to YouTube.

15. "Always One of a Kind," commercial for Dr Pepper's "One of a Kind" campaign, accessed on August 27, 2012, youtube.com/watch?v=0Ix7T_XIA28. Subsequent web-only ads, produced by New York ad agency Code and Theory, feature celebrities offered as "one of a kind" models for us to emulate, leveraging the largely marketing produced cultural phenomenon of celebrity idolization to invite consumers to aspire to their own "uniqueness," ironically by potentially becoming an instance of a rather homogenous type.

16. drpepper.com/promotions/aooak/.

17. Simon Pont, *The Better Mousetrap: Brand Invention in a Media Democracy* (London: Kogan Page, 2013), 52.

18. Pont, 3.

19. Jean Baudrillard, *Symbolic Exchange and Death* (New York: Sage, 1993). Baudrillard drew from Jorge Luis Borges' many poetic formulations of such chains of supplementation which efface and replace the originals in both his short stories and essays, e.g., "Tlön, Uqbar, Orbis Tertius," "Pierre Menard: Author of *Don Quixote*," or "The Circular Ruins."

20. John Dewey, *The Quest for Certainty* (New York: Minton, Balch and Company, 1929).

21. Roland Barthes, *Mythologies*, trans. Annette Lavers (New York: Hill and Wang, 1972), 18.

22. See, e.g., Slavoj Žižek, "10/7/01—Reflections on WTC—Third Version," egs.edu/faculty/slavoj-zizek/articles/welcome-to-the-desert-of-the-real/, or "A Cup of Decaf Reality," lacan.com/zizekdecaf.htm.

23. Umberto Eco, *Travels in Hyperreality* (New York: Harcourt, 1986), 16.

24. Eco, 44.

25. Eco, 41.

26. Douglas Holt, *How Brands Become Icons: The Principles of Cultural Branding* (Cambridge, MA: Harvard University Press, 2004).

27. "Brighter," Discover Card ad in "Life Takes Visa" ad campaign from 2008, accessed on August 24, 2008, adforum.com/creative-work/ad/player/12657333/sxi:5834033.

28. Barthes, 129.

29. McLuhan was perhaps the first to use this term to speak of the way in which new kinds of social groups are formed and fostered by new communication technologies. Marketing guru, Seth Godin, uses the term, firmly within marketing discourse conventions, to indicate a group of people connected to one another around a leader and/or an idea; but in that usage, he is also thinking in terms of the kind of cross-boundary groupings I will explain and analyze.

30. Klein, 15–26.

31. twitter.com/search?q=%23besouthwestern, and southwestern.edu/about/besu.

32. Berger, 140.

33. de Certeau, xiii.

34. Jenkins, 3–4.

II

Mass Moralizing

Chapter Five

The Good Life

By telling
stories,   Adver, ing affects morals

"Advertisers are the interpreters of our dreams . . ."[1]

I want to begin looking directly at the moralizing of and within marketing by pulling together some of the threads of theory and argument offered so far and relating them directly to marketing and the narratives marketing offers to and about us and our worlds. Over the course of that discussion, and the analysis that follows in this chapter and the next, I will focus upon television commercial advertising, not because it is the primary vehicle for mass moralizing, but because it was the most successful and still most common form of media marketing, because it is in many ways still the model for other forms of mass marketing, and because it combines moving image and narrative together into brief but (marketers hope) compelling stories about who we are, what we can or desire to be, and what the world is like.[2] Television commercials attempt to entertain us, to instruct us, to inform us, and to seduce us; and they do so by mirroring the world back at us with life-like "realism." They borrow from and interact with every form and genre of media; and both those other forms, and our lived lives, increasingly reflect their structures and themes.

Much, even most, marketing offers to teach or at least remind us about what matters and has value, offers "lessons," however abstract and spectacular, about how to live. All of the ads we have looked at so far illustrate this point, even if the values we are invited to recall are present only vaguely in the images themselves as in the Benetton ads. Such reminders or lessons are clearly the point of "social" marketing campaigns such as those done by Kenneth Cole. They are no less present in the Jetta ad, speaking in magical vocabulary, reassuring us about our assumed belief that what matters in our lives is the ability to break free from the diminishing consequences of our mundane responsibilities, or in the Jeep ad, whose symbolic object (and earnestly chiding voiceover) communicates the important truth that life is diminished by spectacle and our desire for spectacle, and that we should rather desire simply to "live," "ride," "be." Dr Pepper offers a similar mythic value lesson, also invoking the trap of mundane existence configured as conformist and empty, encouraging us, again, to break free to become our vibrant true selves. Curve perfume also reminds us that what matters is being unique, even if that also means being an instance of a rather cartoonish type, helpfully pre-packaged by them, borrowed from our larger cultural cartoons that are themselves generated, in part, in collaboration with consumer culture.

These ads traffic in magical vocabulary, the same magical vocabulary of our consumer and ideological cultures, borrowing from and enhanced by our journalistic and educational narrative practices. They express themselves by means of glittering generalities, invoking but not always (or often) clearly articulating our dreams or their promises. They also traffic in larger magical structures wherein the world is configured as a problem of some sort, organized by some goal to achieve, or some undesirable feature of our lives to be transformed through consumer activity and market objects, which are themselves always symbolic, increasingly abstract and emotionally valenced, however loosely attached to concrete consumer goods. In doing so, marketing presents the world as largely binary, again borrowing from and enhanced by the hero/villain dynamic of our journalistic and educational narratives. In marketing, however, the consumer is often configured as both. One is the villain in need of salvation if one fails to actualize one's idealized potentialities through market activity, the hero if one does. As Berger has argued, marketing speaks *to* the person it configures as lacking something vitally important *about* the person we dream of being realized through some symbolic good, knowing we are both persons, *needing us to be* both persons. We are twinned, in much the same way as image and thing; we are doubled and conflated, the self dreaming and the dreamed self, both located and realized in the consumer object.

Marketing stories are magical because they are myths, carrying the power of myth to transform what appears before us from the consumer world (this pair of shoes, that car, etc), into symbols that represent hyperreal versions of our dreams and desires. Ads within the marketing dynamic of branding, about Jeeps and bottles of perfume or any concrete consumer object, are presented, *prima facie*, as about what matters in life, about how to live or what kind of person it is best to be. They are about "happiness" or "wellbeing" and how to achieve those through the consumer "good," in both the market and moral senses of the term. They are about the good life, always awaiting us on the other side of the market transaction. Therefore, such ads offer moral lessons, whether or not they explicitly reference moral values or ideas. It is a hyperrealized morality, of course, in which values and ideals are themselves transformed, packaged and repackaged, as consumable goods. As with the concrete object offered for purchase in the ad, but transformed by its symbolic reproduction, morality, a real aspect of our real lives, is thus transformed into market options, consumer choices. The "good" we strive to attain is conflated with the goods we can buy. The moral agency we necessarily enact in our lived lives becomes the moral narratives and clichés of those lives reflected back at us as spectacle which then, because they echo across all spectacle, represent themselves to us as moralized products available through consumer choice.

I have argued that marketing is now simply a dominant storyteller across the world, speaking through a quite limited set of motifs and themes, but with a voice that carries significant authority, however vague or ungrounded, simply by virtue of its mode of presentation. Since morality flows from the stories we tell, and the world-structures and patterns of relations those stories construct for us, then how we tell the stories, what comes to count in them as what matters, what has value and why, shapes our moral possibilities. And if the world and its structures become highly abstracted by the stories we tell, if the motivations for actions and the actions themselves become abstractions, then our morality will necessarily also be abstract. I have been arguing that ads frequently, if not always, operate within an ethical register simply because they offer identity packages and so inflect questions and possibilities of what kind of person to be, and within a moral register because they offer communities to which we may belong, inflecting questions of duty and obligation, however abstract or hyperrealized at both the level of community or the level of obligation. The truth-telling narratives offered in marketing construct particular worlds, with particular elements and objects rather than others, carrying particular symbolic meanings rather than others, which present particular ways of being rather than others as possible and desirable. The result is inevitably a particular set of moral possibilities, configured in particular ways, which drown out alternatives by virtue of their narrative dominance.

Marketing narratives and images therefore produce a reality effect, borrowing from and enhancing that produced by media journalism and education, resulting, in part, from the fact that the images we are shown are true-to-life in representational terms, particularly when they are moving images, appearing to unfold the drama of actual living. The spectacle is the mark of the real, enhanced by the proliferation of the same images and motifs across narrative genres, the homogenization of spectacle. Also like journalism and education, the reality effect of marketing is produced, in another manner, by the selection process. In a kind of veridical circularity, what isn't shown cannot be important, because not shown. In an important way, because marketing is practically univocal, because it is even more insular than journalism or education, always talking with and about itself, always trading in the same myths and narrative themes, its selection process confers additional credibility. It is more coherent and self-referential than either journalism or education, whose individual narratives, however familiar because conforming to established patterns and themes, can seem arbitrary and disjointed.

This authority of "reality" in marketing is further enhanced by the ontological conflation that has occurred in the age of the image. If we take ourselves, and in some senses the world around us, to *be* (in the intransitive sense) primarily in a visual mode, then what matters, what has value will necessarily be spectacle of some sort, something made to be seen by ourselves and others, something valuable only in being seen. The stories we tell the most, and strike us as most important, then, will be about the outward form, the external markings of value(s). These stories will be sensationalized and dramatized, carrying the outward signs of action and promise. We have come to expect our truth-telling stories to display these features, and so the features themselves serve as a mark of truth-telling, or at least as a dynamic that blurs the boundaries of truth-telling across narrative genres.

All of this is further complicated by the fact that marketing narratives tell a very limited range of stories. Most marketing myths are collapsible into each other. Since the stories they tell are located along an extremely attenuated spectrum of human being, and since the identity packages and hyperrealized dream worlds we are offered are thoroughly moralized, our moral choices are located along the same attenuated spectrum of human being. In marketing, these moral/ethical products are presented as something we lack, but can gain, merely by participating in the marketplace and making smart consumer choices. Just as with the promise of a sparkling clean kitchen or a more exciting and appealing self, morality is offered to us not as a necessary and deeply contingent aspect of living our lives, but, through the representation of values and moral sentiments as the point of almost all products we can actually buy, as the thing *we are indeed buying* when we buy products like soft drinks or cars. Morality is represented as something just out of our current reach but attainable by joining the right tribe by means of buying the right stuff.

As Sut Jhally has so clearly expressed, what we really should be asking about is:

> . . . the *cultural* role of advertising, not its marketing role. Culture is the place and space where a society tells stories about itself, where values are articulated and expressed, where notions of good and evil, of morality and immorality, are defined. In our culture it is the stories of advertising that dominate the spaces that mediate this function. If human beings are essentially a storytelling species, then to study advertising is to examine the central storytelling mechanisms of our society. The correct question to ask from this perspective, is not whether particular ads sell the products they are hawking, but what are the

consistent stories that advertising spins as a whole about what is important in the world, about how to behave, about what is good or bad. Indeed, it is to ask what values does advertising consistently push.[3]

This is the question I want to ask in the remainder of this book. Jhally calls attention to how marketing, since the 1920s, has explicitly sought to link products to the real social desires of people: "No wonder then that advertising is so attractive to us, so powerful, so seductive. What it offers us are images of the real sources of human happiness—family life, romance and love, sexuality and pleasure, friendship and sociability, leisure and relaxation, independence and control of life. That is why advertising is so powerful, that is what is real about it." I want to look closely at how our conceptions of the "good" and the "good life" are inflected by the particular formulations of those human dynamics and sources of "human happiness" in marketing. What advertising displays for the consuming public is the spectacle of great dramas, of Suffering, Defeat, Success, Achievement, and most importantly, Acquisition and Wealth, all reduced, more or less, to a pure moral concept: justice—understood as the giving and receiving of what is due—configured in market terms of payment and exchange. In the resulting economized notion of justice, not just consumers, but everyone "gets what they pay for," and, I might suggest, in some sense pay for what they get.

STUFF MAKES LIFE BETTER

So, what are the consistent stories told through advertising about what matters? A central message in almost all marketing, of course, is that consumer products improve one's life. Marketing constructions of personal possibility, like our notions of the good more generally, are thoroughly teleological, driven by and toward idealized goals. The larger metaphysics constructed by such narratives presents life itself as a series of quandaries, of problems that need to be solved or potencies needing to be actualized, all accomplished through market activity. In a culture in which morality itself is frequently presented in quandary terms, as a series of social "issues" or problems begging for a solution, all marketing intersects with morality in this way, perhaps even emerging as a more palatable formulation. If our ideas of morality are attenuated to the model of moral scandal frequently offered in journalism, to what gets explicitly labeled as moral concerns or problems in our public discourse as filtered through mass media—poverty, questions as to the value of life (frequently configured within the narrow confines of death penalty or abortion debates), sexual morality, and questions of integrity (usually glorified in the breach)—then the values which serve as the commodities of marketing may seem to constitute some other kind of and more attractive category of morality or life. In a world in which many have become so ideologically polarized around such a limited number of narrowly construed moral issues, the opportunity offered by marketing to more fully actualize our moral selves, whether or not explicitly so configured, through the consumer process of acquiring material goods, can be quite attractive.

This message is frequently framed in terms that present the consumer object as able to solve problems, or even of enabling a crucial and desirable transformation, and, not infrequently, within explicitly moral registers. Let us look at some specific examples; but I'm sure the reader can call to mind an almost limitless number of ads that offer a consumer object as the solution to "whatever ails you," as the snake-oil salesman's pitch always suggests. A 2002 commercial for Acura, for instance, opens with a picture of an apparently affluent and attractive couple driving their silver car along winding roads near the ocean at night under a full moon. The voiceover explains: "Behind them is a snippy maitre d' and a wilted Caesar," accompanied by shots illustrating this claim in an upscale restaurant. "In front of them is a family drama, playing itself out," is narrated over comical shots of a dog and cat breaking furnishings as they fight. "But right now . . . life is perfect, thanks to a full moon, a powerful engine, and the Autobahn-tested suspension of the Acura RL." While we are told this, we are shown shots of the moon, the woman relaxing luxuriously in her seat, and the car winding further along the road.[4]

A recent commercial for KFC opens with a view of a family in a living room with two teen children, one listening to music through headphones and another engrossed in her smartphone.[5] The mom begins talking excitedly to the camera: "Check it out everybody! Our kids are out of their rooms!" The father adds: "We can actually see their faces!" Mom, gesturing toward son: "Oh my God! He's . . . taller than I remember." There is a cut clearly intended to mimic the kind of rough editing usually found in amateur videos and the mom continues, answering the unspoken question about what has brought about this family miracle: " . . . because we've got the KFC Favorites Bucket." Father: "Everybody gets what they want." Mom: "*We* love this new extra crispy boneless." Both: "Yummmm." Father, wryly acknowledging that KFC can't fix every dysfunctional family dynamic: "Now they still don't talk to us. If somebody's battery runs out, then, you know, maybe we can actually carry on a conversation." Mom, getting back to the real point: "Ten pieces, any recipe, $12.99!" Then, in apparent reference to the fact that the KFC Favorites Bucket lets everyone "have what they want," the mom adds: "And you know what I want? All of us being together." Father, emotionally: "Awww." Mom: "Awww." The kids are shown looking at the parents for the first time, clearly uncomfortable with this expression of sentiment. Father, gesturing toward kids: "They don't care . . ." Mom: "No." Father: ". . . but I care." The end of the commercial invites the viewer to tweet "#HowDoYouKFC?"

There was a series of Jimmy Johns commercials, noted for their use of ethnic (and at least in one case blatantly racist) stereotypes, running in 2008 which depicted various people in various dilemmas—needing to impress a boss in a presentation, coming home from work to an out-of-control family, a car breaking down in a run-down urban setting with what appear to be stereotypical Latino gang members close by, etc.—in which the solution involves the main character remembering to call Jimmy Johns and asking for "help." The delivery person immediately arrives, and all is immediately well. These ads are intentionally facetious, at the very least, presenting the idealized solution to all problems through consumer activity in severely cartoonish terms, but the central message of salvation is not in the least discounted by its express satirical treatment.

One such commercial intended for a Latino audience features a father returning home from work to find his house a disaster zone, with the mother tied to a chair, both her and the house a shambles. The father immediately calls Jimmy Johns, and yells "Ayúdame [Help me]!" into the phone. Immediately the delivery person arrives and the father turns back to the house, with the bag in his hand, to find it the idealized model of the suburban home and family, everyone sitting around the dining table in their best clothes waiting for dinner, as was, we are to suppose, his dream upon initially entering his house. While the problem is solved as if magically, the real argument of the commercial is a subtle inversion of the typical parental bribe: "be good and you'll get a treat later." In this case, people are both bad and good in order to get what they want, and the consumer product is presented as not only able to help one be one's best self, but as the reason to be one's best self, i.e., in order to get more goods.

Another particularly illuminating example from Target during the 2009 holiday season opens with the typical living room Christmas scene of a family in pajamas opening presents.[6] The mom is un-wrapping a large screen TV and exclaims, "Wow!" The dad grimaces and echoes with an undertone of displeasure, "Wow?" Mom: "Thanks, Santa!" Dad, in a stage whisper: "Thought we weren't going to spend too much." Mom, defensively: "But these gifts are from Santa." Dad, exasperated: "I guess Santa forgot we're in a recession." The tension becomes quite palpable and the little girl stops coloring to look at the developing argument. Mom, with a forced cheerfulness: "Well . . . maybe Santa was a little thriftier than you think, hmmm?" Dad, disengaging and unhappy, "Well . . . .maybe Santa . . ." Mom, cutting him off, but still with a forced smile trying to maintain the festive spirit: "Maybe Santa doesn't need any help doing Santa's job." There is a moment of pointedly awkward silence as the camera focuses on the mom's face, and the song lyrics, "chestnuts roasting on an open fire," begin playing. The words "Great Electronics" appear large and mid-screen, followed by, "At

Surprisingly Great Prices" below, and the Target logo over a wrapping paper background fades in.

These commercials all clearly exemplify the consumer product as solution dynamic. While the cartoonish (and at times offensive) Jimmy Johns commercials do very little other than present their product as the solution to any problem whatsoever, the other ads do a great deal more, while doing the same. In such ads we are presented with "problems" that arise from the normal practices of human life, issues of "family life, romance and love, sexuality and pleasure, friendship and sociability, leisure and relaxation, independence and control of life." The "problems" presented are not invented by the ads in order for their products to "solve" them. They are the problems of our daily lives, the "family dramas" with which we are intimately familiar, but which can only be represented in the most simplistic and stereotypical forms in such commercials for rather obvious reasons. In the first place, in thirty seconds, no commercial or ad can unpack the structural dynamics or relational histories that go into a family argument or generational estrangement any more than the typical news story can unpack the larger structural dynamics of a given crime or scandal. Both can only gesture, through the broadest caricatures, at the larger dynamics it hopes we will already recognize, if not fully understand.

BECAUSE STUFF IS *MORE* THAN JUST STUFF

It is not really a question of whether we will believe that a sandwich delivered with stunning rapidity can save us from the threat of street violence, or that a car may provide a peaceful refuge from the petty annoyances of daily life, although we are much more likely to swallow the latter than the former. The fact that the problems themselves are borrowed from our lived lives, yet cartooned, influences the way we see those aspects of our lives. We not only recognize the cartoon versions from our lived experiences, but increasingly come to recognize our lived experiences through the lens of the cartooned versions. The reality of the latter is borrowed from the reality of the former and the two are conflated. If nothing else, through the massive repetition of this formula, we are encouraged to view life itself beyond the marketplace as consisting of "problems" to be solved, whether by consumer goods or our own activity. Once we think in these terms, our ideas about what matters (the problems we face) and what has value (whatever can help us resolve these problems) take on a particular cast that cannot help but influence how we think about morality or the "good" in general.

Such a conflation is why Coca-Cola (and many other companies as well) can dedicate parts of its website to "Coca-Cola Stories," on which the company proclaims that: "Coca-Cola touches the lives of millions of people each and every day. From special occasions to exceptional moments in everyday life, Coca-Cola is there. The brand has become a special part of people's lives."[7] The page invites customers to tell Coca-Cola stories themselves, in their own words about their own experiences, and offers a range of story categories within which to tell them: Romance, Military, Reminders of Family, Special Family Times, Childhood Memories, Times with Friends, A Memory of Home, etc. The stories themselves, deeply tinged with nostalgia for a Norman Rockwell version of American life and values clearly signaled by the artwork on the website, offer formulations that fully conform to marketing versions of the value of Coke. They speak of the pleasures associated with drinking Coke or of nostalgic memories of Coke experiences, even fond memories of particular Coke advertising; but they also speak of moral lessons learned with or through Coke, of thriftiness, the importance of family, of being a good neighbor or a Good Samaritan, of self-sacrifice.

In most of the stories, Coke is advanced as a symbol or even vehicle of these things and even more, a symbol of universal understanding and peace, and even love. Several people write about the buying or giving of a Coke as proof of another's love. Another enthusiastically exclaims, "To me, Coke is love and family!" None of these, as far as I know, were written by advertisers. They are the "stories" sent in by regular people, expressing the value of Coke in their lives, willingly (or heedlessly) adopting the cartoon marketing conventions we have been analyzing as their own sense of the world and themselves.

It is because we have come to see our own life dynamics in terms represented by the flood of ads all mirroring, in caricature, those dynamics back at us at a frequency far surpassing our own direct experiences of them, that commercials can go beyond presenting their products as merely the solution to our "problems," but as the necessary and sufficient vehicles for those life dynamics and transformations. This can happen in oblique ways, as in the 2009 commercial for Jif peanut butter featuring the child actress, Anna Clark.[8] The commercial starts with a shot of an impressive tree house, in front of which is posed a father with tool belt affectionately holding his little girl's shoulders. The voiceover, in the father's voice, starts with: "You know what? This looks just like the tree house I built with my dad," reminding us of the value of family traditions. We then see shots of them working on the house together, and the father says, "Okay, time to go work on the roof." The daughter looks as if she gets an idea and says, excitedly, "Dad, I'll be right back," and runs off screen. A female commercial narrator then voices over shots of the little girl making a sandwich: "It's more than just that great peanut taste. Choosing Jif is a simple way to show someone how much you care." We then watch the little girl walking to the tree house with the sandwich on a plate extended in her arms toward her father. He asks, with touching sentiment in his voice, "You made that for me?" The little girl answers, "Well, you're making this for me!"

Here, Jif peanut butter is not a solution to a problem. It is the "simple" and appropriate symbol of caring, of familial love, a way of giving back to those who have given us so much. The ridiculousness of this claim in no way derails its serious pretentions. We are to believe (and it is probable that no small number of us in fact do believe) that Jif is *more* than peanut butter, more even than a hyperreal symbol for caring and love, but a necessary, or at least deeply appropriate, vehicle for expressing that love, most usually from parent to child, but in this ad, mirrored back from child to parent. Choosy moms choose Jif because it is positioned as instrumental in expressing their love; and if Dad has a somewhat more tangible and impressive way of expressing his, a child cannot do better than to return that love through a primary vehicle these ads suggest it has been shown to her.

A somewhat more satirical version is offered by the various LivingSocial ads. One such commercial starts with a shot of a burly guy in a long beard in a garage who tells us that, "It started about a year ago. I signed up with LivingSocial.com and bought my first deal," which appears to have been a session driving go-karts. We then see him, more trim both hygienically and sartorially, practicing golf as he continues, "I used to feel trapped. But with all these deals . . . 50%, 60%, even 70% off . . . I feel free!" These words narrate a rapid series of shots of him getting shaved, doing yoga, eating cupcakes, and attending a puppet play, at which he cries. We then see him getting a facial, a body wax, and excitedly admiring a pair of red high-heeled shoes, while he says, "The warm rays . . . making me blossom." The last shot is of someone in a red dress and those same heels walking up to a hotel bar, where we eventually see it is him in drag. He faces the camera and tells us, "LivingSocial changed my life. It could change yours too."[9]

Like the Jimmy Johns commercials, this version is an intentionally parodic formulation of the idea that products or services can transform one's life for the better, in this case, offering the familiar promise of freeing us to be our more true selves. But satirical or not, the commercial illustrates the claim almost always genuinely offered, and in no way discounted by its formulation in this ad, that we *need* some consumer good to enable us to break free from the social and personal conventions that "trap" us and prevent us from becoming who we are. We cannot do this by ourselves through our own independent agency; the consumer product is essential to this transformation. It enables it. Its commercial may be tongue-in-cheek, but LivingSocial offers "Change My Life Coaching" on its websites, provided in two 50-minute sessions and aimed at helping the consumer learn how to use LivingSocial to plan and accomplish whatever life transformations they desire. Indeed, one of the primary categories of "deals" they offer is called "LifeMakeovers."

A more serious, certainly more pretentious, and more cinematically impressive version of this message is offered by a commercial for Lancôme, featuring Julia Roberts. [10] In this ad, a new fragrance is presented not so much as necessary to a transformation, but rather as largely interchangeable with it. The commercial opens with a blurry shot of people in shadows and dark clothing but lit with glittery reflections from crystal chandeliers. Glittering words appear on the screen and are narrated: "In a world full of dictates and conventions, could there be another way?" The commercial cuts to a shot of Paris at night, with the roads surrounding the Eiffel Tower lit by means of pulsating spots of light from moving traffic as if themselves a kind of necklace of crystals.

We then move to a scene at some society event where everyone is in black tuxedo or gown under numerous crystal chandeliers in an atmosphere of the most exclusive and fantastical luxury. Into this scene Julia Roberts walks, wearing a glittering white gown and moving through the crowd eliciting some attention from her clearly non-conformist attire (and, of course, from the fact that she is Julia Roberts). She moves steadily until, with significant symbolism, she walks up to a wall completely covered in mirror and views the room behind her. As she does so, thin crystal lines become apparent to her and to the viewer, stretching from above out of camera framing to the wrists of every person in the room (see figure 5.1).

Of course, the self mirrored is the self as seen by an "other." In this commercial, it is the self as "othered" that is configured as bound by social conventions. We can be our true selves when we are ourselves *for* ourselves, not *for* others as spectacle or mirrored, even though we are *always* for others, at least in consumer terms, since we are always *for* ourselves by being other to ourselves as object of spectacle and envy, as is Julia in this scene. This

Figure 5.1. "It's a Beautiful Life," Lancôme commercial.

notion melds seamlessly with the offer of all marketing to be ourselves *for* ourselves by means of giving consumer goods *to ourselves*, such as, in this case, an expensive bottle of perfume. As Julia turns to look at the room directly with an increasingly disturbed look on her face, we see the lines working like marionette strings, controlling the actions of everyone. The music playing in the background to this point switches to lyrics for the first time, a male voice singing, "I wish I could be . . . perfectly free . . ." Julia looks back into the mirror and sees that she, too, is bound by these ethereal strings. She looks at herself, closes her eyes and smiles, as if making a wish or a decision, and wipes the strings from her arm, shattering them. Almost everyone in the room notices this transformational act, looking at her with keen interest as she walks back through the crowd with new purpose and ascends a glass staircase (to nowhere) opening onto the cityscape with the light of dawn just edging above the skyline. At the top of the stairs, she turns, of course, to be admired, and offers us the famous Julia Roberts smile, the dawn breaking over her shoulder bathing her in light, while the words "Life is Beautiful" appear on the screen and are narrated in French.

The final scene shows us a crystal bottle of perfume, spinning in place to shatter the crystal bonds encircling it, with the words "La Vie est Belle" overwritten and a narrator informing us that "Life is Beautiful" is the new fragrance from Lancôme. In this ad the world is configured as both fantasy and nightmare, although with a decidedly softened aspect of horror. We are invited both to envy and pity the inaccessible dream selves presented as enslaved to convention by crystal bonds of light. Our savior is a celebrity, the paradigm of the fantasy self as envied spectacle, who, according to the mythology of celebrity, is already uniquely herself, and so already wearing angelic white in a world of black, and also harboring resources for more fully breaking free in a way we mere mortals do not. She is our avatar, showing us the way to freedom. There *is* "another way"! It is not so much facilitated as simply embodied by both Julia Roberts as minor divinity and the bottle of perfume that is in a very important sense interchangeable with her.

STUFF TRANSFORMS LIFE

A most explicit example of product as essential to transformation is provided by a 2008 McDonald's commercial.[11] It begins with a shot of a father putting on a coat and saying, "Let's go." We then see a boy who says, "Dad, can I talk to you about something?" As they walk down a city street, the father asks, "What's up?" and the boy replies, "Well, you know I'm not little anymore, dad." The father responds, somewhat patronizingly, "Yeah, I can see that." The son argues, "I mean, I can ride a two-wheeler now. What I'm trying to say is . . . Dad . . . am I too big for a happy meal?" The father stops, turns to face his son, and looks like something momentous has just happened. The commercial cuts to a scene at the counter of a McDonald's where the father says, "A Big Mac for me . . . and a . . ." and then looks down at his son expectantly. The boy looks further down the counter where we see another little boy receiving his Happy Meal and looking inside (probably to recall for us the times when such a bag would contain a toy). The son considers for a moment, the father looks at him again, with anticipation for the big decision. The son looks confidently at the server and says, ". . . one for me too." The dad reacts approvingly, nods, and emphasizes to the server, "Two Big Macs," who responds in a tone of collusion and pleasure, "Two Big Macs." We see the ad slogan and jingle "Did somebody say McDonald's?" and the final, intentionally playful shot is of the boy with the Big Mac in his hands in front of his face close to the camera making it look very large, with him looking around it and saying, "Hey, Dad . . . how do you start this thing?"

In this commercial, McDonald's does not present itself or its food as a solution to a problem, nor even as a vehicle for enabling transformation. It offers itself as integral to that transformation, as constituting it in a rather direct sense. Riding a two-wheeler may signify growth, but the commercial clearly represents the movement from Happy Meal to Big Mac as the significant rite of passage out of childhood. In the commercial we are not told that such a central transformation in our lives may happen in a McDonald's, but that it *must* happen in a McDonald's, that the transition to Big Mac simply is that transformation in significant part. Here, "child" and "adult" and even "parent" and "son" take on new, yet the same, meanings, transforming our views about ourselves and the world while invoking and upholding them. It doesn't overturn our perspectives and ideas; it merely asks us to stretch them to include, and then subsume them under, this key symbolic consumer structure. It doesn't ask us to rethink what we mean or understand about leaving childhood behind with all that signifies in our lives and social relations; it asks us to think those things the same, but as essentially requiring McDonald's to achieve.

In a similar way, recent Subaru ads argue that the Subaru brand and their cars do not merely symbolize or express "love," but that they somehow are a kind of love. One 2010 commercial shows a father talking through the passenger window to a very young girl in the driver's seat putting on her seatbelt, giving her advice about how to drive, what to look out for, and what not to do.[12] The girl says in an exasperated tone, "Da-ad!" and we then see that the daughter is actually in her late teens, and understand that the little girl we first saw is simply how the father "sees" his daughter. As she drives off, the father voices over the scene, "We knew this day would come. That's why we bought a Subaru." On the screen, the single word, "Love" appears, and then the Subaru logo and name.

Another ad, from 2011, shows a white Subaru pulling into a car wrecking yard with cars piled high all around.[13] The car stops near another white Subaru, identical except significantly damaged. The man driving gets out, approaches the wrecked car and seems to reflect on the trauma of the accident, surveying all the damage. He retrieves what appears to be a Day-Timer from the back, stands back to look at the car one last time, while the camera focuses through the driver window upon the gear shift lever. He opens the door and unscrews the gear knob, looks at it, and puts it in his pocket while walking back to his car. What is apparently intended to be his own voice narrates over the shot of him driving away, "A Subaru saved my life . . . I will never forget that." The word "Love" appears again, and this time a commercial narrator says, "Love. It's what makes a Subaru a Subaru."

In these commercials (and more generally in many others like them), Subaru is configured as more than symbolizing the attachment one feels for one's family, or, indeed, one's own life. The message of these ads is that Subaru somehow "loves" us as directly as we love those we care about, and so we can trust Subaru (as car and brand and personified emotion fully conflated) to take care of us and the ones we love. Subaru *is* "love," and "love" is what makes a Subaru what it is. It is difficult to know what to make of such a claim, but the mere fact that it can be offered with a straight face, that we do not immediately reject such a claim as making no sense whatsoever, as merely a kind of marketing gibberish, suggests that the ideas such ads borrow and repurpose, ideas about love and family and sacrifice and giving, have already been hyperrealized to the point where attaching them to something like a car can appear reasonable and even appropriate, can be entertained as meaningful in some way, even if we can't quite clearly articulate how when pressed.

The "truth" of these ads cannot be measured in the potential of a product to fulfill their promises about the "good" and the "good life" offered. No product can fulfill the sorts of promises usually offered in most contemporary brand marketing. Nor can it be measured in material terms, such that the truth of the extravagantly beautiful burger in a McDonald's ad can be assumed to hold some material correspondence with the burger we buy and eat. While all such ads borrow their elements—material, emotional, conceptual and moral—from the dynamics of our lived lives, their truth can only be measured in the relation of the ads' narrative worlds to the narrative worlds of our fantasies. The truth of an ad is the truth of our desires. Advertising executive Jerry Goodis puts it this way: "Advertising doesn't mirror how people are acting but how they are dreaming."[14] Berger insists that: "The gap between what publicity [marketing] actually offers and the future it promises, corresponds with the gap between what the spectator-buyer feels himself to be and what he would like to be. The two gaps become one; and instead of the single gap being bridged by action or lived experience, it is filled with glamorous day-dreams."[15]

When a McDonald's ad shows a dad and a young daughter bonding in the drive-through lane, all smiles and excitement, it is claiming that eating at McDonald's with one's child is a way of giving to the child, perhaps repaying the child for neglect, a way to foster warm family relationships. We do not measure this claim against any *real* world configuration of these dynamics, no matter how much the ad borrows from them; we measure it against our desires for this to be true, for it to be possible. The marketing assumption is that believing enough in the possibility that having a cheap burger in a McDonald's playland will constitute good parenting, wanting enough for that to be so, can make it so. No amount of believing can make the cheap hamburger a nutritious meal; so McDonald's shies away from claims of that sort. It makes carefully calculated claims that can be measured not against some testable quantity of the material world, but only against our fantasies.

When ads interact with and seek to shape our moral and ethical ideas as a means for selling products, the question arises quite sharply about what constitutes the distinction between the narrative world of the ad and the *real* world portrayed in or by it, between any idea of "good" personally generated or borrowed from our larger moral cultures and consumer "goods." Any such distinctions break down rapidly in marketing when branding as a marketing strategy aimed at constructing and maintaining meaning systems interacts with and subsumes non-market meaning systems, such that the boundaries between market and non-market are at least blurred, if not erased. What is the *real* portrayed in a McDonald's ad? The items on the menu? The emotions or sentiments communicated by the actors and symbolized by the graphics and music? The dynamics of caring or the significance of shared family moments that are the *actual* things being sold by being tied to the product? Any or all or none of these things?

If morality is in important part, both in our popular conceptions and in our theorizing, about the good, about what we should aim for, about what will foster well-being, or at least bring happiness, then marketing is deeply implicated in our contemporary configurations of those concepts and ideas. In marketing narratives, the world is configured as presenting a series of problems, and personal striving for ends (presented as individualized but increasingly homogenized) primarily assumes the character of searching for solutions to those problems, in order to achieve happiness and realize our best (dream) selves. Well-being is configured as an always just out of reach *telos*—not only goal, but completion or perfection—at least facilitated, if not even essentially realized, through consumer activity and the acquisition of consumer goods.

As Berger argues:

Publicity exerts an enormous influence and is a political phenomenon of great importance. But its offer is as narrow as its references are wide. It recognizes nothing except the power to acquire. All other human faculties or needs are made subsidiary to this power. All hopes are gathered together, made homogeneous, simplified, so that they become the intense yet vague, magical yet repeatable promise offered in every purchase. No other kind of hope or satisfaction or pleasure can any longer be envisaged within the culture of capitalism.[16]

Most marketing configures the good life as a life not only of acquiring stuff, a life enabled to be better, happier, more exciting and fulfilling and even meaningful by having things, but as *lived* through and by means of the market goods we are offered. The good life is not merely enhanced by consumption, but is configured *as* consumption. The good life is the life of consumption, not because consumption makes us happy, or is presented as doing so because it addresses our desires and needs; but because consumer goods are the "good," are at least complicit in the most important life dynamics, if not comprising them in large part. In the next chapter, we will look at how marketing narratives configure the "good" and the "good life" in explicitly moral terms, borrowing from, reshaping, and repurposing our moral ideas which are then offered back to us as consumer good and the point of consumption.

NOTES

1. E. B. White, "Truth in Advertising," *The New Yorker*, July 11, 1936.
2. In addition, I will note sources for viewing the commercials, wherever possible, so that the reader can review them to map my analysis or perform their own. It is easier to do so for television commercials than most other forms of mass media marketing.
3. Sut Jhally, "Advertising at the Edge of the Apocalypse," accessed January 28, 2007, sutjhally.com/articles/advertisingattheed.
4. A similar ad from the same campaign may be viewed here: adland.tv/commercials/acura-rsx-life-perfect-2002-030-usa.
5. "Favorites Bucket Family Time," KFC commercial, accessed February 27, 2014, ispot.tv/ad/7fbK/kfc-favorites-bucket-family-time.
6. "Target: Santa's Job," Target commercial, accessed January 6, 2010, youtube.com/watch?v=GwcMuHsvvYY.
7. "Coca-Cola Stories," accessed January 18, 2001, and again March 30, 2014, coca-colacompany.com/stories/coca-cola-stories.
8. "Anna Clark—Jif Peanut Butter," Jif commercial, accessed June 5, 2012, youtube.com/watch?v=S3UeS8RJqNk.
9. "LivingSocial: It'll Change Your Life," LivingSocial.com commercial, accessed on February 9, 2011, dailymotion.com/video/xoaw8s_adzone-living-social-it-ll-change-your-life_shortfilms.
10. "It's a Beautiful Life," Lancôme commercial, accessed on December 13, 2013, ispot.tv/ad/7L1q/lancome-la-vie-est-belle-featuring-julia-roberts.
11. "Am I Too Old for a Happy Meal?" McDonald's commercial, accessed April 2, 2008, no longer available.

12. "Father-Daughter," Subaru commercial, accessed November 8, 2011, youtube.com/watch?v=6F3-InOdMP4.

13. "Keepsake," Subaru commercial, accessed November 8, 2011, streetfire.net/video/keepsakesubaru-commercial_748699.htm.

14. Joyce Nelson, "As the Brain Tunes Out, the TV Admen Tune In," *Globe and Mail*, April 16, 1983.

15. Berger, 148.

16. Berger, 153.

Chapter Six

Morality for Sale

"You can tell the ideals of a nation by its advertisements."[1]

Much recent marketing explicitly inhabits the role of teacher or sage, relying, it would seem, on our agreement with the sentiments or "wisdom" offered by them to cement an emotional relationship with the brand rather than making the explicit promise to "solve" some "problem" for us. Many ads do this with intentional humor, since a movement toward self-parody by satirizing the typical marketing promises has gained significant traction with consumers it would seem. Marketers understand that we are jaded and recognize the barker when we see him; so marketing often offers self-effacing humor, a kind of Seinfeldian winking at the viewer signaling that they know that we know that they are putting us on. If they can no longer convince us of their claims, they can at least entertain us with them.

Examples of such an approach include the recent and popular AT&T commercials featuring a man in a suit asking young children which is better, "More or less?" or "Bigger or smaller?" with the tagline: "It's not complicated." Another humorous version of this motif is offered by DirecTV commercials with the punch line "Don't Have a Grandson with a Dog Collar," or "Don't Wake up in a Roadside Ditch," which feature a parodied cause-and-effect string of catastrophes in people's lives triggered by the frustration experienced from problems with cable television. There are many ads, though, that seek in apparent seriousness to connect with us emotionally and directly, offering visual and narrative reminders of what matters to us, to instruct us about what is most important in life.

One such ad, for Carter's clothes, offers a series of delightful vignettes of parenthood, accompanied by the requisite mellow acoustic music, beginning with shots of a newborn infant coming home and ranging through the usual stereotypical and myth-resonant images of crib and mobile, blowing bubbles by the backyard inflatable pool, eating from a highchair, birthday parties, marking growth on the kitchen door jamb, chasing lightning bugs at dusk, and walking to the school bus together.[2] A young girl's voice narrates over these images: "I was born on a cold September Sunday. When you brought me home, it was a whole new world. That first night was a 'doozy,' but you got the hang of it, and so did I. And together we grew, and grew, and grew. Some days were fussy, but others were all smiles. And even now, many moons later, when you hold my hand, I hold it right back. Because the day I became yours, you became mine." On screen the following words appear: "When a child is born," and, after a short interval, "so is a mom." The little girl then concludes: "From the first night home, to the first day of school, and every first in between, count on Carter's."

This commercial appears to have achieved an emotional resonance with consumers judging from the amount of social network buzz generated by it.[3] A Cheerios commercial, sometimes mentioned in the same social media buzz, and offering a message similar to the Subaru or Jif commercials, elevating Cheerios to a symbol, if not even vehicle, for "love," also goes right for the heartstrings.[4] A mom and little boy are shown eating a bowl of breakfast cereal together and the little boy asks, "Mom, did Nana ever give you Cheerios when you were a little kid?" The mom responds, "Yeah, she did." The boy asks, "Were Cheerios the same back then?" The mom responds, in an indulgent tone clearly indicating that she's performing her motherly duty of patiently answering her child's meaningless questions, "Cheerios has pretty much been the same forever." The boy looks contemplative for a moment, then says, "So . . . .when we have Cheerios, it's kind of like we're having breakfast with Nana." The mom (and, the marketers hope, the audience) tears up at this point, and she nods and says, "Yeah." She kisses the boy on the head and says again, "Yeah." Then the Cheerios branded yellow appears on the screen with the single word: "Love" with a single cheerio for a period, and we hear the mom whisper in the background, "You're so sweet." Here, the fact that Cheerios, at least in one form, has resisted the marketing impulse to offer a "newer," "bigger," "better" version of itself, is presented as elevating its value (we can "count" on it, as we can on Carter's), and the commercial further suggests that its constancy enables it to serve as a connection to those we love no longer with us. Even in the face of death, Cheerios maintains the bond of love.

This idea of sentimental connection via material object was not invented, of course, by the brand marketers at General Mills or Subaru. The notion of a keepsake is as old as emotional bonds themselves, in all likelihood. Almost any material object can serve as symbol or reminder of or connection to those whom we love and who may be absent in some way. What these commercials argue is that such sentimental connections are not only more readily and easily available through, *but are made particularly possible by* the constancy and ubiquity of a consumer good. Cheerios, in this case, is not primarily for eating, or, at least, if it is, that does not exhaust its symbolic and emotional significance. Because of its longevity and constancy, both as product and as a feature of our consumer lives, it possesses a status far beyond its material existence as loops of (purportedly) toasted oats. It is among life's common but important "little things" that matter because they make life better. However, this commercial and those discussed above which offer their products as essential to living our lives well all seek to work upon us at a level far beyond that instrumental message. Such ads primarily call upon and colonize our sense of connection and loss, of love and family ties, to remind us that caring and being cared for is what is most important in life. Whether or not Cheerios or Subaru or Jif is instrumental in expressing or even instantiating love, they remind us that love is what matters, is the most important thing, is what life is all about.

Marketing, at some level, always presents its products as instrumental to our happiness or well-being. It is not so much a question as to why we would buy them otherwise as it is a question of why money would be spent marketing them otherwise. If some consumer good is *actually* necessary for us, clearly essential to our lives, we will buy it. No marketing will be necessary. Marketing seeks to present a particular brand of consumer good as more instrumental than another, or as instrumental in a way we may not recognize or acknowledge without their assistance. The development in marketing most significant for our inquiry is this new mode of offering the message of instrumentality couched in terms of narrative reminders about what matters, that aims to connect directly with us emotionally and morally, expressing or mirroring the values the marketers assume we hold and hold dear. In the process, however, those values are, if not entirely transformed, at least stretched, to include new consumer and material registers. "Family" signifies all the things it has always signified, but it signifies them in slightly different, more caricatured form, and includes material elements we may not have regularly associated with the core ideas and emotions attached to the concept: fried chicken, cars, breakfast cereals.

LIFE LESSONS

A good example of this new dynamic are the various Rice Krispies commercials shot in black and white *cinema vérité* style.[5] One such commercial features a dad in robe and three of his young daughters coming downstairs to eat some breakfast cereal. Echoing the famous Rice Krispies motto "Snap, Crackle, and Pop," the father asks what sound the strawberry included in the cereal makes. The girls, giggling, offer various absurd, nonsensical sounds, which the father encourages or repeats. After we are allowed to simply enjoy this family scene for a bit, a narrator tells us: "Sometimes the best way to get 'em talking is just to speak their language. Rice Krispies with real strawberries. Childhood is calling."

A similar commercial by Wal-Mart shows a family van with car-topper pulling out from a Wal-Mart parking lot to "hit the road" for a family vacation.[6] A family of six is shown looking out the windows or perusing maps as they travel through typical vacation country of forests and hills or coasts. We see tourist attractions, hotels and hotel swimming pools, and finally the beaches of Florida, where the family romps through the dunes or swims in the ocean. All along catchy acoustic guitar music, apparently written for the ad, plays in the background with the repetitive lyrics, "Gotta get away, get away, get away . . . ." The commercial is shot in the slightly yellow and red saturated colors that recall early 8mm home movies or Kodachrome film. All of these elements seem designed to trigger nostalgia in people who were children themselves in the seventies. Along the way, we see the kids eating snacks from a plastic bag with the Wal-Mart brand, and we see the van pass a Wal-Mart tractor trailer on the highway; but the outward cues to the brand are minimal. We are invited to just enjoy the spectacle of the family vacation in all its nostalgic glory for more than 50 seconds before the screen fades to a single color frame (a turquoise only found in Kodachrome prints) with the words, "Wal-Mart saves the average family $2500 per year." These words are then replaced with the question, "What will you do with your savings?" Finally, Kodachrome turquoise fades into the regular Wal-Mart branded blue and the marketing theme for these ads appears in the words: "Wal-Mart. Save money. Live better."

A central feature of these commercials is manufactured nostalgia, borrowing from elements of our lived pasts or merely from our hyperrealized cultural myths. Marketing weaves its way into those fantasies by constantly referring to its own past formulations in nostalgic terms. Our idealized past selves are integrated with idealized past marketing motifs such that the recollection of the latter constitutes or at least invokes the former. It is a closed system, in which the mirroring of past mirrorings is meant to call to mind our own idealized pasts in rich emotional tones. Having been inundated with such marketing for over half a century now, each of us can be relied upon to have already formed emotional and mythic associations with commercial jingles or catch-phrases. These have become common elements in our culture, much to the delight of marketers, and most of us recognize them, even if we are too young to recall their actual employment as marketing. But it is not enough to simply recall these elements, to rehearse them straightforwardly. They gain mythic power by being integrated into the larger myths of our culture, myths of family dynamics and relationships, myths about how to live and live well, and what matters in the good life.

In these ads, we are not primarily intended to directly connect a given consumer product with the ability to realize our mythic dream selves (although it is certainly fine with the marketers if we do so), as if Cheerios or Rice Krispies or Jif or Subaru, but no other consumer products, are directly instrumental in expressing love or family caring. We are invited to inhabit a narrative world in which key human dynamics are depicted, in cartoon but nonetheless often emotionally powerful terms, as integrally involving particular consumer products. It is enough if those powerful myths we already inhabit about what it means to be a family or demonstrate our caring are invoked richly enough by the brief narratives of the commercials in a way wherein the particular consumer product finds a space, a little corner of our psyche, where it can live and grow, however tenuous its connection. The emotions are not generated by those narrative worlds, of course, and even less by the material goods busily situating themselves in those worlds and our myths, but merely called forth for and from us through already established resonances, and hopefully ghosted upon the brand, if not also the object.

Wal-Mart may save us money, which may indeed allow us to afford some things in our lives otherwise not possible (setting aside the clearly moral and significant question about what costs to others such savings entail). But it is the way they explicitly suggest we spend that savings (while cutely pretending to be open-ended about it in the final question)—invoking a mythic ideal of the family vacation, where we (finally!) get to spend "quality" time together in a car and hotel rooms on our way to some hyperreal destination (if not destiny)—that comprises the central feature the marketers rely upon to arrest our attention and insinuate themselves into our dreams. Wal-Mart is not primarily teaching us economics, here; it is teaching us values, or at least situating itself as able to remind us which values already do or should matter to us. These commercials present their brand identities as at least as wise as or even, perhaps, wiser than us about moral and life values, able to recall for us our hopes and dreams, and perhaps call us to our better angels.

Wal-Mart's primary competitor, Target, offers a series of commercials explicitly coaching us in this way. One such video opens with the Target logo itself unfolding as if it were a pop-up book or greeting card, to show an idealized world in which live characters encounter a plethora of consumer options, such as a whole "tree" of flat screen TVs which eventually collapses into just a few, and then only one, while a narrator tells us: "In a world of countless little choices, among mountains of megapixels and a gaggle of gigabytes, shouldn't you spend less time sifting through the nonsense, and go straight to the happy ending?"[7] The final shot is the idealized world zoomed out to reveal the caption "simply what matters" framing the lower part of the image, which then folds itself back into the Target logo. The explicit argument is the somewhat surprising, and perhaps commercially risky, claim that

Target actually presents the consumer with *less* "choice," *less* consumer "freedom," that its advantage is that it offers *fewer* consumer options. The primary argument, however, is the moral lesson that "simple" is better. In a knowing tone, the narrator invites us to recognize, with Target's help, that too much stuff, and too many choices, is a problem (which Target handily solves), a recognition grounded in an underlying truth we all know, or should: that our lives will be better, happier and both more free and care-free, if we avoid needless complication.

One among many clear and telling examples of this kind of life-lesson coaching is an artistic Louis Vuitton video, with stunning visuals and haunting music, which offers to teach us one true meaning of life.[8] Launched in 2008 as part of its "Core Values" marketing campaign, the video features a collage of images with no discernible central theme or clear indication of the consumer good being marketed. Over these images a series of statements and questions are projected: "What is a journey? . . . A journey is not a trip . . . It's not a vacation . . . It's a process . . . A discovery . . . It's a process . . . of self discovery . . . A journey brings us face to face . . . with ourselves . . . A journey shows us not only the world, . . . but how we fit in . . . Does the person create the journey . . . or does the journey create the person? . . . The journey is life itself . . . Where will life take you?" The final shot is simply the words "Louis Vuitton," almost as if source citation for the wisdom offered. In this video, not atypical of luxury marketing in general, the goal is clearly not so much to sell us luggage as it is to suggest to us that a particular luxury luggage maker not only understands us, not only is very much like us in some sense, but understands life, understands the meaning and value of life, and is happy to share that wisdom, or, at the very least, show itself to "belong" with and to the already wise "tribe" of fellow "life-travelers" to which it is speaking, an audience whose own wisdom presumably includes appreciating all that is finer in life.

VALUE LESSONS

Many marketing narratives become direct teachers of morality by offering to teach or at least remind us about "values." It has been a marketing and corporate chestnut for several decades now to articulate "core values." My own university has articulated such a set and has emblazoned them in gold letters on the wall of the student center and on the backs of our business cards. Our set of core values is very little different (only slightly more pedagogically oriented) than those on the wall of the local Mama Fu's restaurant. The concept of "core values" was perhaps given its strongest impetus within the business world by the Jim Collins bestseller, *Built To Last: Successful Habits of Visionary Companies*. My own university's foray into core value articulation was inspired, in part, by this work. The concept has caught fire, spreading almost everywhere in our culture.

A Google search for "core values" will quickly return millions of entries, page after page listing the core values of every kind of business or organiza-tion, including schools, churches, government offices and departments, and social groups. Every group, it seems, has a set, including most media outlets. One of first entries you are likely to find in your search is a helpful definition of the term by, of all sources, the National Park Service:

> The core values of an organization are those values we hold which form the foundation on which we perform work and conduct ourselves. We have an entire universe of values, but some of them are so primary, so important to us that through out [sic] the changes in society, government, politics, and technol-ogy they are STILL the core values we will abide by. In an ever-changing world, core values are constant. . . . They are the practices we use (or should be using) every day in everything we do.[9]

You may be forgiven for perhaps not knowing you have "an entire universe" of values, but such a claim, including the admonition that such values simply do, or at least *should* (a tacit admission that we may sometimes fall short of moral perfection), underlie everything we do, is a commonplace in both marketing and non-marketing moral discourse in recent years. The website proceeds to articulate how core values are "essential tenets" that "clarify who we are," "articulate what we stand for," and "guide us in making decisions."

The website for the business journal *Inc.*, famous for its lists of the 500 or 5000 fastest growing companies, offers an article written by Kevin Daum, that asks, "If your company has core values, shouldn't you?"[10] The article offers a 5-step process, including exercises, whereby you, too, can articulate your own set of core values, arguing that you don't really know your own values until you have articulated them in writing and tested them in daily decision-making. Daum urges all of us to use our core values as a way of "keeping true" to ourselves and "staying out of trouble." Brett and Kay McKay, lifestyle bloggers and husband and wife author team of bestselling self-help books on the *Art of Manliness*, offer a page on their popular blog called, "30 Days to a Better Man Day 1: Define Your Core Values."[11] Defin-ing one's core values is the first step because, the authors argue, it is the one thing we can control in our lives and worlds. Doing so will give us "a sense of purpose," give us confidence, keep us from making bad choices, and make our lives simpler. A common feature of this article and many other books and articles about core values, is the apparently arbitrary restriction that we are limited to a set of five.

The very idea that we as individuals or groups, or that brands or corpora-tions or institutions, can "have" core values is a fairly recent phenomenon, speaking in terms of moral or ethical theory. It wasn't until the mid-seventies that developmental psychologist Clare W. Graves pioneered the use of the term "values systems" to talk about the emergence of cultures and understand why we make the choices we do.[12] The notion of a "value"—of a belief or idea, or even material thing or state of affairs—that we hold dear (and thus, as it were, value) as a basis for action is not new, of course. But the idea that we can have a set of these, more or less consistent, and definitely constant, that not only guide us in our actions, ethical or moral or otherwise, but anchor who we are, keep us true to ourselves, and express those "selves" to the outer world has taken on new and widespread cultural capital in the past few decades. It is no longer really a question of whether we *can* have such values, but an expectation that we *must* have them. We are not complete persons without them. We are not able to stand up to life's tidal forces and remain true to ourselves without *something* in which we "believe" to ground and guide us, as NPR's revival of the insipidly inspirational 1950s radio series by Edward R. Murrow, *This I Believe*, coaches us.[13]

We are constantly being preached to about "values," about what we should "believe," what we should "stand for," and marketing has not shied away from the pulpit. Indeed, in a good bit of marketing, it is the "values" that are the thing most ostensibly on offer as the consumer product we are to invited to desire to complete ourselves. It is not inconsequential that we generally think of values as primarily culturally transmitted, as taught, either from parent to child or through social institutions. In our contemporary cultures, marketing narratives have increasingly assumed that role of cultural transmission, not only as teacher of values, but as purveyor of culture more generally. It does not invent the culture it peddles, of course; it merely borrows, cartoons, and repurposes it. Once again, however, the boundaries between culture borrowed and culture purveyed are blurring, with each element, teacher and pupil, market and consumer, mirroring each other until any clear distinctions become increasingly difficult to discern.

An illustrative example is a 2007 Jack in the Box commercial where "Jack," the brand spokesperson with the Styrofoam head, pops in front of a camera filming a young man filling his car at a gas station and says: "Hey oil companies, I don't want to tell you how to run your business, but prices are nuts! And don't give me 'when demand is up, prices go up,' because I've got millions demanding my value menu, and I keep prices low." He then presents his "Big Deal" menu item and its "value price" of just $2.59, saying, ". . . and that's less than a gallon of gas. And that's with premium, not regular." He concludes, "So, here's a tip: If you want to keep customers happy, give them what they want, at prices they can afford." He starts to exit from the camera frame and then stops, saying, "And, oh, one more thing, see you on the golf course."

This commercial offers what it hopes will be a humorously framed highlighting of the economic value of the franchise's "Value" meals, and does so by chiding oil companies in both business and moral terms. The implicit claim is that oil companies, unlike Jack himself, have forgotten their "values," and it is going to hurt both their bottom line, and in some sense, the moral balance of the world at large. Even though Jack is a corporate giant himself (acknowledged with the quip about the golf course), he remains a champion of a "value" that any consumer can understand and appreciate: ensuring consumer "happiness" by giving us what we want. In this commercial, it is difficult, if not impossible, to disentangle the various and numerous meanings of the term "value" being proffered. This is not a problem, however. Indeed, it is incredibly helpful to marketing interests if our own sense of "value" is as thoroughly pluralistic and entangled.

Such a message is not lost on oil companies. Chevron, for instance, has run a series of commercials and launched a website dedicated to enlisting and then defusing our frustration over gas prices, the perceived injustices of "big business," and our concerns about our environment and our own welfare. Oil companies may make a lot of money, but Chevron wants to reassure us that they still share our values. On its website, www.chevron.com/weagree, up for several years now, we are told that we "might be surprised to see how many things we can agree on." The site offers a series of propositions such as "The world needs more than oil," and "Protecting the planet is everyone's job," each with the invitation for us to click on an "I agree" button which will record our "vote" and show us how many others "agree." While the "I agree" button is clearly configured as a "vote," there is no alternative option offered. We are invited to "vote," but as with most propaganda, our "choices" are structured so as to allow only a single outcome for our "free expression." Tabs at the top of the page invite us to explore these issues, and presumably our points of agreement, further.

One commercial running as part of this marketing campaign opens with a split screen reminiscent of the typical television news format presenting arguing experts which shows a working man in a warehouse on one side and an attractive company spokesperson on the other.[14] The man starts with, "Oil companies make huge profits," in a clearly belligerent tone. The spokesperson nods and admits (in what we are undoubtedly supposed to take as refreshing candor), "Last year Chevron made a lot of money." The man leans into the camera and quite pointedly asks, "Where does it go?!" We are then shown one of the "propositions" from the web campaign stating: "Companies should put their profits to good use." The shot returns to the spokesperson full screen, now identified with the word "Emily" (in cursive, to personalize her), who says, "Every penny and more went into bringing energy to the world." We are returned to the split screen to see the now mollified worker explain, in appreciation of that claim, "The economy is tough right now . . . everywhere." The spokesperson begins talking over his last words, further blurring their ideological differences and making them seem to both be speaking to the same point, "We pumped $21,000,000,000 into local econo-mies, into small businesses, communities, equipment, materials." The man, now identified as "Building Contractor" (she gets a name, he gets a label), says, almost in unison with the spokesperson who also says, "That money can make a big difference to a lot of people." The words "We Agree" are stamped in red across the split screen. Argument resolved! Frustration de-fused!

Beyond the clever use of vocabulary ("pumping" money into the econo-my), the blurring of the boundary between benefiting others and themselves with the subtle manipulation of the categories of the recipients of their lar-gesse, and the overall clear purpose of the campaign to defuse negative brand perceptions driven by cultural narratives of price-gouging oil companies, a favorite economic and ideological scapegoat, the commercial offers a telling illustration of cartooned moral outrage channeled into equally cartoonish moral agreement and harmony. The overarching message is that, accounting ledger disparities aside, we are all in this together. And, deep down, we all share the same values and want the same things for ourselves and the world.

Honda Insight offered a 2009 commercial that also made this point quite explicitly along a slightly different register. Using a song by Rabbit called "Together," in which the catchy tune with the refrain "We are all in this together" played over a set of cleverly composed images, we are taught that we are not alone and our differences don't matter as much as we might think.[15] The commercial uses "sleight of hand" cinematography, framing scenes in a parking garage with camera angles that repeatedly present a single person and their Honda Insight but then "reveals" them to be several people. In many of the shots, the people revealed are ethnically diverse from those we originally see. The opening lyrics of the song reinforce this visual message of racial harmony or virtual equality: "Let's all paint the town, red and white, black and brown." At the end, a narrator announces, "The Honda for everyone is here. The Insight—designed and priced for us all." The consumer up-side of sharing the same values is, apparently, being able to have all our needs and desires satisfied by one consumer good, precisely because such goods are able to share our values. We are not just in this together; we are one, in the quite specific sense that we are all the same. Of course, marketing must treat us as if we are all the same, no matter how much it pretends to cater to our individuality. It is just unusual for marketing to be this honest about its reductionism. It can only do so safely by elevating the idea of sameness to the status of moral ideal.

We can find many such examples without straying outside the automotive industry. For instance, Toyota offered a commercial in 2007, featuring beau-tiful images and moving music, in which young and photogenic children representing several ethnicities in picturesque settings (only some of which featured a silver SUV) speak directly to us through the camera lens: "Before you know it, I'll be walking down the aisle. Someday soon, I'll be away at college. Right before your eyes, I will take my kids to the same places you took me. Don't wait."[16] Once that message has sunk in a little, a commercial narrator makes sure we get the point by reminding us, "They grow up fast. Enjoy it while you can." The words "Get the feeling" appear on the screen, followed by the Toyota name, and the final voiceover, "The eight-passenger Sequoia." The explicit message is that a particular SUV from Toyota can help us "seize the moment" by offering enough room to take the whole family, and even their friends, to special and rather mythic places (much like the Wal-Mart commercial), rather than let those precious opportunities slip past irretrievably. The underlying message, as with the commercials above, is an express reminder about what matters, a reminder that we can and do get too busy in our lives and should stop and care for what is most important before it is too late. It offers that wisdom *through* the "mouths of babes," but *from* a car manufacturer.

An even more explicit version of the motif can be found in a more recent commercial by Buick.[17] The commercial shows the typical series of "slice of life" shots with which we should by now be familiar, many of them in this case featuring actual cars. Most of them depict some act or behavior clearly meant to indicate caring, or giving, or simple good deeds, such as the opening scene of a man holding a newspaper over a women to shield her from the rain. A commercial announcer asks us the following questions and offers the following moral advice: "How will the value of your days be measured? What will matter is not what you have, but what you gave. What will matter is not your success, but your significance. What *will* matter is how long you'll be remembered, by whom, and for what. A life of meaning, and purpose . . . and happiness. That's the greatest luxury of all." Once we have absorbed this solemn moral advice, we are then asked, in typical rhetorical fashion, "What if there was a car company that felt the same way? That car company is Buick."

We may, of course, ask what it means to be offered such wisdom from a car company, what it is that particularly equips them to offer it, or even to possess it, what is it that making a car teaches them such that they can in turn teach us? This particular commercial anticipates that question and explains that Buick is growing faster than any other major brand in America by making vehicles of "substance and quality," with "a look and feel that says, 'come as you are.'" So, the answer to our query would appear to be that Buick is wise because Buick is good, better than others at what it does, and this authorizes them to preach to us. The commercial offers the common luxury marketing bromide that seeks to distinguish the "luxury" on offer as distinct from what we are used to, but in this case, not by being a different or better kind of luxury, but by being luxury "the way it should be," that accepts us "as we are." *Our* kind of luxury, it assures us. Buick claims to know the true meaning of luxury, not just what *it is*, but what *it should be*. Such a morally charged luxury is one that makes no demands upon us, and that we "deserve" simply by being who we are, as we are.

Buick is able to speak of luxury in such moral terms because it has just claimed to understand and be happily willing to communicate the meaning of life itself. What is most unusual, though, is its offer of some kind of warrant, some credential, authorizing its claims. Such authority is usually simply assumed, and, apparently, unquestioned by most consumers. The point, of course, of the glittering generalities marshaled as the content of the wisdom offered is precisely to avoid such questioning. The magic words "value," "meaning," "purpose," "significance," and, of course, "happiness" do not need to be analyzed, and certainly not in automotive terms, to secure our "agreement" and approval.

Car companies are not the only marketing narratives situating their brands as able to offer such life or value lessons, of course, and almost all such messages are steeped in magical terms. A particularly interesting example is offered by Domino's Pizza, interesting because it offers its value lesson after a clever critique of typical marketing hype. [18] The commercial shows typical scenes of daily life transformed by getting a pizza with the voiceover: "We *could* tell you that carrying out Domino's on a Monday will bring out the 'weekend' you. That Domino's will make the mundane, magical. Or that Domino's will make a Tuesday feel like Friday. But *that* would be a lie." Setting aside my appreciation for the use of the terms "mundane" and "magical," it is interesting to note the clear admission of the falsity of most marketing claims. It's not as if Domino's has always eschewed such usual claims in scrupulous attention to marketing honesty itself. It offers that admission here, of course, to situate itself as a kind of moral authority. Even if it has itself transgressed, it *knows* right from wrong, and wants you to know it knows. This first part of the commercial, like the Buick commercial above, provides a kind of warrant or credential for the life wisdom that follows.

The commercial switches gears at this point, shifting away from the cartoonish images and music of the first part, to a scene of a family enjoying pizza, yes, but as a way of enjoying each other, all happy together, creating and achieving one of those "special" fantasy family moments idealized in most marketing that addresses the family. We are then told: "The *truth* is that pizza alone won't make your weeknight special. It's what you do with it that will." This wisdom is followed by the rather more commercial advice to carry out a large three-topping Domino's pizza for $7.99 "only Monday through Thursday," and "make the most of your weeknight."

The images are quite telling in this commercial. The idealized family of four, father in business attire, mom wearing the familiar "Father Knows Best" sweater, one of each gender of child, is apparently watching slides projected on a screen in the backyard. We are not shown what they are watching, but it is obviously, even cartoonishly, delightful to them. We are meant to surmise, I believe, that they are watching scenes from some family event or vacation and reliving the moment together. In this commercial, we are expressly counseled to make our lives special by experiencing our lives as spectacle, rather than in some direct activity (with the exception of the activity of consuming the product for sale). The ad could not be more explicit in its adoption of the conventions we have analyzed wherein it is only the dream self (or family) as image, as projection, literal in this case, of our mythic fantasies, that is the goal we should strive to achieve as the means to happiness. The specific wisdom offered in this example may be short and sweet, but its larger framing echoes the dominant message of almost all advertising.

Whether merely gestured toward, as in this case, or made the explicit point, as in the Buick commercial, we are constantly subjected to lessons about "values," about what matters in life, as a way to attach us to brands and sell us things; and the lessons are consistent and perhaps surprisingly narrow in range. There are, apparently, only a relatively few "values" that really matter and about which we need to be reminded, just the ones, it would seem, with which we have strong emotional connections already, like family or "freedom" or individuality, i.e. those values embedded in or triggering our moral sentiments. As is the case in the intersection of marketing and the "good life," "values" are at least reconfigured, stretched and cartooned, if not also significantly altered and deeply inflected, by their use as mythic symbols intended to attach us to brands, by their presentation as wisdom from voices whose only claim to authority are the credentials of the marketplace.

It is easy to dismiss such messages, to argue that no one really takes them seriously, or even pays much attention; but such an argument would miss the point. First, we do take them seriously, precisely to the extent that we take the values being presented, however cartooned, seriously outside their consumer incarnations, which we almost universally do. Family *does* matter to us, as do the other values marketing borrows and mirrors. More importantly, however, the cartoon versions, precisely to the extent that we recognize in them the values that do matter to us, enter into dialogue with those values, borrow emotional resonance and conceptual significance from them, and so color them, mingle with them. They are able to do so *because* the values we hold outside the marketplace are *no less* symbolic and mythical. Yes, family is real and signifies actual biological and social relations we inhabit in the world; but "family" as a "value," the idea or ideal of family, even the emotional power of family, are, in part, grounded in and expressed through mythic symbols constructed with and through our larger cultures. Marketing does not transform these values into myth or symbol. It merely adopts them, already mythical and symbolic, and repurposes them. These commercials work, when they do work, because the values they offer to teach us, however cartoonish, are the *same* values we already hold, in much the *same* form as we already hold them. I will be arguing, in this next section and in the final chapter, that something like this point is true about morality more generally as well.

MORAL LESSONS

Some moralizing marketing narratives go beyond the offer to remind or teach us about life or values to inhabit the role of moral teacher even more definitively. Such marketing presents itself as moral teacher or even guardian, as Bourdieu puts it, of our cultural moral values while at the same time inhabiting the same and more usual marketing role of fostering brand loyalty and selling us things. It is, in part, because those two roles are conflated, that teaching us moral lessons is inextricably tied together with selling us things in these narratives, that morality itself becomes a kind of consumer good, which we "acquire" through market activity rather than habit or practice or self-development, or rather than possess through nature or upbringing.

One form such direct moralizing takes in some marketing involves attaching a brand to a moral ideal that we are assumed to hold, usually, again, in the vague terms of glittering generalities. In such narratives, the brand becomes a kind of moral cheerleader, presenting itself, as does Louis Vuitton in the example above, as sharing our moral values, as belonging, together with us, to a particular and explicitly moral tribe. Such presentations can be general and aimed primarily at generating nebulous warm feelings, or they can target specific moral concerns and invite us to share their sense of righteousness, or insinuate that they share ours. An example of a more general moralizing can be found in the many Coca-Cola multi-cultural ad campaigns, from the "I want to buy the world a coke" campaign of the 1970s to the "We are the world" campaign of the 1980s, to the recent Super Bowl "security cameras" commercial. Coca-Cola marketing has a knack for exciting our feel-good impulses, invoking ideals of multicultural unity and harmony, in ways that seem to resonate strongly in American culture at least. The original "Hilltop" commercial jingle of 1971, "I want to buy the world a Coke," was turned into a full-length song by The Seekers, articulating and popularizing the desire to teach the world to sing together in perfect harmony. The popularity of the commercial jingle not only inspired its translation into mainstream popular music, but ensured its rise to hit status in the US and the UK.

The most recent iteration of this moralistic marketing by Coke is the 2013 Super Bowl commercial featuring footage from security cameras around the world. The version that first aired featured the song "Give a Little Bit," by Supertramp; but a version posted by the corporation on YouTube features a remix of the Jackie DeShannon song, "Put a Little Love in Your Heart."[19]

Both songs, of course, model the longstanding brand message of giving to the world as a means of making it a better place, of, in general terms, "being nice." As with most of their ad campaigns, this one has generated a good deal of positive sentiment in popular culture. TED, the "Ideas Worth Spreading" website, features the ad in their "Ads Worth Spreading" section, which was created "to highlight the ads people want to see and share with their friends."[20] On its own website, Coke tells us that the commercial was intended as a "reminder that acts of kindness and bravery are taking place around us all the time."[21]

The commercial works by means of a conceptual reversal, similar to the Chevron commercial above and drawing from the way most journalism titillates our impulses to moral judgment, in which we are at first invited to think or fear the worst, in the expectation that security cameras will capture and display the worst human behavior (as they are of course designed to do). Those expectations, required by the dynamic of the ad, are quickly upended and we are invited to watch a series of actions that Coke clearly intends to model the "best" of which we are capable. The commercial starts with the caption, "On security cameras around the world . . ." on a field of branded Coke red, then shows us several cameras themselves, before showing the caption, again on red, ". . . we found . . ." The images that follow are repeatedly captioned to play with and then against our expectations. We are shown "People stealing . . ." but what they steal are "kisses." There are "addicts" and "dealers," but they are "music addicts," and "potato chip dealers" giving handouts to those in need. There is fighting and attacks, but the fighting is for fun with umbrellas, and the attacks are "attacks of friendship." We are shown an "honest pickpocket" picking up and returning a wallet. The charade is then dropped, and we are shown images labeled with terms meant simply to arouse admiration and good feelings, like "Love" and "Kindness." The commercial goes on to show us "Friendly Gangs," "Rebels with a Cause," "Peaceful Warriors," and a series of "Heroes," along with just a "Lot of Crazy People," having a lot of fun and being happy. It ends with the invitation: "Let's look at the world a bit differently," followed by an image of a Coca-Cola bottle and the campaign invitation to "Open Happiness."

Even though this commercial speaks in glittering generalities and clearly intends to elicit warm feelings, as does almost all Coke marketing, it does so by calling upon us to expect the worst and then offers itself as moral tutor, teaching us to fight against our expectations to look at the world "differently." It assumes, correctly, that we don't have high expectations for our fellow human beings, that we are trained, by journalism and many other cultural narratives, to be afraid of each other, which is the reason we have so many security cameras in the first place. It then suggests that the problem is not so much bad behavior, but precisely those expectations. If we can just turn that apprehensive frown upside-down, just learn, as Coke clearly has, to see the world as at least "half-full" of kindness and caring and heroism and hope, then we and the world will be the better for it. We need not worry overmuch about social and structural inequalities, conflict and hate, crime and suffering; we just need to look on the bright side of things. We just need to open ourselves to the good in the world, primarily by opening a bottle of Coke. I am clearly being trite in my analysis; but in the ad itself, such trite sentiments are presented seriously, and Coke is presented as essentially enabling the change of perspective that can change the world. We do not have to struggle to make the world better; we can just "open happiness" by buying and drinking a can of colored corn-syrup.

A commercial from Verizon Wireless offers a similar lesson about prejudice it hopes will inspire and resonate with us, at least if we happen to be teenage girls.[22] A series of ethnically diverse young women in various settings speak directly to the camera and inform us, in rather serious tones: "Air has no prejudice. It does not carry the opinions of a man faster than those of a woman. It does not filter out an idea because I'm 16, and not 30." We are told that, "Air is unaware if I'm black, or white," pointedly presented by two girls of opposite skin color to that referenced by the speaker, and further told that it "wouldn't care if it knew." The sermon continues: "So, it stands to reason my ideas will be powerful if they are wise . . . infectious . . . if they are worthy. If my thoughts have flawless delivery, I can lead the army that will follow." The final shot is of a Verizon branded red screen with the words shown and narrated, "Rule the air . . . Verizon," accompanied by a ruletheair.com website address, which merely redirects the searcher to the regular Verizon Wireless smartphone portal.

In this commercial, "air" is a magical solution to the problem of prejudice, yes, but it is also configured as a moral being itself, "not caring" about race and open to what is good or wise or powerful without respect to gender or age. One can see how such a message, however obvious its pandering, may be viewed as potentially appealing to young women, a group often systematically devalued or ignored, at best, outside the allotted cultural and consumer registers of sexuality. In this commercial there is an at least tacit acknowledgement that the effort to make the world better may be a bit of an uphill fight against entrenched cultural patterns of bias and preference, but it can be done, and even led from perhaps an unexpected front, through the moral superiority of a hyperrealized brand product, "air." The reason we would buy Verizon, of course, is that it "owns" more of that "air," or at least makes it more accessible to more people. We can set aside the question as to whether Verizon itself, through its business practices, is as unprejudiced as "air." What is most significant for our analysis is the explicit role of moral teacher inhabited by the brand, as channeled through teenage preachers. Verizon presents itself as unified in "cause" with at least a particular segment of the consumer population, which includes not only young girls, but anyone who "cares" about these "issues;" and also as uniquely situated to aid us in the struggle to improve things.

A series of commercials from Hyundai go a bit further, scolding us rather directly about losing our moral values, and presenting itself as moral champion and model. These commercials were part of Hyundai's 2007 "Think about it" marketing campaign, in which even the campaign slogan blurs the boundary between marketing and moral rhetoric. One ad for the campaign shows a shot of a road at night with the dividing line stripes passing by rather hypnotically, then cuts to the face of the driver and then his view out the windshield at the road.[23] A narrator tells us: "Instant gratification has us in a stranglehold, so much so that we don't want to fix things anymore. Just replace them. Don't like your nose? Get a new one. Don't like your job? Get a new one. Don't like your spouse? Get a new one. Whatever happened to commitment, to standing by our decisions?" While we listen to this reproach, we see images of a man with a ridiculously large nose, a "boss" in an office chair menacingly pointing his finger at us, and a woman in a bridal gown, all superimposed upon the road in front of the car as if conjured by the driver's imagination. The commercial finishes with shots of the driver in the car moving along the road. The shots of the driver always show him contemplative (or perhaps just sleepy), apparently "thinking about it." The final shot is of the words "10 years / 100,000 miles powertrain warranty . . . Think about it."

Here, Hyundai rather directly accuses the audience, or at least some unspecified segment of the population, of having lost sight of a key moral value: commitment. The examples selected by them to illustrate that loss are cartoonish in both category and detail. We don't usually think of commitment in terms of noses or even jobs, primarily, although the commitment of marriage is a category staple, of course. Even should these examples strike us a clearly appropriate cases, however, their incarnation in the ad is severely cartoonish. No one would be happy with the grotesquely large nose shown on the first subject. The "boss" is the typical cartoon image of a petty tyrant. Indeed, it is very interesting that they decided to illustrate the concept of spouse by means of a bride, an absolutely consumer-driven synecdoche of marriage, a hyperrealized symbol of its inception that has little or nothing to do with the actual work or practice, let alone the "commitment" of being married. What could it mean to be "committed" to such cartoons? In such a representation, commitment itself is necessarily cartooned. Still, Hyundai offers itself seriously as a shining counter-example to our rampant fickleness.

The commercial must assume, of course, that we do indeed still value commitment, or why would we care that they do. And while commitment is configured finally in the commercial as the longest warranty in the business, a promise to stand by the consumer who buys Hyundai's product, there is no real distinction made between that distinctly market form of commitment and the broader moral concept. Indeed, they are actively conflated. Jeff Goodby, a principle at the advertising agency responsible for the ad, has said that the point of the ad is to get people "to pay attention to something that's true," which, he admits with self-deprecating humor, is not usually one's job in advertising.[24] The "something that's true" to which we are supposed to attend is the idea that there is something wrong with society generally, a moral illness that has us in a "stranglehold," but that "a different way" is possible, as Lancôme also promises. It is interesting that the particular moral illness adduced in this ad is "instant gratification," something that if it is indeed a problem, has been created in no small part through the widespread growth of consumerism in our cultures. Thus, Hyundai offers to correct, or at least model a correction, to a moral problem it has at least some part in creating.

All of this explicit moral sermonizing still participates fully in the configuration of both the moral and consumer worlds as comprised of problems that require solutions; it is just that these ads present a moral value, attached in some way to a brand, as the solution, instead of, or at least in addition to, the consumer good for sale. In these ads, we are invited to buy that good—a soft drink, phone plan, or car—not because that purchase or the product purchased will directly solve the problem presented, but because the brand itself, through its products, instantiates or fosters a moral rather than merely material and consumer good that can do so. So the product we are invited to "buy," in both an epistemic and consumer sense, is the moral value on display.

As Naomi Klein explains, brands are in the business of selling *themselves*, using the products they make as marketing tools, rather than the marketing as a tool for selling the products. She cites Nike CEO Phil Knight: "For years we thought of ourselves as a production-oriented company, meaning we put all our emphasis on designing and manufacturing the product. But now we understand that the most important thing we do is market the product. We've come around to saying that Nike is a marketing-oriented company, and the product is our most important marketing tool."[25] In these ads, as in the case of Nike athletic shoes, the product is the *symbol* of the "good," in both a material and moral sense; and it is the "good" itself that we are configured as desiring. Clearly, they are not wrong about that. It is a construction in which we participate, if not even primarily originate.

COLONIZING MORAL "ISSUES"

Some marketing moralizes about hot-button moral "issues" head on, representing themselves as occupying the "right" side of some moral "debate." In doing so, they amplify and further entrench our sense that some "issues" are essentially "moral," coloring our sense both of the categories and of the particular issues. Some do so somewhat satirically, but others are quite serious. American marketing seems to be more comfortable offering such lessons with a touch of humor. One clear example, albeit somewhat difficult to coherently parse, is found in the 2008 Skittles Piñata man commercial.[26] The commercial opens onto a scene in what appears to be a teacher's break room, where a "man" who appears to be made of crepe paper like a traditional piñata, enters the room using a crutch, one arm in a cast and sling, and sporting a bandage on his head. Everyone in the room is immediately and obviously uncomfortable. The piñata man approaches another man at one of the tables and slaps a bag of chocolate Skittles on the table top and asks: "Is this what you were looking for? New chocolate flavored Skittles?" The man whom he addresses replies, "I'm *really* sorry." The piñata man continues: "What did you think was going to happen, Stephen? Did you think you were going to hit me with that bat and little chocolaty candies would come pouring out?" The man at the table hesitates, and then quietly says, "yes." The piñata man says "I have to buy my Skittles downstairs," and adds, in a rising tone of indignation, ". . . like everybody else," as he turns to address everyone in the room, who all quickly attempt to appear busy doing something else. The piñata man turns to leave and then stops and yells: "I'm just like everyone else!"

The commercial is absurd, and clearly intended to be. A piñata man, whatever he is, is so very clearly *not* just like everyone else. The commercial lampoons the phenomenon of prejudice, of harmful stereotypes, and the sometimes vicious attacks perpetrated on those who are "othered" by them. It is difficult to believe it intends its moral message to be taken in any way seriously. If not offended, we are, presumably, supposed to be amused by the parody of outrage and righteous indignation; but it cannot work unless it works both ways, and in its wry, if extreme, portrayal of "difference" as something to ignore or disregard, it speaks rather directly to our traditional and familiar moral ideals. No matter how satirical the whole, the individual elements—the tone of indignation, the discomfort and guilt over transgressing moral boundaries, the moral sermonizing itself in a fantasized apotheosis of the oppressed speaking truth to power—are all indistinguishable from their straightforward and familiar counterparts in actual human situations. It is a fascinating commercial because it presents the brand as inhabiting the role of moral teacher without any serious moral intent, and yet it cannot escape that role once invoked, which says something quite interesting about the role itself. Moralizing, even when satirical, necessarily presents a moral lesson; and moral lessons are always serious, even when they are not.

Even PSA marketing in the US can seem a bit uncomfortable with straightforward moralizing. For instance, a commercial produced by Keep California Beautiful, a non-profit organization which, according to its website, is "dedicated to alternative waste management, beautification, community networking and outreach," offers a moral lesson on recycling framed with sardonic humor.[27] The ad offers what could be an outtake from an episode of *The Sopranos*. We are shown an older model Cadillac pulling up to a wharf on the waterfront at night. There are no captions or narration, not even any musical soundtrack. We see two men in the front seat from behind, wearing leather coats, one taking a sip from a water bottle. They pop the trunk, get out and look around, and then move to the trunk to take out a carpet roll or rug obviously wrapped around a human body. They throw it into the water, and as they turn to leave, the man with the water bottle finishes the drink and starts to throw it on the ground. He notices a recycling bin nearby, and instead throws the bottle in it. The following words appear on the screen as the men get back into the car and pull away: "Redeem yourself. Recycle." Again, while clearly intended to be humorous, juxtaposing murder, organized crime, and littering as comparative moral evils, the ad has a serious purpose: to convince us of the moral value of being good stewards of our resources and planet. The moral issue and lesson, *per se*, are, of course, genuine, and it is worth considering how the humorous framing in these ads inflects the serious issues portrayed. However absurd it may seem in this instance as well, we are rather seriously being invited to "redeem" ourselves, to make up for whatever other misdeeds of which we may be guilty by at least being ecologically conscientious. Indeed, that message is rather facilitated by the extreme analogue chosen in the ad: those among us who aren't "mobsters" are presumably closer to redemption through such seemingly small good deeds.

Not all marketing that seeks to colonize moral "issues" is framed with disarming humor presumably intended to soften the sting of the moralizing they present. Many inhabit the practice quite straightforwardly, even earnestly, although it is more common outside the United States. A 2009 commercial for Banco Provencia, airing in Argentina, addresses the "issue" of prejudice again, in this case as a matter of gender heteronormativity.[28] The commercial opens with a view of a small picturesque town (including horse-drawn cart) and an elderly gentleman getting out of a (silver) car and approaching someone who appears, from her clothing, to be a hairdresser or beauty salon owner. She seems surprised to see the gentleman, and addresses him by name: "Mr. Lopez. How strange to see you around here." The elderly man gets right to the point: "I'd like to know, when the bank granted you credit to open the salon, did they ask for your identity card?" She responds that they did. He says, "But the document shows that you are a man." She crosses her arms and says again, "Yes." He says, "And they granted it anyway." She just nods. He continues, "This is the same bank that granted me credit to buy this car. That made me think. And so it encouraged me to come and apologize to you for treating you badly all this time . . . for not knowing how to treat you." The woman seems to be touched by his statement. The man then hands her a carved wooden ballerina, which he invites her to take. She asks, "For me?" He says yes, and then, "I'm sorry," and she thanks him. The man returns to his car and the following words appear on screen: "Your life changes when there is a bank disposed to change." The final shot is a black screen with the Banco Provincia logo, and the words written and narrated: "You have a life. You have a bank."

Setting aside the irony of presenting the overthrow of heteronormative prejudice by means of a gift that thoroughly re-inscribes gender stereotypes (an irony that may have been intentional on the part of the ad agency), the commercial not only directly offers its brand identity as moral teacher, but goes further to suggest that its normal and regular business practices—the straightforward lending of money—can "make us think," leading us to change the way we look at the world, grow more tolerant, like the bank itself, apparently, and even motivate us to act on those transformations to repair the harm we may have caused to others. Banco Provincia can teach us not only how to live better, but how to think about our lives, reflect on their meaning and practice, and motivate us to repair our wrongs, all merely by being nothing more than a bank. The moral value of others can be amply demonstrated by nothing more than the egalitarian treatment of a financial institution in its lending practices. The person we may have considered "bad" is redeemed by getting credit, the same as us. In an important sense, this ad argues that "having a bank" isn't an addition to our "having a life," it is a necessary corollary, essential not merely to our fiscal well-being, but to our moral well-being.

A rather notorious example is the McDonald's ad, aired in France in 2010, which generated a great deal of media discussion by addressing the "issue" of homosexuality.[29] The commercial shows a young man looking at his class picture in a McDonald's restaurant while his dad orders their meal. He receives a call from his lover and tells him that he was thinking about him too and misses him. He sees his father coming and says he has to hang up. The father asks about the class picture, remarks that his son looks just like him when he was a teen, admits he was quite the ladies' man, and speculates that his son could "get all the girls" if it weren't sadly the case that his class is all boys. During the father's soliloquy, the young man shows facial expressions that signal his disinterest in his father's womanizing and bemusement over his father's cluelessness. The screen then fades into the words, "Come as you are."

The explicit marketing proposition is that McDonald's, perhaps like Banco Provincia, is "tolerant" of a range of "lifestyles." There was some media head-scratching over why such a message seemed necessary or appropriate. Nicholas Graham, of *The Huffington Post*, wondered whether French gay people had been feeling unwelcome in McDonald's, for instance. Others have wondered if McDonald's was seeking a new market segment. Such puzzlement misses the point, I believe. As Stéphane Xiberras, president and creative director of BETC Euro RSCG and the person responsible for the ad, explains, the motivation for the ad was to tell little stories about life that happen in what the marketers desired to present as a "neutral space," meaning, presumably, not just a space of tolerance, but a space free from moral judgment altogether.[30] Nathalie Legarlantezec, brand manager for McDonald's in France, says the campaign wanted to reflect society "as it is today." She goes on to explain that they intentionally eschewed presenting the young man's sexual orientation as a "problem," even though McDonald's acknowledges that such a person might still find "difficulties" or "complications" resulting from his or her sexual orientation. She explains that she decided to "tell the story" because she found it beautiful and emotionally intense.

The point is rather directly that the ad bothers us in some way, if only because of the tension portrayed between father and son. Xiberras admits that if society were really fine with homosexuality, then the commercial would have no impact at all. It would be boring, or at least appealing merely on the level of any media depiction of romantic interest. That is clearly not the central dynamic of this ad. It is the father as ignorant of this important facet of his son's life and his son as in some way uncomfortable with his father knowing about it, that the ad clearly presents as a condition of society needing further "work," as Xiberras puts it. And McDonald's is presented as, if not leading us in that work (since that claim would be patently absurd), at least as a place where we can take refuge from it, or from the "complications" of the world outside its "PlayPlace" boundaries.

McDonald's and most of the brand identities busy explicitly or implicitly preaching to us about morality conjure an ideal moral world in which we all live together in tolerance and harmony, free from the troubling and harmful consequences of not only our own worst impulses, but also their own problematic practices (and such misdirection is often precisely the point). There is no more dogmatic or frequent moralistic demand than that we all be morally non-judgmental. But such a demand and such an ideal moral world is not alien to any supposed non-consumer imaginaries. If we balk at accepting the proposition that consumer products can help us realize such a world, we are less reticent to entertain the possibility that the brand identities which manufacture or sell those products "share" our "values," in some way hold the self-same moral ideals and goals. And if we are going to buy stuff anyway, why not buy from those who are like us, from those we can trust and "count on" because they see the world the way we do, feel about it the way we feel, and touchingly remind us about what is most important and meaningful?

What is at work in all of these moralizing narratives is a conflation of what we take, or at least often seem to want to take, to be non-consumerist morality or ethics, non-market values and meanings with their consumerist versions. The conflation works both ways, however. Both now borrow from and inform each other. One is not distorted or manipulated by the other. They have become indistinguishable, if they were ever actually distinct. In borrowing from, and then adopting the role as communicator of supposed pre-consumerist values and moral ideas, those values and ideas have received new contours, new registers, new dimensions or facets; but they have not become new and utterly different things.

This kind of moralizing in marketing is possible because of the new prevalence of brand marketing, the symbolic character of consumer objects, the conflation of material and meaning systems and structures, and the structural and ideological collaboration of what Steven Heyer, COO of Coca-Cola has called the "trinity in brand building—content, and media, and marketing."[31] Because of these dynamics, filtered through the largely homogenous but at the very least mutually reinforcing mass narratives we daily consume, material consumer objects and their associated brand identities are able not merely to stand for values or ideas or emotions, but in an important sense *be* those things, at least symbolically. As Heyer says in his address, "creating value around this bottle [rather than in the content inside it] is the secret formula of Coca-Cola's success. Coca-Cola isn't black water with a little sugar and a lot of fizz anymore than one of your movies is celluloid digital bits and bytes, or one of your songs is a random collection of words and notes. Coca-Cola isn't a drink. It's an idea. Like great movies, like great music. Coca-Cola is a feeling."

Heyer speaks of this kind of marketing of ideas and feelings, of moral "goods" rather than consumer products, not as the generation of intellectual property, but rather of "emotional capital," which he says creates "value for people that lives beyond and extends the immediate moment of consumption" and "enriches people's lives," and which consumers and corporations both can "spend" in leveraging the marketplace or our own happiness. Heyer could not rhapsodize in these terms, however, if it were not the case that ideas and values and our emotions already lend themselves to such uses, to such attachments, if it weren't always already the case that "things" can be ideas or feelings, and so, in some sense, that feelings and ideas are things. Brand marketing didn't invent some new ontological possibility in the world; it merely recognized important structures of moral and broader human dynamics and bends them to its needs.

As I have noted, Berger suggests that consumer choice has supplemented political or social choice, the act of consumption substituting for the democratic act.[32] I want to argue that consumer choice, with its always implicit and often explicit registers of personal identity and community formation, has come to stand for moral choice. The ethical question of who one desires to be, what sort of person one will actualize, the moral question of to which group or community one belongs, and so owes responsibility and obligation, are sublimated by the consumer questions that carry the exact same significance. Whatever else they are, marketing, journalism, even our educational systems are moral systems. They valuate the world and interpret it in morally charged terms. They construct, borrow, fashion and refashion interconnected and relational systems of moral symbols, values, and entities.

I do *not* want to argue that one system of moral values (more to be desired or better in some moral or extra-moral sense) is being replaced by another and more consumerist system of values (of a worse or more shallow sort). I want to argue that our historical and cultural systems of values are being (re)configured *as* consumerist. I think current and dominant marketing discourse practices invite us to inhabit our old familiar world, the world of our traditional cultural narrative frames, attenuated significantly, adopted and adapted, but still recognizable as our values and our meaning systems. The radical change is that it invites us to do so in ways that make of those values and meaning systems commodities, market goods, to be purchased as a way of becoming who we are, as opposed to allowing them to remain non-commercial ways of living and being which, through actualization in our activity, shape who we are in the living (rather than in the consuming).

Is this a change for the worse? I don't know how to address that question without invoking some perhaps impossible moral rubric that would necessarily stand apart from the very system I am analyzing. But I do, obviously, think we are participating in dynamics that are reshaping the way we think and act in the world, and being aware of that change, of those dynamics, is important, if only to keep open the possibility of direct and effective agency on our part. It is fair to ask, and important to be able to ask, whether we want a world in which everything is consumer or consumable product, and in which every choice, even choices about who to be and to whom we owe obligation and responsibility, is a market choice. The final chapters will take up this question more fully.

NOTES

1. Norman Douglas, *South Wind* (London: Martin Secker, 1917), 54.
2. "The Day You Became Mine," Carter's commercial, accessed November 3, 2012, youtube.com/watch?v=Gza-yfENn_4.
3. A Google search will turn up a great deal of conversation about this ad, most of it quite positive. For instance, a blogger who blogs about "Life Sublime," lifesublime.ca/blog/, tells us on her Facebook page, "They got me with this one . . . a commercial!!! Love it!": accessed April 30, 2014, facebook.com/Life.Sublime/posts/163543017121102. Another blogger who writes about the loss of her daughter as a form of therapy, highlights the commercial for her readers: accessed April 30, 2014, bonnielaubian.blogspot.com/2013/04/the-day-i-became-yours-you-became-mine.html. An entry on a website called *The Bump*, about pregnancy, writes: "Has anyone seen the new Carter's commercial? That line sends me over the edge into a land of tears. It's a commercial but such an emotional 30 seconds." This entry started a conversation universally praising the commercial and talking about the emotional power of it: accessed March 30, 2014, forums.thebump.com/discussion/12081600/the-day-i-became-yours-you-became-mine.

4. "Nana," Cheerios commercial, accessed May 1, 2014, youtube.com/watch?v=CSNAdo9Czns#t=17.

5. "Childhood is Calling," Rice Krispies commercial, accessed April 30, 2008, splendad.com/ads/show/3134-Rice-Krispies-Childhood-is-Calling-Speak-Their-Language.

6. "Live Better," Wal-Mart commercial, accessed September 28, 2007, adage.com/article/ad-review/long-awaited-wal-mart-ads-obvious-brilliant/120476.

7. "Simply What Matters," Target commercial, accessed April 13, 2008, video no longer available.

8. "Journey," Louis Vuitton video, accessed April 3, 2008, youtube.com/watch?v=QPzxmIWWep0. This video and a longer version were only available on the website and through related social media. The longer version may be viewed here: youtube.com/watch?v=NQlueM5ETYU. Louis Vuitton first made a television commercial in 2012.

9. "What are Core Values?" National Park Service webpage, accessed on May 2, 2014, nps.gov/training/uc/whcv.htm.

10. Kevin Daum, "Define Your Personal Core Values: 5 Steps," *Inc.*, accessed May 2, 2014, inc.com/kevin-daum/define-your-personal-core-values-5-steps.html.

11. Brett & Kate McKay, "30 Days to a Better Man Day 1: Define Your Core Values," *The Art of Manliness*, accessed on May 2, 2014, artofmanliness.com/2009/05/31/30-days-to-a-better-man-day-1-define-your-core-values.

12. Clare W. Graves, "Levels of Existence: An Open System Theory of Values" *Journal of Humanistic Psychology*, 10 (1970): 131-155. An interesting recent discussion of Graves' ideas in light of "core values" can be found in Said Elias Dawlabani, "The Psychosocial DNA of Capitalism," *Huffington Post*, accessed September 6, 2013, huffingtonpost.com/said-elias-dawlabani/the-psychosocial-dna-of-capitalism_b_3882188.html.

13. See thisibelieve.org

14. "We Agree: Profits Help Create Growth and Jobs," Chevron commercial, accessed on November 11, 2011, youtube.com/watch?v=lEazYJkzjMg.

15. "Together," Honda Insight commercial, accessed on November 18, 2009, youtube.com/watch?v=pEuei5gvtqg. For a discussion of the cinematography, see motion.kodak.com/motion/Products/Customer_Testimonials/Commercials/Sleight-of-Hand_Achieved_In-Camera_for_Honda_Insight_Spots/index.htm.

16. "They Grow up Fast," Toyota Sequoia commercial, viewed on ABC, October 1, 2007.

17. "What Matters," Buick commercial, accessed on August 12, 2011, youtube.com/watch?v=OrviER_pGws.

18. "Powered by Pizza," Domino's Pizza commercial, accessed on November 6, 2013, ispot.tv/ad/71WM/dominos-pizza-powered-by-pizza.

19. "Security Cameras," Coca-Cola commercial, accessed on May 7, 2014, youtube.com/watch?v=DKy4utFUN-k.

20. "Ads Worth Spreading," TED, accessed on May 7, 2014, ted.com/about/programs-initiatives/ads-worth-spreading. The "Security Cameras" commercial is located here: ted.com/initiatives/aws/security_cameras.html.

21. "Coca-Cola Security Cameras: Big Game Commercial 2013," Coca-Cola, accessed on May 7, 2014, coca-colacompany.com/videos/coca-cola-security-cameras-big-game-commercial-2013-yte8m5d6xenwa.

22. "Rule the Air," Verizon Wireless commercial, accessed on August 15, 2010. Rebecca Cullers wrote an article about the commercial, "Ad casts Verizon as cure for Racism, Sexism," on *Adweek*, accessed August 18, 2010, adweek.com/adfreak/ad-casts-verizon-cure-racism-sexism-12343. Due, perhaps, to media critiques, the original ad is frequently marked "private" by websites referencing it, but can be found on YouTube posted, frequently, by consumers who appreciate its messages, such as youtube.com/watch?v=QNSDbkBG_IY.

23. "Hyundai—Commitment," Hyundai commercial, accessed on October 29, 2007, splendad.com/ads/show/1602-Hyundai-Commitment.

24. Stuart Elliott, "A Brand Tries to Invite Thought," *New York Times*, September 7, 2007.

25. Klein, 22.

26. "Piñata," Skittles commercial, accessed June 19, 2011, adweek.com/video/advertising-branding/funniest-commercials-skittles-pi-ata-132704.

27. keepcabeautiful.org/about-us/. The ad, "Mobsters," was produced by BBDO San Francisco, accessed April 4, 2008, adforum.com/agency/9575/creative-work/6696848/mobsters/keep-california-beautiful-keep-california-beautiful.

28. "Transgender Apology," Banco Provincia commercial, uploaded to YouTube by the online financial industry brand publication *The Financial Brand* (thefinancialbrand.com), accessed April 1, 2010, youtube.com/watch?v=Wu7nKR0t5zQ.

29. "Come As You Are," McDonald's commercial, accessed June 1, 2010, huffingtonpost.com/2010/06/01/gay-mcdonalds-ad-in-franc_n_596361.html.

30. Maxime Donzel, "McDonald's dit ne pas cibler les gays avec sa nouvelle publicité," *Yagg.com*, accessed May 8, 2014, yagg.com/2010/05/28/29999.

31. Steven Heyer, "Keynote Remarks: *Advertising Age* Madison + Vine Conference," Beverly Hills Hotel, Beverly Hills, California, Feb. 5, 2003, adage.com/article/news/steve-heyer-s-manifesto-a-age-marketing/36777.

32. Berger, 149.

Chapter Seven

Morality as Consumption

"Philanthropy is about feelings, not facts. It is about icons that move us, not arguments that persuade us."[1]

"Getting involved in something, helping others, improving the fabric of the universe—I believe if you do that, even just a little bit, I think you'll find your life gets better, too."[2]

"The individual who burns with desire for action but does not know what to do is a common type in our society. He wants to act for the sake of justice, peace, progress, but does not know how. If propaganda can show him this "how," it has won the game; action will surely follow."[3]

Perhaps the most interesting intersection with morality in marketing is to be found in "cause" marketing that goes beyond offering moralized identity packages as commodities to portray the act of consumption itself as moral activism. The latter is, of course, made possible by the former. The marketing project of branding—of cultivating deep emotional attachments to the symbolic face of commodities—commodifies those very emotions, blurring the boundary between the private/personal and the market, between personhood and consumer object, with significant impact on both our moral and metaphysical structures. If we see ourselves primarily, or at least frequently, in market terms, as instances of market-derived identities configured through mythic images and narratives whose character is ineluctably spectacular, then our encounter with "others," particularly others in "need," almost always as spectacle presented through the same market-inflected and market dominated communication media, must inhabit the same existential mode. "Others" are market objects too. Our engagement with them is appropriately expected to occur in and through the marketplace.

Žižek calls this way of thinking "cultural capitalism" and locates its in-ception in the late 1960s. In a book and also a RSA lecture delivered in 2009, both entitled *First as Tragedy, Then as Farce*, he develops the idea that charity is integral to the current form of capitalism in the current global economy.[4] He argues that there are new "global citizens" whose primary, almost exclusive, interaction with the world is through business and humani-tarianism, with the result that more and more frequently and broadly the two are brought together as one activity. He cites a number of examples of the way that blending has been practiced in the regular consumer marketplace, such as Starbucks's insistence that when you buy a cup of its coffee, you buy into a larger effort to do something good for the environment through their "Shared Planet Program," or that when you buy a pair of TOMS shoes, you do something good for others in need. Žižek argues that this form of capital-ism offers the consumer the chance to buy redemption (echoing the PSA message from Keep California Beautiful), at the very least from being merely a consumer. The very act of self-interested consumption is at the same time an act of redemption that connects one to the broader world in ways that accomplish "good."

In his lecture and book, Žižek refers to an "old form" of charity, in which a capitalist makes money "in the morning" and then gives part of it back "in the afternoon" through charity, a form in which the activity of the market-place and that of humanitarian or ecological activism were at least more clearly distinct, if not fully separable. However, his analysis offers a narra-tive about charity that already fully participates in the construction of caring as shifted from direct action to those near us in need to "causes" one "sup-ports" with money when one has achieved sufficient material well-being. Such a notion exhibits the same dynamic he is critiquing: humanitarianism envisioned as primarily, if not exclusively, occurring through economic ac-tivity.

The broader phenomenon that Žižek refers to under the rubric of "cultural capitalism" goes by many related names, such as "conscious consumerism," which urges us to be a consumer in the most responsible way, with an emphasis on limiting that role as much as possible.[5] It is also called "con-scientious consumerism," or "ethical consumerism," or even "green" consu-merism. All these "movements" share an emphasis on the social conse-quences of consumption and valorize whatever is organic, recycled, cruelty-free (or free-range), and procured through "fair-trade," preferably locally. There are "ethical" investment strategies and specific financial market prod-ucts which limit their portfolios to companies who have approved social sensitivities. An earlier example of this cultural consumer impulse (before the 1960s) might be the exhortation to buy union-made goods, or even, in a sense, general interest in kosher products.[6]

These movements gathered steam in the US in the 1970s by emphasizing the protection of life in food harvesting practices and caring for the planet we all "share," such as buying tuna captured with methods that protected dolphins.[7] Early activism in these movements frequently took the form of boycotts or protests, but dedicated organizations soon developed. In 1982, *Green America* (originally *Co-op America*), was formed "to harness economic power—the strength of consumers, investors, businesses, and the marketplace—to create a socially just and environmentally sustainable society," thereby expressing the union of economic and social forces and both consumer and social "goods" in the way to which Žižek calls attention.[8] The central assumption of this particular mission statement and these movements in general is that the only forces powerful enough to instigate or institute social change are market forces, or that, at the least, such forces are simply more effective. Well-meaning ideas or intentions, stirring humanitarian or environmental rhetoric, by themselves, are inadequate to properly move us to do the "right" things. This way of thinking accepts as given that we are market-driven and consumer oriented at our core.

The term "green" is so broadly used today (even strictly within the marketplace and not in its broader political formulations) that it is in danger of becoming vapid; and many analysts question both its marketing and environmental effectiveness.[9] Market rhetoric about green marketing promotes the idea of recruiting or enlisting all "stakeholders" in the process of marketing the product, with the result that consumers participate in marketing as ideologically committed parties, promoting the product as a way of promoting moral or social values.[10] "Green" marketing is a clear example of a social concern that has been largely co-opted by marketing and repurposed for increasing sales and fostering brand loyalty. There is even a term for this co-option: greenwashing—the outward adoption of "green" practices, or at least rhetoric, with the primary motivation of increasing profits.[11]

Recent trends have broadened the focus of ethical consumerism beyond the environment to include almost any activity or decision that could be considered to have moral implications, which doesn't exclude much consumer activity. John McMurtry argues that there is no purchasing decision that is not ultimately moral or does not involve moral choice.[12] An early instance of broader ethical concern connected to brand identity, and one that strongly influenced the direction of the ethical consumerism movement as well as corporate business models, was Ben & Jerry's Corporate Social Responsibility (CSR) reports first produced in the 1980s. Ben & Jerry were early adopters of the notion that "business can be a source of progressive change," by "behaving in a socially responsible manner, and dealing with other business parties who . . . behave in the same manner."[13] However one views that possibility for corporate behavior, probably the majority of corporations now have some form of CSR policy or corporate philanthropy which they frequently trumpet on websites and other marketing material.[14] Since bought out by Unilever in 2000, however, Ben & Jerry's CSR has been largely reduced to the typical set of "values" and lists of "issues" they "care about" along with reports on corporate philanthropic activity.[15]

Efforts to put social responsibility and ethics at the heart of a business strategy have generated significant interest and discussion over the past decade or so. A catch-all label for this approach is "doing well by doing good," and operates under the idea that not only is there social pressure from a range of what are often referred to as "stakeholders" to which businesses and brands must be accountable if they wish to be successful in the marketplace, but that putting some kind of "social responsibility" into business strategies just makes good business sense as well. A central and growing moral theme in capitalist culture is that businesses have a responsibility, even obligation, to deliver on social and not merely financial metrics, with the assumption that both are ultimately tied together, as the phrase "doing well by doing good" cleverly expresses, since both terms are interchangeable across moral and economic contexts.[16] If integrated into a business strategy, such efforts are inevitably highlighted in the corollary marketing strategies, as we shall soon see.

Not only has there been a trend toward presenting corporate and brand identities as "caring" about the world, but there has also been corresponding movements to hold those corporations and brands accountable to social "concerns." For instance, in 1989, the popular non-profit magazine *ethical consumer* was founded in the UK, and since 2009 continues as a multi-stakeholder co-operative publishing both in print and on the web with the mission of making "global business more sustainable through consumer pressure."[17] It publishes information on the social and environmental behavior of corporations and brands, including a version of the increasingly popular ratings systems, so prominent in consumer culture recently, that assesses the ethical behavior of companies along nineteen criteria. The webpage that explains that rating system opens with the following heading in bold: "Ethics made easy - a simple way to find the products that reflect your principles."[18] It proclaims: "You are unique, so are your ethics. Everybody has their own unique set of ethics and beliefs, so we've developed cutting-edge website tools which make for the world's most sophisticated and convenient ethical rating system. In just a few simple steps you can personalise our product guides to produce a shopping list that accurately reflects the issues that are most important to you - be that animal testing, climate change, sweatshop labour, GM crops, nuclear power or whatever." "Whatever," indeed.

This particular example highlights quite a few of the dynamics we have been analyzing so far and adds a few more important elements. First, it claims to offer "personalized" tools for analyzing the business practices of the companies with which we're interested in shopping, but that necessarily also locate ourselves and our consumption practices along a pre-packaged morally evaluative spectrum. Thus, it reinforces the idea that moral concern for how we behave in the world is intimately connected to our consumer activity. It reminds and reassures us that we are "unique," which is good (if also somewhat complicating), but nonetheless configures us along an attenuated spectrum of "issues" that are both already reified into concrete moral categories, if not also moral commodities, and that further entrenches those particular categories along with the idea that morality consists of such sets of a few select "issues." It offers us simplicity and ease, noting that they have done the work for us (developing "cutting-edge" analytic tools), since we are presumably quite busy otherwise occupied with more pressing demands, and that participation in their process (through buying and using their magazine) is all that is needed to be the responsible moral people we obviously would like to be, if only it weren't so darned complicated and time-consuming. It is "ethics made easy."

It is also ethics made consumerist. It assures us that not only can its process help us find the products that "reflect our principles," but, more importantly, it assumes without question, and asks us to assume, that products *can reflect* principles, that each thing we buy has at least a symbolic, if not even more concrete, moral character. We are offered help at preparing shopping lists that go beyond identifying our consumer needs to select items that will meet and fulfill our moral needs. Indeed, those are configured as the same. Both it and all the examples we've discussed locate morality and social activism firmly within economic registers. Doing good doesn't just require money; it is *about* spending and buying, whether directly (buying a particular product because its brand identity "cares" about what we care about or promises to make a difference in the world through our consumption) or indirectly (buying as leverage, exerting the only force that can make businesses accountable to our moral priorities). Such consumerist ethics may not even strike us as odd in any way, since charity, as it is most commonly understood, is about giving money to "causes," about helping others, usually at a distance, through economic and consumer activity. Given this economic character, it is not difficult to see how and why efforts to incorporate charity and activism into the more general consumer process would occur, and be expected to have seductive power in our moral consciousness.

MAKING A DIFFERENCE: FEELING GOOD (ABOUT YOURSELF)

People want to make a difference. As much social science research makes clear, we are in some important ways commonly driven by sympathy and an impulse to altruism in our behavior and actions. Those same impulses to "care," however, are also experienced as self-interest, and sometimes the impulses and opportunities for egoism and altruism clash. When presented with the choice between fulfilling some desire and deferring that desire in order to further the interests of others or some larger community, frequently the choice to defer is deferred. As *ethical consumer* recognizes, people at least feel quite busy. Many of us feel that we are stretched thin, over-committed, or at least heavily engaged in daily routines and practices with precious little time to spend specifically aimed at helping others or "making a difference" in the ways typically conjured by that phrase. We also live in an age in which opportunities for spending our time, largely in ways that are self-gratifying, have exploded. Almost all marketing, as is obvious, affirms and feeds these impulses to gratify ourselves. This clash may create cognitive dissonance. We are bombarded with messages urging us to give in to our impulses to make ourselves happy and yet we also feel a moral responsibility, if not even natural impulse, to do something good, to improve ourselves and our communities, or even, in broader terms, our world.

I would argue that this tension is not as sharply drawn as it might at first appear. The impulse to do something good is not so neatly differentiated from the impulse to gratify ourselves, or simply to avoid feeling bad about ourselves. I'm not talking about the case of those occasional individuals whom we believe derive a great deal of pleasure from helping others such that they choose "selfless" activities over many other possibilities for self-gratification. I'm talking about how the impulse to do good is itself an impulse of self-interest, at least according to a range of social science theories.[19] The emotions we feel which prompt us to make a difference or do something good are either gratifying in themselves (sympathy, love, pride, gratitude) or create a discomfort that begs for resolution through some specific act (guilt, pity, shame, disgust, embarrassment, blame). If evolutionary theories or even just much contemporary psychological research about our emotions are at all correct, then it is not really possible to draw a clear line between our impulses to gratify ourselves and our moral impulses to help others or do good.

The impulse to make a difference and the relation of that impulse to our own sense of well-being and impulses for self-gratification is not lost on Madison Avenue. Recently, a particular kind of marketing has spread that offers to resolve any last remaining vestige of this tension. No longer are we to choose between making ourselves happy and doing good. Our lack of time or opportunity is no deterrent. We are told that making a difference *is* what makes us feel good; and we can do good in the world *by* making ourselves happy, through buying things we already want. In this new message, one hears echoes of Chernyshevsky's formulation of rational egoism: "Yes, I will always do what I want. I will never sacrifice anything, not even a whim, for the sake of something I do not desire. What I want, with all my heart, is to make people happy. In this lies my happiness."[20] It is the marriage of egoism and altruism. In this marriage, charity has been further commoditized and fully integrated into straightforward consumer activity. It has become something marketed and sold. Therefore, both it and ourselves as difference-makers, as doing good in the world, are something we can purchase; and that purchase is a "deal," because we get something we like and want in the bargain. We love deals. There is a new kind of cause marketing that invites us to become a new kind of moral being, activist consumers, who, *through our consumption*, make the world better.

I want to look in detail at several examples of this kind of marketing, the TOMS "One for One" campaign and Dove's "Campaign for Real Beauty," in particular. But before turning to those, let's take a look at some other instances of this type of marketing to get a clearer sense of how it works. An illustrative example can be found in a 2008 press release from Trevelino-Keller (the "country's fourth fastest growing PR firm") which announced that a shopping center in Atlanta, The Corner–Virginia Highland, had become the first "Carbon Neutral Zone" in the US, a status it achieved by purchasing "carbon offsets."[21] The press release begins with this contextual introduction: "Climate change is one of the most daunting challenges of the twenty-first century, but the recent growth and popularity of American eco-consciousness has created a new sense of urgency to address this problem. Today the green movement took a significant step forward as the first 'Carbon Neutral Zone' in the United States was announced in Atlanta."

The title "Carbon Neutral Zone" certainly sounds impressive, and although the further discussion (one cannot really call them "details") provided in the press release of the process of procuring "carbon offsets" is somewhat confusing, we are assured by it that this "first-of-its-kind" ecological initiative will "set the standard for American companies looking to adopt sustainable business practices and reduce their carbon footprints," and allow all those participating in and patronizing the "zone" to express their care for the environment together. Should the reader be curious to learn more, though, a little research into the Chicago Climate Exchange and the details of this "zone" will reveal that the retail shops participating did not alter their practices or energy-use patterns in any way, but merely paid money through the Chicago Climate Exchange to other energy users who weren't polluting as much. These other companies also weren't required to alter their energy-use in any way. They were merely already more energy-efficient and leveraged that efficiency as a kind of trading share in a pollution exchange market (that closed at the end of 2010). As a result, these shops were able to present themselves as ecologically conscious and as leading the fight for a more "sustainable" system without doing anything other than spending a little money, thus providing a paradigm for the "activism" envisioned by this kind of marketing. The green movement's "significant step forward" seems, in this case, to have been rather a new kind of walking in place, a new guise for the same old consumer activity.

Sometimes the marriage of consumerism and activism is serendipitous for a particular brand. In early 2010, Procter & Gamble began running commercials for its dish detergent brand, Dawn, which highlighted the fact that it seems to be the soap of choice among non-profit groups that work to repair the damage caused to wildlife from oil spills. It did not originate this environmental connection. Indeed, according to a *New York Times* article, it rejected all requests to donate Dawn detergent to such groups until 1989.[22] Eventually, however, someone in the company must have realized that there was some benefit to be gained from the connection and commercials highlighting Dawn's unintentional environmentalism were produced. One such commercial showed oily ducks, otters, and penguins being washed with numerous bottles of Dawn detergent in the background, accompanied by the caption: "Thousands of animals caught in oil spills have been saved using Dawn. Now your purchase can help."[23] We are then shown a bottle of Dawn with a new label element which reads, "1 Bottle = $1 to save wildlife." The commercial ends by reminding us that Dawn is "Tough on grease, yet gentle," with some fine print about a $500,000 cap on donations and the requirement to visit dawnsaveswildlife.com, where we will learn that "the little things we do can make a big difference."

When we visit the website, as we must for our purchase to "help," we are shown an idealized natural world featuring adorable ducklings and are told: "Everyone has the power to change the world—even by doing something as simple as washing the dishes." On the main Dawn website, one can watch another commercial about the rescue effort connection in which we see more images of oily wildlife and lots of bottles of Dawn over which a narrator tells us: "To help save wildlife affected by oil spills, rescue workers have opened up a lot of Dawn. They rely on it because it's tough on grease, yet gentle. But even they'll tell you, Dawn helps open something even bigger."[24] We then see lots of cleaned wildlife released from cages, presumably freed back to the wild. Another version shows a number of animal parents and offspring in various adorable scenes with the caption: "Even a mother can't protect them from oil spills. That's why rescue experts turn to Dawn. It's tough on grease, yet gentle."[25] The ad ends by urging us to "Do more than dishes."

The power or opportunity to "change the world" just by doing the dishes is perhaps a new, and undoubtedly incredible, bit of news for most readers. We are supposed to be surprised (given the tone of the narrator) that opening a bottle of Dawn to wash our dishes actually opens up "something even bigger." Procter & Gamble was apparently surprised as well. But once they realized that, through no particular environmental intentionality of their own, their particular combination of surfactants and detergents is actually, well, tough on grease yet gentle in ways that give it value in rescue efforts, those efforts immediately became something Dawn "cares" about and remain an integral part of their marketing campaign still. This marketing makes a specific point of informing us that not only can consumer products have unintended or hidden moral value, but that our own consumption of those products, simply by virtue of keeping them in business through our patronage, shares that moral value, even without intentionality on our part. Certainly we are invited to "care" about the poor oily animals, or at least invited to think better of Dawn if we already do so; but the key point of this example is the way in which our regular consumer activity is configured as good for the world even if we don't particularly care, or don't know that we do or should. We can do good and do the dishes at the same time, because, in some directly economic sense, those are the same thing, even if we remain unaware of what the good is or how it is accomplished.

Another interesting example of "doing well by doing good" is found in Clorox Company's "Filter for Good" campaign featuring the Brita brand. As Jack Neff, at *AdAge* reports, the Oakland based Brita company was approached by the city of San Francisco with a request to develop a filtered water bottle that could replace the usual plastic water bottles.[26] When the green movement was gaining momentum in the mid-1970s, Perrier began a $5 million marketing campaign initially aimed at making imported bottled water a status symbol. The idea of pure, bottled water struck a chord in the environmental movement, however, and production and sales of bottled water has grown dramatically worldwide in the intervening years, now generating more than $100 billion in annual revenue. According to typical PR material on the subject, the global consumption of bottled water has increased by a factor of five since 1990, and enough plastic water bottles are produced each year to encircle the planet 190 times.[27] That's a lot of bottles, and that many bottles headed for landfills or littered around the environment has generated a "green" backlash (not to mention the significant controversy over the actual quality or production methods of many bottled water brands); hence the request from the city of San Francisco.

In 2009, Brita joined with Nalgene, a prominent maker of BPA-free reusable water bottles, and created the "Filter for Good" PR campaign under the guidance of Suzanne Senglemann, who was charged with increasing the company's profitability while improving its environmental impact by focusing more on the health and environmental benefits of their products rather than the taste.[28] They created a website, filterforgood.com, where, as Senglemann puts it, people can go "to go get information on where to purchase the products or, more important, what they can do to make a difference." This website is featured on both Brita's and Nalgene's home websites as well. Nalgene's page dedicated to the campaign is low-key, but urges browsers to buy the product to make a difference:

Want to reduce the amount of waste you produce? Want to help reduce global warming? Purchase this commemorative FilterForGood bottle. Brita and Nalgene are teaming up to promote the importance of clean water and show how small changes can make a big difference for people and the environment. Nalgene & Brita have teamed up to create the FilterForGood pledge. It's a simple commitment to reduce your personal waste by giving up bottled water, even if it's just a few days each week. Together, filtered water and a reusable bottle are an ideal solution for going green at home and on the go. It's an easy change that can make a big difference.[29]

The promotional website, filterforgood.com, redirects to Brita's dedicated page, which is quite a bit splashier. This page has a number of prominent graphical elements inviting the viewer to "join the movement" which it reports has over 430,000 members, and tallying the number of water bottles "saved" from ending in landfills (almost 430,000,000 at the time I last accessed the site). As is typical of many marketing and PR campaigns, the website highlights celebrity involvement and endorsements. Early in the campaign, Bono, of U2, worked out an arrangement to replace all water backstage at his concerts with Brita filtered water, an example soon followed by the Sundance Film Festival and, in a paid arrangement, NBC's *Biggest Loser* series.[30] Its website prominently displays the involvement of many other celebrities and celebrity venues, such as Dave Matthews, Jason Mraz, and the popular South-by-Southwest music festival.

Early in the campaign, Brita produced a series of PR videos. One such video, in 2009, documented a PR event, the "Brita Climate Ride," in which over 150 "activists, experts, and everyday people" rode bicycles from New York City to Washington, D.C. to "raise awareness about climate change and renewable energy."[31] The video, entitled "My Hope for the Future," features a number of people in bike-riding gear sharing their hopes for the future, which all turn out to involve one or several of the now familiar concerns of these movements: a greener, more local, more sustainable, and/or more communal world working together for change. One young woman then tells us that her hope for the future is that "everyone realizes they can make a difference in small ways, something as simple as using a Brita pitcher and reusable bottle at home."

What is most interesting for me in these campaigns is shown clearly in the video's "branding" of "hope for the future." Brita is following widespread PR and marketing practices in its campaign, offering to help us "make a difference" by doing something "small" and not too demanding of our time, energy, or pocketbook. It ties into long-standing "concerns," even using magical words borrowed from the movements themselves, such as the notion of "saving" bottles (albeit from landfills) which echoes the now nostalgic refrains to "save the dolphins" or "save the whales." It cleverly insinuates its own marketing into the larger ethical consumerist movement, equating a "hope" for more reusable water consumption with all the other "hopes" of the green movement. But it does more than this as well. It offers a particular formulation of "care," in this case the very importantly personalized "*My* hope for the future.*" As we will see when we look at TOMS, part of what is at work in these campaigns is an effort to "brand" the very act of caring. When Brita gathers a group of people for a PR event and invites them to share their hopes, and then offers those to us through brand marketing, the hopes themselves take on, in at least some small way, the character and imprimatur of the brand.

MAKING THE WORLD A BETTER PLACE,
ONE PURCHASE AT A TIME

This is certainly what the TOMS or the FEED Projects + Target's "FEED USA" campaigns hope to accomplish. The FEED USA campaign title echoes the name of the United States' largest domestic hunger-relief (and celebrity darling) charity organization, Feeding America, which operates a national network of food banks, and with wh FEED is partnering.[32] FEED Projects is a retail outlet founded on the popular new idea that consumer products can be vehicles for social change. The company was formed in 2006 by Lauren Bush, granddaughter to President George H. W. Bush, and Ellen Gustafson, one-time "spokesperson" for the UN World Food Programme, with a new business model often labeled "social entrepreneurship" which claims to balance the usual business priority on profit with social responsibility.[33] It sells bags (many in burlap), and now accessories (mostly woven bracelets) and apparel (mostly T-shirts), and a portion of each sale is donated to the UN World Food Programme, UNICEF, and other partner programs, through which the company claims to have provided over 75,000,000 meals by mid-2014. There is an "impact" and a "story" as product description categories on the website for every item. The "impact" informs the consumer how many meals his or her purchase will provide. The "story" for the FEED 5 woven bracelet, for instance, reads: "Making a difference, one weave at a time."[34] Its mission statement proclaims that "FEED is proud to help FEED the world, one bag at a time." The company also formed a non-profit wing in 2008, called the FEED Foundation, "dedicated to ending world hunger—one child at a time."[35]

This emphasis on "one at a time" seems to be both a nod to the conventional wisdom that change comes in "small steps," and perhaps also a built-in apology for continuing the crusade indefinitely. The effort to eradicate any given social problem in one fell swoop would not make for a very sustainable business model. Instead, this model and its marketing focuses upon the "good" each individual purchase can accomplish, helping us to feel better about ourselves even under the circumstance where we face the same social problems over the course of time without apparent reduction in severity. We have done our part, we can say, perhaps several times over, having purchased the bottle of Dawn, or the Nalgene bottle, or the clothing or accessory item again and again, each purchase a separate "act of charity." As FEED Projects explains on its "Mission" webpage, "the impact of each product, signified by a stenciled number, is understandable, tangible, and meaningful."[36] Thus, FEED makes a huge and complex problem easy to understand and to address, one purchase at a time. Social activism made easy, and consumerist.

Such an approach is tailored to an awareness of the world that is itself episodic. As we discussed in chapter 2, journalistic narratives about the world focus on the anecdotal and dramatic, on images of individual hungry children or oil-covered animals from the latest environmental or social crisis. It cannot and so does not address itself to larger social structures or systems that are ultimately the root causes for these crises. Therefore, social entrepreneurs are relieved of the burden of doing so as well. They may offer rhetorical gestures toward the *idea* of systemic or structural dynamics, but the business model itself, "one for one" as TOMS so accurately labels it, is the idea that a single purchase will provide a single "good" to address some localized and concrete rather than systemic and structural "need." If the need strikes us as dauntingly large, so much the better, since that means many purchases will be required to address it.

FEED Projects also highlights the country of origin of some of its products, such as its bracelets, simultaneously presenting itself as engaged in "fair-trade" and "fair-labor" relationships and also providing the exotic appeal of having an object made by hands one has also in some small way "helped" by means of one's purchase. Through the object, one is able to touch or feel more directly connected to the beneficiary of one's "help." The object bought is the symbolic surrogate for the other in need whom one "cares" about, and its use is a constant reminder of the other, but more importantly, of the "care" one experiences and the "good" one has done, something no mere donation to a worthy cause can hope to provide. It is, of course, a fetishized "other" and a fetishized "care." It is interesting that FEED Projects, as is also the case with TOMS, focuses upon children. Blake Mycoskie is on the Board of Advisors for FEED Projects. The humanitarian pull on our emotions that children in particular exert has long been recognized in philanthropic and humanitarian organizations. Almost all the PR material for FEED, including numerous videos of Ms. Lauren Bush touring the US or the world, feature shots of her with children, and the marketing focuses upon providing school meals.

In late 2012, the company launched "FEED USA," a joint venture with Target, offering more than "50 lifestyle products" whose purchase includes the opportunity to "help fight hunger."[37] The campaign webpage and press releases speak of FEED's history of fighting global hunger, but then coming to recognize that even in the US people "do not have dependable access to enough food." The page offers us information about the problem, "hunger by the numbers," which alerts us that "1 in 6 Americans" (by which, I assume, they primarily mean people in the US) are "affected by hunger," and that 17 million children are living in "food-insecure households." The explanation offered for the "lack of dependable access" to enough food is "limited money and resources," which is, frankly, a laughable attempt to "explain" the dynamics behind the broad and pervasive structural problems of poverty and hunger anywhere, but particularly in a wealthy industrial country such as the US. As already noted, there is no attempt to communicate any real analysis of the socio-economic systems and structures underlying this phenomenon.

It is, of course, impossible to say whether the company newly became aware of the phenomenon of hunger in the US, or simply recognized a new marketing opportunity. It is not clear how the association with Target came about, at least not from either's PR releases.[38] Target appears to consider the collaboration to be one of its "designer" partnerships, in which Target markets a particular product label for a limited time. Target claims to have longstanding interest in the issue of hunger, however, and has donated food and produce from its grocery sections to Feeding America for over a decade.[39] As Target's president of community relations, Laysha Ward, says in a *USA Today* article written as part of its PR rollout: "This for us isn't a cause of the moment. It's something we believe in and have stood for since the beginning of time." Perhaps not quite that longstanding, but Target certainly recognizes the popularity of "cause" marketing. As Ward also says, "People are time starved and they're looking for easy solutions and they certainly want to make a difference." That about sums up the central assumption of cause marketing.

As should be clear by now, cause marketing is both a bit of a gold mine and a liability for business. The much cited 2010 study by Cone Communications, a PR firm that specializes in cause marketing, reported findings that would be very hard for any marketing agency to ignore:

Americans' enthusiasm for cause marketing . . . continues to strongly influence their purchase decisions:

- 88% say it is acceptable for companies to involve a cause or issue in their marketing;
- 83% want more of the products, services and retailers they use to benefit causes;
- 85% have a more positive image of a product or company when it supports a cause they care about; and,
- 80% are likely to switch brands, similar in price and quality, to one that supports a cause.

Not only are consumers willing to switch among similar brands, they are also willing to step outside their comfort zones. When it supports a cause:

- 61% of Americans say they would be willing to try a new brand or one unfamiliar to them;
- 46% would try a generic or private-label brand; and,
- Nearly one-in-five consumers (19%) would be willing to purchase a more expensive brand.

The data signal a ripe opportunity for companies to engage consumers on a new level—one that fulfills both their needs for goods and to do good.[40]

More than 8 out of 10 people surveyed want the things they buy to perform a kind of double duty, making a difference in the world in addition to providing consumer satisfaction. Of course, less than half are willing to forego a designer label to do so, and slightly less than 2 out of 10 are willing to spend more in the process.

This means, for all practical purposes, that some effort at social responsibility is simply the cost of doing business in this new consumer environment; but it is also an opportunity, and can be made the core business model, as is the case with FEED Projects and TOMS. The most coveted consumer segment is known as Millennials, those eighteen to twenty-four-year-old consumers who grew up with "community service" as either an educational requirement or an expected element of their resumes. It is a group that is not only socially conscious, but has been trained, in a sense, to express that consciousness as an element of normal life practice, even if the time and energy dedicated to it is miniscule relative to other activities. In a rather direct sense, they have been trained to expect social activism of themselves, but for it not to cost too much.[41]

Target speaks directly to this consumer segment explicitly in this new language of social activism. In mid-2013, once the "collection" became available in stores, Target produced a series of commercials to highlight the products. One commercial tells us about one such Millennial named Kate. We see her engaged in a range of activities, but the point of the images is clearly just to present an attractive young woman doing things we are supposed to find appealing and fun. It is the "story" the narrator tells us that is the primary argument of the ad:

Kate needs plates, and a cute tote-bag, and a shirt for her date. So, Kate comes to Target, who's making products with FEED, to give meals across America. Kate's plates give Mike a treat [we will meet Mike in other commercials]; her bag gets her mentioned; and her shirt gets Mike's attention. But her shirt *also* gives 16 meals, her bag gives 28 meals, and her plates give 50. So now, Sean gets lunch [we see a picture of an appealing young Asian boy], a family gets dinner [we see a family at the dinner table passing food], and lots of people smile [Kate and her friends laugh together]. Kate did a great thing; and the people she feeds will too. Well done, Kate. Enjoy the plates.[42]

The clear argument of this ad is that we can get the things we desire to create the idealized world we desire and *also* do good without doing anything more than simply shopping. The pleasure is at least doubled—there are more "smiles" generated—because we get both the attention for which we long and to feel good about ourselves for making a difference and doing a good thing; and we get to enjoy the plates! We do not have to spend one second or one bit of energy or money we weren't going to spend anyway on ourselves in order to do something "great" and make a difference in the world. It is particularly interesting to note the specific choice of words used to talk of Kate's philanthropy—"the people *she* feeds"—as if Kate is directly giving them food or even personally spooning it into their hungry mouths. As long as the products we buy and the businesses we patronize "donate" some nebulous amount (however "clearly stenciled" on the products) to some ambiguous "cause," then it is precisely the same as if we were doing it ourselves. Consumption *as* activism. Well done, Target. Enjoy the profits.

ONE FOR ONE

As Žižek has noted, there is perhaps no clearer example of this business model and the idea of consumption as social activism than TOMS shoes. TOMS was also founded in 2006, by Blake Mycoskie, whom the company refers to as the "Chief Shoe Giver," a celebrity of sorts from his appearance on the second season of *The Amazing Race*. Blake's "story," as told on the company's website at every conceivable opportunity and in many biographies, explains that it was during a vacation to Argentina in 2006 that Blake became aware of the "need" for shoes for children in the rural areas of the country, and founded his shoe company in order to "help."[43] As Blake says, he was "struck with the desire—the responsibility—to do more."

The company was founded on a business model like that of FEED Projects, in which a portion of the profit from every sale is set aside as a donation to some humanitarian organization. An earlier webpage for the company puts it succinctly: "One person buys. One person is helped."[44] TOMS, however, personalizes that model more fully. The consumer is offered a more direct relation to the person in need by means of a simple one for one correspondence between product bought and product given. The company promised to give a pair of shoes to some child for every pair bought, and so each shoe purchase offers the consumer the opportunity to feel as if he or she has given a pair of shoes to some specific (if unknown) child in need. The CSR page on their website explains the overarching idea: "At TOMS®, we believe we can improve people's lives through business."

As the 2013 "Giving Report" explains, TOMS is founded in the idea that it is possible to transform "everyday purchases into a force for good around the world."[45]

A promotional video from 2011 lays out the central argument this business model hopes will persuade consumers to shop with them.[46] In it, we are told that we make, on average, 612 decisions every day, some big and life-changing, but most of them pretty small. We are asked "what if" one of the small decisions could be a big one as well? We are then told that in 2006, Blake Mycoskie made a decision that "changed everyday purchases into a force for good." The video ends with the question, both graphically and narrated: "Would you change one daily decision to help change a life?" That is a seductive hypothetical: the idea that we could just change one small decision, buy this brand of whatever rather than another and the world could become a better place. This business model hopes all of us would do that if given the chance, and why wouldn't we? Such an invitation works as both an enticement and a shaming. If we wouldn't change one small decision in order to help, what kind of person are we?

That basic idea of "One for One" became a "movement," to use the company's own term for it, that now drives everything the company does. Its webpage dedicated to the trademarked phrase explains: "We're in business to help improve lives. With every product you purchase, TOMS will help a person in need. One for One."[47] That "movement" situates itself firmly within the larger green and ethical consumerist movements, expressing concern for and adherence to practices that focus on the environmental and social impacts of their products and operations, including fair labor, sustainable and environmentally friendly (even vegan) materials, and "giving back to the community." Their CSR page presents the obligatory promise for this business model: "Our efforts are focused on making sure that we operate in a manner that's consistent with our brand values." These values are not explicitly articulated at any point, but the overall ethos of the marketing and frequently repeated origin narratives lead the consumer to understand, however vaguely, that they are the same general values of the larger movements, i.e., the desire to make the world a better place.

It is a business model and "movement" that has generated significant attention and praise. The company has worked to formulate its movement with the usual signposts of social activism, including annual events to "raise awareness" about issues, such as "Day Without Shoes" or "World Sight Day." There are a number of "TOMS Campus Clubs" at universities and high schools in the US and Canada.[48] Blake's bio page on the company website attests to some of his accolades:

> In 2009, Blake and TOMS received the Secretary of State's 2009 Award of Corporate Excellence (ACE). At the Clinton Global Initiative University ple-

nary session, former President Clinton introduced Blake to the audience as "one of the most interesting entrepreneurs (I've) ever met." *People Magazine* featured Blake in its "Heroes Among Us" section, and TOMS Shoes was featured in the Bill Gates *Time Magazine* article "How to Fix Capitalism." In 2011, Blake was named on *Fortune Magazine's* "40 Under 40" list, recognizing him as one of the top young businessmen in the world.[49]

In 2011, Blake published *Start Something That Matters*, a #1 *New York Times* bestseller, which offers, as his website tells us, "his own amazing story of inspiration, and the power of incorporating giving in business."

Yet even while his particular model of social entrepreneurship has garnered attention and praise, there have been questions about labor practices and manufacturing locations, as the company's CSR page also acknowledges:

> As we've disclosed previously in our Giving Report, our shoes are made in China, Ethiopia and Argentina. We are aware of the challenges associated with overseeing a global supply chain and our global staff actively manages and oversees our suppliers and vendors to ensure that our corporate responsibility standards are upheld. On an annual basis, we require our direct suppliers to certify that the materials incorporated into our products are procured in accordance with all applicable laws in the countries they do business in, including laws regarding slavery and human trafficking. We also clearly define appropriate business practices for our employees and hold them accountable for complying with our policies, including the prevention of slavery and human trafficking within our supply chain.[50]

The fact that the company feels the need to reassure its consumers (twice in the same paragraph, and twice more further down the page) that they are paying careful attention to the issue of "slavery and human trafficking" says something significant about the locations chosen to produce the shoes, which now includes a new plant in Haiti.

The shoes consumers buy are produced in China. The "giving shoes" are produced in the other countries, and the company promotes that fact as its way of providing jobs in the locations their philanthropy targets. Fair enough, I suppose; but it is also fair to ask how any company would go about holding a particular plant accountable to the "applicable" laws and local labor practices, much less the company's own "brand values," in a country such as Ethiopia. Present PR material merely identifies "outside experts" and "respected third parties" as agents for assuring conformity to standards, including a "respected international inspection and consulting firm" to audit the manufacturers on a periodic basis through visits, both announced and unannounced. Previous versions of their website, however, have mentioned the international auditing firm, Intertek, who claims to be the "global leader in the testing, inspection, and auditing of consumer goods."[51]

I am not raising these concerns to call TOMS' practices or integrity into question. I am not particularly interested in the possibility of hypocrisy or bad faith.[52] There is a more important point which this juxtaposition of praise and concern brings to the fore for us than just the perhaps inevitable complications arising from the combination of a large for-profit business, with its "global supply chain," and the moral impulse to do good and make a difference. It is not the moral character of this or any company that is at question in our analysis, but the nature of morality itself as inflected by both their rhetoric and practices and our adoption of their model of "caring."

We can *both* admire Blake and his company for the "good" they do, hold it and others like it out as a model for a more morally and socially conscious way of doing business, *and also* be suspicious of their motives and actual accomplishments *because* there is practically no way to measure either their sincerity or the degree and quality of "difference" our participation in their consumerist model of philanthropy accomplishes. Such a juxtaposition is made possible by virtue of the way philanthropy is configured now, not only by these new business models, but by our larger "cultural capitalist" understanding of charity, wherein the sheer distance of those in "need" and the global manufacturing chain or humanitarian organizational network intercalated between their need and our "giving" makes it virtually impossible to hold either claims or activity accountable.

We buy things. That's what we experience directly: the goods we desire and the normal consumer exchange. There is no difference for us, as activity, in buying TOMS shoes or FEED bags than in buying any other pair of shoes or clothing accessory. We do not see children fed or shod. We do not know how many are "helped," or where they are, or how; not really, not even when the "numbers" are helpfully stenciled on the product we buy. The TOMS website offers helpful "Where We Give" maps on most pages with the countries in which the "giving partners" operate color coded by the kind of "giving" that happens there. It is a map of the whole world, though, and roughly half of it is colored in some fashion; so it doesn't narrow down the location of the beneficiary of one's individual consumer philanthropy very much. The casual consumer of the product doesn't even really know if TOMS or FEED does the "giving" themselves, or sub-contracts it through other humanitarian providers; and they don't need to know, either for whatever giving process occurs to happen, or to feel good about themselves. We are simply sold things, with this single but all important difference, things with a story attached. That's why Blake's "story" is plastered all over the website, all marketing and PR materials, and his book, and is the centerpiece of every speaking engagement. It's the story we are being sold and asked to buy. It is the story that is the sole conveyer and site of the "morality" that we purchase and exercise in our consumer activity.

That is also why TOMS has branched out to tell new stories of new possibilities for "giving." On the website, the menu at the top lists the usual product categories where the consumer can directly shop for the products which interest them, but also the new "Marketplace," which we are told is "a new destination for making a difference," TOMS' new "platform" for partner social entrepreneurs where one can "Shop by Cause" or by the region of the world they'd like to "help," or at least from which they'd like to obtain exotic goods.[53] The menu also lists two additional categories, however, "Stories," and "One for One." These categories and pages represent the primary marketing effort and are where the central moral persona of the business is presented and sold. That stories are the most important element of TOMS is made clear by the presence of a dedicated page (a kind of blog about the company's persona and philanthropic activities) on the same level as any of the retail pages.

On these pages, the consumer will learn about the new initiatives TOMS has developed under its "one for one" model, first, in 2011, eyewear that offers the "gift of sight," and just this year, coffee that offers the "gift of water." As I am writing this chapter, TOMS has just announced a new animal initiative, started by TOMS' "Chief Animal Lover," Heather Mycoskie, in which funds from the sales of special shoes will be earmarked for the Virunga National Park to support a population of mountain gorillas.[54] Every page on TOMS' website highlights the stories. The Giving Report is replete with stories. The Marketplace page depends upon them. Even the regular online retail pages for shoes, with the usual selection of styles and options accompanied by descriptions and reviews, features a large "One for One" image and link for "learning more," where, if we click, we will be told the stories. The new retail page for coffee highlights them even more prominently. The main One for One page links to separate pages for "The Gift of Shoes," "The Gift of Sight," and "The Gift of Water" where the TOMS story is front and center.

Each of these pages spells out the idea of the "movement," tells the consumer what is given and where, and how it all works and what the purchase "supports." The top element of every page, however, is a selection of "giving in action" stories, including videos, where the consumer can participate, even if vicariously, in the "good" their purchase is about to accomplish. On the "Gift of Water" page, dedicated to the latest market initiative from TOMS, giving, for each bag of coffee bought, "a week of clean water to a person in need" in each of the five countries from which TOMS sources its coffee beans, we are invited to read "Josephine's Story." The quick 3-slide presentation introduces us to a ten-year-old girl from Rwanda who "treks" up a mountainside four hours every day for water. The second slide vaguely references violence which can occur in a struggle for the water available and shows a picture of an unidentified person with blood on her hands and legs filling a 5-gallon container from a spigot. The final slide shows Josephine again, and tells us that "Water For People," TOMS' partner humanitarian organization in this initiative, worked with the "local government" to bring access to improved water closer to home, changing Josephine's life for the better, and concludes by assuring us that "it's a story [TOMS] can recreate in communities all over the world—thanks to people like you."⁵⁵

This is a "story" only in the loosest sense of the term. We "meet" Josephine only in the sense that we see a picture and read her name. Other than her difficulties with getting water, we know nothing about her, and learn nothing from her "story." The story is really about TOMS and the consumer, and tells the same story all the TOMS stories tell: a story of TOMS and us together making a difference in the world through our consumption. On this page we are invited to learn more about "Direct Trade," which is the name TOMS gives to its supply and manufacturing process. In this story we find on the linked page, "Follow the Bean," we again meet a Josephine from Rwanda, although we do not know if it is the same person, and in this instance she is a mother of eight and the owner of one of the few female-owned and "best-running" farms in the region. We are shown a clearly staged picture of Blake with someone we must assume is Josephine, and are told that "it's important for us [meaning, presumably, both TOMS and the consumer] to get to know our farmers personally and learn their amazing stories."⁵⁶ The "amazing story" that follows (with the exception of learning that Josephine lost her husband in the genocide in Rwanda) is just the usual marketing hype surrounding the artisan-like crafting of any connoisseur or gourmet item, but it is noted that "the women who sort the beans take pride in knowing that their work will be appreciated all over the world."

TOMS eyewear feature a distinctive stripe on the frame, and we are told that "every stripe tells a story" (see figure 7.1). The stripe that is most obvious, because white, is discreetly located on the part of the frame usually covered by the wearer's ear or hair, but the point of it, of course, is to announce to everyone that one's eyewear is more than just eyewear, that it is a kind of social activism, and that one is a kind of social activist for buying the sunglasses. It is interesting that the glasses tell this "story" most obviously when they are not actually in use. John Whitledge, Creative Director for TOMS Eyewear, says: "When I design something, I always start with a story."⁵⁷ The story, we are told on the ad image, is this: "The hand-painted stripes symbolize the three elements of One for One. The first stripe on the temples represents you [the consumer]. The stripe on the tips represents the person you are helping give sight to. And the middle stripe is TOMS, bringing the two together." This "story" presents TOMS as essential to connecting with those in need. Without TOMS, how would the two ever come together, at least in today's busy world? As Blake tells us on one of his promotional videos, TOMS is "able to give someone the opportunity to wear a pair of shades, knowing that there is a greater purpose . . . When they see the stripes,

Figure 7.1. "Every Stripe Tells a Story," TOMS eyewear.

and those colors, it will be a reminder that they have impacted someone's life in a One for One way."[58]

In the 2011 promotional video released to announce the eyewear initiative, entitled "Next Chapter" (continuing the story metaphor), Blake makes the central claim that his marketing is advancing in direct and clear terms.[59] One for One, he tells us, is not just about TOMS; it's about us. "One for One is much bigger . . . than TOMS. It's what *you* think we can do to make the world a better place, using the One for One model." We are then shown a bunch of people cutting out words and images from magazines or individual artwork and gluing them to cardboard tubes while they tell us, much like the PR video for Brita, what they care about and hope for, many using the phrase, "my One for One . . . ." In case we didn't get the message clearly, the final few people simply say, "*this* is *my* One for One," and Blake asks us: "What is *your* One for One? Show us at Facebook.com/TOMS."

One of the most interesting PR videos features Ben Affleck telling us about *his* "One for One."[60] He informs us that his "One for One" is the Eastern Congo Initiative, "because everyone has the right to be healthy and safe." He tells us about the organization he founded (without mentioning that he founded it) and the many things it seeks to accomplish in the region as well as his hopes for the future. The video ends with him reminding us who he is and that "this is [his] One for One." The central feature of all of these videos, and the One for One "movement" itself, is the attempt to "brand" the very act of caring about something under the TOMS aegis. We don't merely care about this or that, hope for something or another, this strategy informs us; we "have" a "One for One." What is yours? Caring is proprietary, and belongs to, or is at least "sponsored" by TOMS, or FEED, or they would like for us to think so at any rate.

This is an incredibly subtle and important shift in thinking to which we would do well to critically attend. It is, essentially, the "story" we are asked to listen to and inhabit, and it is *about us*: *we* are the story. The concrete details don't matter, and so we aren't really ever told them. The story is not about those details, not really, not even about those in "need" except as an opportunity to motivate our consumption. The story is simply a large and nebulous narrative of caring, and what is important in it is the overarching brand identity of our caring, and the idea that we can accomplish it, primarily, through purchasing a particular brand of consumer good. That is what we are buying and buying into when we decide to make a difference in the world by buying something from TOMS or FEED, by buying Dawn or Brita rather than some other brand.

What all of this adds up to is the complete collapse of "making a difference" into consumption and the consumer experience, offering the opportunity to feel good to the consumer without placing any demand on him or her outside the normal consumer exchange transaction. This story, its allied business model, and its concomitant marketing depend upon and require the prior existence of the "cultural capitalist" model of philanthropy. Doing good and making a difference is *already* almost exclusively constructed as an economic transaction, about giving money to "causes" or the organizations who champion them, anonymous donations to anonymous recipients, without any real knowledge of those in need or their problems, or any real understanding of the social or economic dynamics that are the causes of those needs. Raising "awareness," under this rubric, is *always* merely about bringing the "problem" to people's attention, never about the complex genealogy of political and economic power systems behind them. Once we are "aware," we are to excise any sense of guilt produced by that awareness, and exercise any "caring" excited by it, by giving some money to someone who will "help." These new social entrepreneurs just make it easier for us to do that, since we weren't necessarily going to look for some specific organization to give to, even if we have been raised to be "socially conscious" and "have" something we "care" about, but we are going to buy some shoes or bags or coffee or dish soap at some point.

JOINING THE GOOD FIGHT

Some marketing campaigns, however, do not merely present some cause as needing our consumer attention, but as a kind of branded caring that directly (or at least vicariously) engages us in the front-line battle with some social problem. One of the most telling examples is perhaps Unilever's brand Dove and its "Campaign for Real Beauty." Let me note at the start that Unilever also owns the Axe brand of body scents whose marketing ranks among the most egregiously misogynistic of any mainstream brand. Again, I am not interested in the parent company's clear hypocrisy or what might be characterized as pandering, about which Dove may have little say. My interest is strictly the example of Dove's moralism, positioning itself as leading the fight to "address" what it presents as a pervasive social and moral problem.

In 2004, while trying to think of a new way to market a cream that supposedly reduces cellulite, Dove's marketing firm, Olgivy, came up with an idea it called "Celebrate Real Curves." One of its first ads explains: "Firming the thighs of a size 2 supermodel is no challenge. Real Women have real bodies with real curves. And Dove wants to celebrate those curves" (See figure 7.2). The ad shows six young women in white underwear that are

Figure 7.2. "Real Women Have Real Curves," Dove.

indeed somewhat larger than the typical professional model. The marketing apparently struck a chord with consumers since there was a rather immediate sales increase for Dove products. Soon ads with various somewhat larger sized young women in white underwear were everywhere. Realizing they had struck pay dirt, Ogilvy contracted with their Irish PR subsidiary, Wilson Hartnell, to start a PR campaign around the marketing which it called "Campaign for Real Beauty." The current website for the campaign invites us to "imagine a world where beauty is a source of confidence, not anxiety," and presents the history of the campaign as a leading agent in "widening the definition of beauty."[61]

WHPR received an award for excellence from the Public Relations Consultants Association in 2005, and the document WHPR wrote detailing the campaign attached to that award is unusually informative and interesting.[62] The campaign began in Ireland, with the "ultimate aim," according to the document, "to generate a widespread debate on society's attitudes toward beauty." They admit that the important goal for them was "to position Dove as a ground-breaking brand that is leading the debate on society's definition of beauty." Setting aside the fact that a debate on society's definitions of beauty has been going on for significantly longer than a decade, without any input from Dove, the firm did commission a "study" by Behavior and Attitudes, Ireland's largest independent *market* research company, which surveyed 300 Irish women and discovered that only 1% were "comfortable" describing themselves as beautiful, and that almost 80% believed that "the media should do more to represent a wider definition of beauty."[63] Olgivy had launched the initial marketing campaign after commissioning a similar global study on beauty and "well-being" by StrategyOne, another market research firm, in collaboration with Dr. Nancy Etcoff, of Harvard, and Dr. Susie Orbach, of the London School of Economics, both noted scholars and social critics who have written about the impact of beauty standards on women. This study interviewed over 3,000 women from ten countries, and found that somewhere between 1/3 to 1/2 of the women (varying by country) did not "feel comfortable" describing themselves as beautiful, that only 2% would choose the word "beautiful" to describe how they look, and that between 60% and 90% want "the media" to do a "better job of portraying women of diverse physical attractiveness—age, shape and size."[64]

These results are hardly surprising, of course. As Lauren Dye has noted, according to the American Society for Aesthetic Plastic Surgery, approximately 11.7 million surgical and nonsurgical procedures were performed in the United States alone in 2007. Of those surgeries, 91% were performed upon women.[65] With these sobering statistics in hand, WHPR set about promoting the campaign, including an inaugural press event, with a "panel of experts," and a series of "road show" events in which visitors to a PR/marketing trailer could "learn more about the campaign" and "cast their votes" relative to the marketing's primary ads (see figures 7.3–7.5). The initial ads for the campaign portraying women with precisely those three parameters in play—age, shape and size—featured large "tick box" billboards showing a model and the option to choose between two ways of describing her, such as "fit" or "fat," "grey" or "gorgeous," and "wrinkled" or "wonderful."

The campaign certainly did spark a debate which continues today. Whether that debate is the one WHPR envisioned is open to question. There has been a great deal written about the campaign, including a fair number of critiques which focus on the fact that Dove sells beauty products, after all, and started the campaign to sell a "firming" cream (to treat a "problem" that only exists because beauty companies declared it to be a problem), that the women in the ads are mostly young (when not intended precisely to raise the issue of age), mostly light-skinned with good skin tone (no cellulite in sight), and are in their underwear. This last point is important, I believe, and demonstrates that no matter how much Dove wants to stretch the "definition" of beauty a size or two, they still fully participate in the mainstream cultural ideal of women as visual objects. These women are "happy" with their bodies, as the ads takes significant pains to portray, but they all know that their bodies are what matter, that their bodies are what makes them sexy or beautiful and provides what power they enjoy, rather than what they know or can do, and the ads do not make any attempt whatsoever to portray such qualities. The women just stand there, in variously provocative poses, to be gazed at. The ads do not really offer some new "definition" of beauty; the women in them are presented as beautiful in *the same old way*, i.e., grounded in how they look to others.

Figure 7.3.   "Wrinkled or Wonderful?" Dove Campaign for Real Beauty.

Figure 7.4.   "Fat or Fit?" Dove Campaign for Real Beauty.

The campaign raises the issue of beauty as a problem, playing off wide-spread female insecurity over appearance, but they raise it without challenging the larger cultural ideal in any substantive way. These ads remain thoroughly enmeshed in the traditional definitions, and, indeed, require them. At best the ads suggest that curves or being grey or having freckles can be counted as beautiful "too," along with the normal qualifiers of beauty we have been taught. Mostly, though, the initial ads invite us to ignore the very qualities the ads shove in our face in order to "vote" for the option we know we are supposed to choose if we are enlightened. "Grey or gorgeous," "fit or fat," "wrinkled or wonderful" are exclusive binaries, not conjunctions. Most of us conform readily to the clear expectation, according to the results of the "voting," because the clear implication is that one of the binaries is negative. It is a longstanding rhetorical practice to present two, and only two, options with a clear bias against one, in order to enlist the support of the audience.

What is more important for our analysis, however, is the way Dove has used the intervening decade to present the initial campaign as a moral "cause" of continuing concern both for them and for us, even if we suspect that their concern might have dissipated before now had the campaign failed to achieve its marketing goals. Dove has a website "mission" page, like TOMS and FEED, and invites those visiting to "learn more" about the "issue" or "problem" of society's definition of beauty, to visit the sites of their "partners," which includes the Girl Scouts, Boys and Girls Club, and Girls Inc., and to "get involved" in their "self-esteem workshops." Almost every page references the "research," and the number of women who describe themselves as beautiful has apparently risen from 2% to 4% (not much to show for a decade of campaigning).[66] The problem appears to be intractable,

□ grey?
□ gorgeous?

Why can't more women feel glad to be grey? Join the beauty debate.

campaignforrealbeauty.co.uk *Dove*

Figure 7.5. "Grey or Gorgeous?" Dove Campaign for Real Beauty.

despite Dove's best intentions to drive the "debate" and "help the next generation of women develop a positive relationship with the way they look," or, indeed, despite the increased sales of their beauty products.[67] As they admit, "there is more to be done," and to help in that work, there are videos, lots and lots of videos.

Some of the most widely viewed have been television ads, such as the 2006 Superbowl commercial "Little Girls," or the web videos produced in the hope (since realized) that they would go viral, such as "Daughters," "Evolution," "Onslaught," and "Amy."[68] In these videos, we see that the "campaign" rather quickly shifted away from "celebrating" curves to the larger issue of self-esteem. It wasn't until 2010 that Dove officially launched its "bold, new vision," the "Movement for Self-Esteem;" but even in 2006, we see the shift had largely taken place. The Superbowl ad, which received, of course, a great deal of attention and went a long way toward cementing the Campaign both as a marketing tool and in the public consciousness, was called "True Colors," and featured a cover of the popular song by that title, whose lyrics are perfect for the ad's central message. It showed various pre-teen and teenage girls, looking serious, or perhaps sad, with printed captions over them, such as "hates her freckles," "thinks she's ugly," "afraid she's fat," and "wishes she were blonde." The video fades to a branded white screen with the caption, "Let's change their minds." We then see happy young girls (who, not incidentally, are slimmer, blonder, and more conventionally attractive) before the screen fades to white again with the words, "we've created the Dove self-esteem fund." We then see all the original girls, now happy, even joyous, while the captions preach: "because every girl deserves to feel good about herself . . . and see how beautiful she really is."

The final white screen pleads: "Help us. Get involved at campaignforrealbeauty.com."[69]

It is not easy to learn much about the "Self-Esteem Fund." If you visit their current Mission page, there is a place to click to "Learn More" about how "Your Purchase Helps Support Self-Esteem," but although the connected page informs us that "The Dove Self-Esteem Project invites all women to join us in creating a world where beauty is a source of confidence, not anxiety," and that every time we buy a Dove product we help them and their charitable partners "provide inspiring self-esteem programming for girls," that is basically all that we can "learn."[70] The only link on this short page is for "Where to Buy Dove." Visiting any of the sites of the "charitable partners" will uncover many references to the Campaign, with prominent branding visible, but most of the "activities" or "events" seem primarily to involve Dove's promotional material. There is a Dove webpage called "Dove Self Esteem Toolkit & Resources" with "Articles for Parents" and "Resources for Teaching," but many of these are the same as or very little different from the regular product or campaign promotional materials.[71] There are promising activities offered, such as the "Why I'm Brilliant" game, but even this activity starts by asking the young girl to find a photo of herself and put it at the center of what will eventually be a collage ultimately highlighting more than her looks.

To learn about any of this requires some digging, whereas the "problem," as opposed to the "solution," is front and center in the promotional material. The viral videos such as "Daughters," "Onslaught," "Evolution," and "Amy" all highlight the media or social dynamics that Dove suggests are the cause of female insecurity about their looks, or simply note that insecurity in sharply poignant terms. The Mission tab directs to two main pages, one on Self Esteem and one on Real Beauty. The current promotional video highlighted (in the sense that it pops up to cover the rest of the page) on the Real Beauty page is called "Mirrors."[72] About two thirds of the video shows adult women looking in every possible reflective surface to check their appearance, presumably quite critically, judging from their expressions. We then see the branded white screen and the question: "When was the last time you smiled back?" The final segment shows very young girls looking in mirrors and giggling, being goofy, and clearly having fun seeing themselves. The video, of course, suggests that something is lost, something which allows us to feel good about ourselves, somewhere along the way from childhood to adulthood. It does not say what that is, or what is responsible, or what to do about it.

"Amy" and "Daughters" are further examples that merely highlight the problem. In "Daughters" we see young women, seemingly interviewed at random "on the street," as it were, talking about their insecurities concerning their appearance and mothers talking about how hard it is to combat the powerful feelings of inadequacy without any mention of what might be responsible for them. In the more recent video "Amy," a teenage boy rides his bike to Amy's house and calls for her, over and over again, waiting, while the sun sets and no one ever appears. Eventually a caption tells us: "Amy can name 12 things wrong with her appearance. . . . He can't name one." The final caption is: "Sent to you by someone who thinks you're beautiful" (intentionally mimicking viral email language the company hopes will be repeated by the viewer). No one who has experienced the almost universal self-doubt and pain experienced by young women in relation to self-image, either directly or indirectly, can be unmoved by these videos. There most certainly is a problem, a very big problem. That is not in question.

Dove does make some gestures toward articulating some of the causes of the problem. Both the "Onslaught" and "Evolution" videos suggest that it is the rampant photoshopping of marketing images of women, and the subsequent bombardment of those images through mass media, which lead to impossible standards of beauty and distort young women's expectations for themselves and society's attitudes toward beauty as a whole. They are not wrong about this, of course. Indeed, it's obvious, and many others have offered penetrating analysis of the causal dynamics and the often devastating consequences. Dove simply packages the most superficial elements of that analysis into an emotionally powerful narrative. The final admonition of the "Onslaught" video is: "Talk to your daughter before the beauty industry does." Of course, Dove is part of the "beauty industry;" and it's been talking too, for a long time, in precisely the same terms. That they can now sermonize to that industry, and to us, seemingly without any appreciation of irony, clearly demonstrates the degree of autonomous, even anonymous, authority conferred by inhabiting an explicitly moralistic voice, even when the moral lesson is spoken by, in some sense, offending parties.

The most recent viral video is "Real Beauty Sketches," produced in 2013.[73] The video is certainly powerful and very well done. In it, we are introduced to a number of women, mostly younger, and very much mostly white, and a sketch artist formerly with the LA Police department. The women are asked to describe themselves to the sketch artist, who does not see them. He draws the face they describe, and the women leave. Then the artist asks another person who just met each woman to describe her and he draws what they describe. The main part of the video shows the women viewing both sketches and having strong emotional reactions. In each case, the sketches produced from the women's self descriptions are clearly less conventionally attractive and don't represent the women very well. The sketches produced by the descriptions of others are much more faithful to the women's actual appearance. One of the final scenes involves the sketch artist asking one of the women, "Florence," whether she thinks she's more beautiful than she says she is. Florence thinks about it a moment, nods and says, "yeah." Florence then goes on to remark that she should be more grateful of her "natural beauty," and reminds us that beauty "impacts the choices in the friends that we make, the jobs we apply for, how we treat our children . . . it impacts everything . . . it couldn't be more critical to your happiness." The final message, on branded white: "You are more beautiful than you think."

Dove selected from among what all the women said, in response to viewing the sketches of them, to let us hear Florence tell us that beauty is everything, the most critical component determining one's potential for happiness. In allowing her to tell us this, Dove tells us this. Such a claim is not in "debate" with society's definition of beauty. It accepts it fully as the most important thing about a woman. It doesn't offer a counterargument. It merely encourages us to think ourselves as closer to the ideal than we currently do. That is, in its own way, a powerful invitation, and one worth making to a group so battered by the ideal that they are, indeed, their own harshest critics. It would be perhaps better, though, to invite them to reject the ideal, to construct their own hierarchy of qualities and abilities where how one "looks" doesn't, in fact, determine everything.

However powerful the messages, though, at best, Dove just shows us the problem, not what we can do about it, at least not directly. Its invitation to buy a bar of soap or a tube of cream in order to help make the world a better place is, unlike FEED or TOMS, clearly secondary, if not even more tertiary, and it doesn't make it easy to see how its "giving" works. Rather, the Campaign is an explicit invitation to join a moral tribe, one that is configured almost completely on the basis of vague, if powerful, sentiments, and a general agreement with their "concern." It is basically an invitation to recognize that one is already and has long been part of the tribe of the self-image insecure, the beauty industry wounded. It's a big tribe. Dove just wants us to know that it understands us, and our pain, and would like us to feel better, primarily by identifying ourselves with their brand as a way of "fighting back."

Dove configures itself as doing something to help us feel better primarily on the ground that they mention the problem. Its campaign of mentioning it may indeed have sparked a "debate," but it has never participated in that debate in concrete terms, nor, indeed, articulated exactly what the terms of that debate are. It gestures, vaguely, toward cultural or media causes of female insecurity, and invites us, ambiguously, to feel better about ourselves, primarily by thinking ourselves more like the ideal model it really doesn't ever directly challenge than we might otherwise, or, at best, by stretching that model to include just a bit more territory—frizzier hair, slightly larger size or different shape, somewhat older—as long as one is still otherwise attractive by the standard measures. As the blogger, Jazzylittledrops, has noted, there are women that look like the pictures on the left in each pair in the "Real Beauty Sketches" video.[74] What is Dove saying about and to them?

It is important to notice that Dove doesn't once mention any of the products it sells in these videos or the Campaign in general. It doesn't have to. It has branded this concern for self-esteem and "real" beauty. It owns it. It only has to show the Dove logo, which has become more about the campaign than the soap or cream. It has achieved what Rob Walker has called total *murketing*, the seamless connection of a social or moral concern with a brand.[75] *Murketing* is possible because in important ways, moral concern has become free-floating, de-contextualized, abstract, able and ready to be attached to almost any product or brand. This has happened, in part, because of the developing public character of activism, whose primary dynamic, or at least most familiar face, is the mass media call for attention to some problem.

This development has been driven in part by changes in communication technology that increasingly bring the conditions of distant and largely alien elements of the world to our awareness as spectacle, i.e., as something we view without a corresponding ability to interact, to learn from direct engagement, or to effect change except through hypermediated "responses." Boltanski has noted: "It is action above all that is the problem. The spectacle of the unfortunate being conveyed to the witness, the action taken by the witness must in turn be conveyed to the unfortunate. But the instruments which can convey a representation and those which can convey an action are not the same."[76] Except, in the consumer process, they are. We cannot reach out to and interact with the person in need any more than we can with the "person" who makes the material goods we need and use. In our world, contact with either the supplier of our wants and desires or with the person in need of our largesse operates through a chain of intermediaries of whom we know little or nothing, and with whom we have a single relation: we pay them.

One result of these developments is the increasing centrality of emotion and attitude over direct activity, and concern for distant others over engagement in one's own community. In academia, for instance, "activism" is not infrequently parsed as a kind of "solidarity" largely expressed through emotional attachment to "issues" and moral attitudes channeled through "protests" with no clear link to or effect upon those about whom we are concerned. In short, such configurations of activism are little different from the market-driven and market-oriented moral identity packages we have been analyzing.

Given this almost ubiquitous, and even totalizing, character of modern "caring," it is worth asking if such a thing as "public action" in response to moral need (suffering, disaster, crime, corruption, hate and hate-crimes, etc) is even possible. It is worth looking at the power and social relations structured by these new invitations to "care"—to ask who gets to care, about whom and what, and for what reasons. The key idea of conscientious consumption, of course, is to broaden awareness and re-ground consumption in a moral register, reminding all of us that all of our consumer choices have moral consequences in a variety of ways, impacting the environment, people, and the future of economic and social systems. Fair enough; but it is worth asking about the character imparted to caring in general by this emphasis on consumer morality, on taking care of ourselves, each other, and the planet as configured primarily as consumer choice.

Lilie Chouliaraki has written insightfully about this new character of caring. She invites us to reverse the assumption that the spectacle of suffering places an impossible moral demand upon us (imploring us to care in situations where we have no power to act), and instead invites us to consider whether the ubiquity of modern spectacles of suffering aren't in fact altering our sense of moral demand itself, that the norms of morality itself are in tension rather than us as individual spectators.[77] Rather than the good Samaritan who acts to relieve suffering in concrete and direct terms, the modern spectator Samaritan enacts moral obligation through the exercise of emotion, a feeling of pity. What Walker calls *murketing*, accomplished by means of moral care as consumer activity, seeks to fill the vacuum of actual action with its surrogate—buying things—as a way to act upon those emotions and express that pity in concrete terms, harmonious with the modern form of charity, which, as we have noted, almost exclusively occurs through monetary dynamics involving anonymous others and anonymous intermediaries.

Chouliaraki also argues that the spectatorship of suffering has altered the emotion of "pity" from a "natural sentiment," perhaps of love and care, as she suggests, but perhaps of a more fundamental socio-biological character, to a socially constructed disposition, or, I would argue, identity package, which locates both actors (pitier and pitied) firmly within a limited and primarily economic range of possibilities and norms.[78] The practices of journalism (her focus), she argues, and of marketing I would add, both in terms of discourse and image, construct both parties within a "narrow repertoire of participatory positions" which include very few options beyond indifference and a variety of vicarious "activisms" meant to concretely express the emotional reactions elicited by the spectacle. For her, the "public" engaged and aroused by these spectacles are not empirical entities, but "symbolic act[s] of cultural identity" that carve an ephemeral "we" out of a collection of spectators.[79] They are tribes. Within this larger and new dynamic, I would add, marketing is busy (re)shaping our moral norms through a staging of possible relations to "others" in "need" that do not allow us to guide, much less control, the outcomes or experience the effects of our "activity" beyond the immediate and personal experience of consumption. Thus, consumption takes on a new and higher dynamic, whereby the usual activity is elevated to activism, and the buying and consuming of goods also counts as an act of social "good."

The primary dynamic in most activist marketing configures moral action as primarily, if not exclusively, brand selection. We do good by choosing one brand over another, and not by any other overt action on our part, aside from the consumer activity in which we were already going to participate: buying things. Such a configuration of moral action integrates fully with brand marketing in general, since that strategy seeks to construct morally charged meaning systems as brand identities. Most brand identities aren't as explicit as TOMS or Target/FEED or Dove at presenting themselves and the consumption of their products as moral activism; but all brand identities seek to inhabit and present identity "personas" that feel good to us and strike us as admirable, even enviable, offering to confer those very qualities upon us through participation in their brand.

We obviously and clearly recognize that on some level, such marketing is a kind of propaganda, a way of making us feel good about the brand and ourselves without making many, if any, demands upon us. Acknowledging this character offers a further perspective on the deeper dynamics whereby morality lends itself to market use. As I will argue in the final chapter, morality in consumer culture has become, if it has not in some sense always been, a kind of sociological propaganda, in Jacques Ellul's sense: a simplified, abstract idea propagated to satisfy our need for meaning and importance and to respond to our sense that the world is problematic, with a proposed solution involving the recovering of values or value systems largely configured as market options. In the final chapter I will focus on the question of how morality is configured in the popular consciousness, both in light of all the moralizing we have been analyzing, and as inflected by it; but I will also take up specifically the important and interesting question of how morality already works in that consciousness such that it can be put to use in the ways we have seen: to gather us into moral "tribes," to offer us moral identities as consumer goods, and to sell things.

NOTES

1. Lilie Chouliaraki, *The Spectatorship of Suffering* (London: Sage, 2006), 147. See also *The Ironic Spectator* (Cambridge: Polity, 2013). Together, these works offer an illuminating analysis of the moral implications and invitations presented by mass media spectacles of suffering, particularly through broadcast journalism in her first book, but expanding to include celebrity appeals and events in her second. Clearly, given my analysis so far, I am rather firmly in what she would call the "pessimistic" analytical camp; and, unlike her, I will not offer any normative prescriptions for what we could or should do about the phenomena I am analyzing.

2. Ben Affleck, accessed on May 27, 2014, toms.com/easterncongo.

3. Ellul, 209.

4. Slavoj Žižek, *First as Tragedy, Then as Farce* (London: Verso, 2009) and "First as Tragedy, Then as Farce," RSA Animate lecture, November 24, 2009, accessed on November 13, 2013, thersa.org/events/video/archive/slavoj-zizek-first-as-tragedy,-then-as-farce.

5. As explained on the webpage "Conscious Consumerism," by *The Center for a New American Dream*, accessed on May 19, 2014, newdream.org/programs/beyond-consumerism/rethinking-stuff/conscious-consumerism. Conscious consumerism, with its emphasis on simplification and living a life as minimally consumerist as possible, seems antithetical to market-

ing on its face, but the appeal has been incorporated into much marketing rather directly, as we have seen in some of the examples already analyzed. It is perhaps the least influential of the related ethical consumerist movements, but it has achieved a significant popularity among certain elements of society. *Huffington Post*, for instance, uses "Conscious Consumerism" as a tag and news category (see huffingtonpost.com/tag/conscious-consumerism/), and the articles so tagged on their website connect to a broad range of related topics. *Huffington Post* also uses "doing well by doing good" as a tag, as does *Forbes*.

6. However one interprets or understands *kashrut*, the Jewish dietary laws have always involved a moral component, such as the insistence on separating the meat of an animal from milk, which many rabbinical commentators regarded as having an ethical aspect, or slaughtering animals by methods that ensure respect and compassion.

7. This "cause" made a central appearance with all the now familiar corporate dynamics in the 1978 movie *Heaven Can Wait*, demonstrating that such movements had achieved popular recognition and a kind of cultural capital by the end of the decade.

8. *Green America*, accessed May 10, 2014, greenamerica.org/about/.

9. An early and popular "guide" to participation in the movement for the consumer is Julia Hailes, *Green Consumer Guide*, published in 1987, and in a new edition, *The New Green Consumer Guide* (New York: Simon and Schuster, 2007). For questions as to its effectiveness and apologies in response, see the special issue dedicated to the topic in the *Journal of Marketing Management*, 14 (1998) or Toby Smith, *The Myth of Green Marketing* (Toronto: University of Toronto Press, 1998).

10. See, e.g., Jaime Rivera-Camino, "Re-evaluating green marketing strategy: a stakeholder perspective," *European Journal of Marketing* 41 (2007): 1328–1358; or J. Joseph Cronin, Jr., et al., "Green marketing strategies: an examination of stakeholders and the opportunities they present," *Journal of the Academy of Marketing Science* 30 (2010).

11. The term was first coined by Jay Westerveld in a 1986 essay about the hotel industry according to Jim Motavalli, "A History of Greenwashing: How Dirty Towels Impacted the Green Movement," *AOL Daily Finance*, accessed Feb 15, 2011, dailyfinance.com/2011/02/12/the-history-of-greenwashing-how-dirty-towels-impacted-the-green. See also Richard Dahl, "Green Washing: Do You Know What You're Buying?", *Environmental Health Perspectives*, 118 (2010): 246-252.

12. John McMurtry, *Unequal Freedoms: The Global Market as an Ethical System* (West Hartford, CT: Kumarian, 1998).

13. "Ben & Jerry's Corporate Social Responsibility," accessed on May 19, 2014, bjsocial-responsibility.weebly.com/. See also Brad Edmondson, *Ice Cream Social: The Struggle for the Soul of Ben & Jerry's* (San Francisco: Berrett-Koehler Publishers, 2014).

14. For a critique of these practices, see David Henderson, *Misguided Virtue: False Notions of Corporate Social Responsibility* (London: Institute of Economic Affairs, 2001).

15. E.g., "Issues We Care About," accessed May 19, 2014, benjerry.com/values/issues-we-care-about.

16. Nancy Koehn, "A Brief History of Doing Well by Doing Good," video blog interview on *Harvard Business Review*, accessed June 25, 2012, blogs.hbr.org/2012/06/a-brief-history-of-doing-well.

17. *Ethical Consumer*, accessed May 10, 2014, ethicalconsumer.org/aboutus.aspx.

18. "Quick Guide to Using *Ethical Consumer*," *Ethical Consumer*, accessed May 19, 2014, ethicalconsumer.org/home/quickguide.aspx.

19. There is an impressive amount of both scholarship and popular literature over the past several decades that attempts to look at moral philosophy, or the origins of morality itself, in terms of evolutionary theory. Richard Dawkins' book, *The Selfish Gene* (Oxford: Oxford University Press, 1989) was one of the first to introduce this possibility into the popular conversation. I will highlight the following that have served to inform my own thinking on the matter: Jerome H. Barkow, Leda Cosmides, and John Tooby, *The Adapted Mind* (Oxford: Oxford University Press, 1992); Richard Wright, *The Moral Animal: Why We Are the Way We Are: The New Science of Evolutionary Psychology* (New York: Vintage, 1995); Matt Ridley, *The Origins of Virtue* (New York: Penguin, 1996); William R. Clark and Michael Grunstein, *Are We Hardwired?: The Role of Genes in Human Behavior* (Oxford: Oxford University Press,

2000); Leonard D. Katz, ed., *Evolutionary Origins of Morality* (Bowling Green, OH: Imprint Academic, 2002); Michael S. Gazzaniga, *The Ethical Brain: The Science of our Moral Dilemmas* (New York: Harper Collins, 2005); Frans De Waal, *Primates and Philosophers* (Princeton, NJ: Princeton University Press, 2006); Marc D. Hauser, *Moral Minds* (New York: Harper Collins, 2006); and Frans De Waal, *The Age of Empathy* (New York: Random House, 2009). Much of this scholarship focuses upon the central role of emotions, or what Adam Smith called the "moral sentiments," in our moral attitudes and behaviors. Among works that first looked at evolutionary theory or evolutionary psychology in particular relation to ethics and morality and the role emotions play in both, see Iris Murdoch, *The Sovereignty of Good* (New York: Routledge & Kegan Paul, 1970); Bernard Williams' seminal essay, "Morality and the Emotions" in his *Problems of the Self* (Cambridge: Cambridge University Press, 1973); and also Robert Frank, *Passions Within Reason* (New York: Norton, 1988); Antonio Damasio, *Descartes' Error: Emotion, Reason, and the Human Brain* (New York: Penguin, 1994); and James Q. Wilson, *The Moral Sense* (New York: Simon & Schuster, 1997), or, for more recent engagements, Carla Bagnoli, ed., *Morality and the Emotions* (Oxford: Oxford University Press, 2012) and Robert C. Roberts, *Emotions in the Moral Life* (Cambridge: Cambridge University Press, 2013).

For more technical surveys of the debate over the moral role of emotions in the social sciences, see Elliott Sober and David Sloan Wilson, *Unto Others: The Evolution and Psychology of Unselfish Behavior* (Cambridge, MA: Harvard University Press, 1998); Ulliga Segestrale, *Defenders of the Truth: the Battle for Science in the Sociobiology Debate and Beyond* (Oxford: Oxford University Press, 2000); Samir Okasha, *Evolution and the Levels of Selection* (Oxford: Oxford University Press, 2006); and E. G. Leigh, Jr, 'The Group Selection Controversy' *Journal of Evolutionary Biology* 23 (2010).

For more general surveys, see Jonathan Haidt, "The Moral Emotions" in R. J. Davidson, K. R. Scherer, & H. H. Goldsmith, eds., *Handbook of Affective Sciences* (Oxford: Oxford University Press, 2003), 852–870; Jesse Prinz, "The Emotional Basis of Moral Judgments" *Philosophical Explorations* 9 (2006): 29–43; June Price Tangney, Jeff Stuewig, and Debra Mashek, "Moral Emotions and Moral Behavior" *Annual Review of Psychology* 58 (2007): 345–372; James Blair and Katherine Fowler, "Moral Emotions and Moral Reasoning from the Perspective of Affective Cognitive Neuroscience: A Selective Review" *European Journal of Developmental Science* 2 (2008): 303–323; and Elizabeth Horberg, Christopher Oveis, and Dacher Keltner, "Emotions as Moral Amplifiers: An Appraisal Tendency Approach to the Influences of Distinct Emotions upon Moral Judgment" *Emotion Review* 3 (2011): 237-244.

20.   As translated from Nikolai Chernyshevsky's *What is to be Done?* in the introduction to Fyodor Dostoevsky, *Notes from Underground*, trs. Richard Pevear and Larissa Volokhonsky (New York: Alfred A. Knopf, 1993), xiv.

21.   Trevelino-Keller's claim to the status of fourth fastest growing PR firm, a somewhat unfocused bit of PR itself, may be found on its website: trevelinokeller.com, accessed May 10, 2014. The press release, "First Carbon Neutral Zone Created in the United States" may be found at www.verus.co2.com/Docs/Verus_VAHighlandsPR%20REV4.pdf, accessed May 10, 2014.

22.   Leslie Kaufman, "Ad for Dish Detergent Becomes Part of a Story," *New York Times*, June 15, 2010.

23.   "Dawn Animals Commercial," commercial for Dawn Dish Detergent, accessed May 20, 2014, schooltube.com/video/249f1df7bd72a1887cc8.

24.   "Open," Dawn dish detergent commercial, accessed on May 20, 2014, dawn-dish.com/us/dawn/commercials. Dawn has also posted the commercial on YouTube, youtube.com/watch?v=RFStdNtTkNI.

25.   "Saving Wildlife," Dawn commercial, accessed on May 20, 2014, ispot.tv/ad/7Vq3/dawn-saving-wildlife.

26.   Jack Neff, "Brita's Marketing Grows from Grassroots Efforts," *AdvertisingAge*, accessed November 20, 2009, adage.com/article/cmo-interviews/brita-s-marketing-flows-grassroots-effort/140519.

27.   "Facts on Water Worldwide," *AquaAccess*, accessed on May 21, 2014, aquaaccess.com/downloads/WaterStatistics.pdf.

28. Neff.

29. Nalgene "store" webpage for "Filter for Good," accessed May 21, 2014, store.nalgene.com/category-s/35.htm.

30. Neff.

31. "2009 Brita Climate Ride: My Hope for the Future," Brita PR video, accessed on May 20, 2014, dailymotion.com/BritaFilterForGood.

32. Feeding America, at feedingamerica.org/. The organization changed its name to Feeding America in 2008, after being named as an "Idol Gives Back" charity organization on *American Idol*.

33. See, e.g., the Center For the Advancement of Social Entrepreneurship at Duke's Fuqua School of Business, caseatduke.org/.

34. Feed 5 Woven Bracelet, retail web page accessed May 21, 2014, feedprojects.com/shopping_product_detail.asp?pid=49994&catID=3675. Interestingly, the "story" for the original FEED 1 bag, designed by Lauren, includes the interesting final comment, faithfully echoing the rhetorical binary of "truth-telling" narratives: "The bag is reversible, too, since we know there are two sides to every great story." Accessed May 21, 2014, feedprojects.com/shopping_product_detail.asp?pid=49368&catID=3673.

35. "About Us," *FEED Foundation*, accessed May 21, 2014, thefeedfoundation.org/About-Us. Lauren Bush, Jenny Johns, and Kristina Fell serve both as managing directors on the Board of Directors of FEED Foundation and as executives in FEED Projects. There are only two other members of the Board for the foundation.

36. "Our Mission," FEED Projects website, accessed May 21, 2014, feedprojects.com/our-mission.

37. "FEED USA," FEED Projects + Target campaign website, accessed May 21, 2014, feedprojects.com/target.asp.

38. See, e.g., "Target and FEED Partner to Fight Hunger in the US," or "Target and FEED Partner on Exclusive Collection to Fight Hunger in the US," Target press releases, accessed May 11, 2013, corporate.target.com/discover/article/Target-and-FEED-partner-to-fight-hunger-in-the-U-S and pressroom.target.com/news/target-and-feed-partner-on-exclusive-collection-to-fight-hunger-in-the-u-s.

39. Hadley Malcolm, "Target Partners with Lauren Bush," *USA Today*, accessed on May 11, 2013, usatoday.com/story/money/business/2013/03/11/target-lauren-bush-feed-partnership/1967139.

40. "Cause Marketing Remains Strong: 2010 Cone Cause Evolution Study," Cone Communications PR release about a 17 year study on consumer interest in cause marketing, accessed on May 11, 2013, conecomm.com/cause-marketing-remains-strong.

41. They are also accustomed to using communication technology to accomplish much of their life activity. As I was writing this chapter, I came across a bumper sticker advertising the website, howgiving.com, with the slogan, "automate your thoughtfulness." A quick visit of the website revealed its pitch to Millennials: "It's about giving. HowGiving is a desktop and mobile app designed to make us the givers we truly intend to be. By automating the process of reminding, then guiding you quickly through the purchase process of a card, flowers, or a gift, you transform from . . . *well you* . . . into the big giver you were meant to be! In addition, you can calculate your own Charitable Donation Percentage on each purchase to be designated for the charity or cause of your choice." This site does not present consumption as moral activism, but it does offer to "automate" one's charitable and more general "giving," offering the consumer a cheap and easy way to morally improve themselves, all through a handy app.

42. "Feed USA: Kate," accessed May 14, 2014, http://www.ispot.tv/ad/7toS/target-feed-usa-kate.

43. "About TOMS," accessed on May 22, 2014, toms.com/about-toms#companyInfo.

44. "Our Movement," accessed on June 22, 2011, toms.com/our-movement.

45. "Corporate Responsibility at TOMS," accessed on May 23, 2014, toms.com/about-toms#corporateResponsibility, and "2013 Giving Report," accessed May 23, 2014, toms.com/static/www/pdf/TOMS_Giving_Report_2013.pdf.

46. "TOMS—Change One Decision to Help Change a Life," accessed on May 27, 2014, youtube.com/watch?v=LGO1TFH1seo&list=PLvSoqFwcrRNi-Vh01q0YDfWPLlLHW_rkJ.

47. "One for One," accessed on May 22, 2014, toms.com/one-for-one-en.
48. See tomscommunity.com/TOMSCampusClubs, accessed on May 23, 2014. TOMS has also produced a video for YouTube, one of many it posts there, extolling the virtues of TOMS campus clubs in evangelistic tones through the earnest testimonials of college students who have joined: youtube.com/watch?v=G9DVVyBKlYs. They have also posted an "Employee" video, youtube.com/watch?v=Ojs2VPQlZR8&feature=kp, which presents the opportunity to work at TOMS in similarly evangelistic and earnest tones.
49. Blake was invited by my university's former president, Jake Schrum, to give our 2011 Shilling Lecture. This lecture series has featured such speakers as Jane Goodall, Thomas Friedman, Wangari Maathai, Bill Bradley, James Baker III, Benazir Bhutto, Desmond Tutu, President Jimmy Carter, and William Sloane Coffin. Blake's lecture was titled, "The New Rules for Tomorrow's Business: A Student's Guide to Making a Difference in the World."
50. "Corporate Responsibility at TOMS," accessed on May 23, 2014, toms.com/about-toms#corporateResponsibility.
51. "Auditing Services for Consumer Goods," accessed on May 23, 2014, intertek.com/consumer/auditing/. Mention of Intertek was made on an earlier version of the company's "Questions" page, "FAQ," accessed on October 24, 2011, toms.com/faq. This version included the question, "How does TOMS ensure its manufacturers adhere to human rights standards?" which ended its response with the following: "For more information: intertek-labtest.com/services/auditing/intertek_compliance/?lang=en." There is no such question or response on current versions of the website as of this writing. Intertek is a large global auditing firm which offers quality, compliance and testing services for many of the world's transnational corporations and even many governments. The company's services have received some journalistic and legal attention in the past, including cases involving laboratory fraud, slave labor, and the inspection of contaminated grain. See "Regulations and You: the long arm of the lab laws," *Today's Chemist at Work* November (2000), accessed October 24, 2011, pubs.acs.org/sub-scribe/archive/tcaw/10/i11/html/11regs.html; "Fresh allegations of 'human slavery' emerge from the tomato fields of Immokalee," and "Guilty! On eve of trial, farm bosses plead guilty to enslaving Immokalee workers in tomato harvest . . .," *Coalition of Immokalee Workers News*, accessed on October 24, 2011, ciw-online.org/blog/2007/12/no_slave_labor/ and ciw-on-line.org/blog/2008/09/guilty-on-eve-of-trial-farm-bosses-plead-guilty-to-enslaving-immokal-ee-workers-in-tomato-harvest/; and "Insurer pays cereals board for bad grain," *Daily Nation*, Kenya, October 24, 2011.
52. It is reasonable to ask, though, even should one accept this model of philanthropy on its face, how many children could be shod or fed if the apparently substantial profits of these companies were more directly channeled into providing the "aid" that is the central marketing element, if not also *the* primary consumer "good" being offered. None of these companies claim, as part of their social responsibility, to have adopted business models that substantially reduce the enormous salaries usually paid to top executives, for instance. One can fairly ask why only *one* pair of shoes for each pair bought? Or, indeed, why buy such an expensive shoe in the first place rather than sending the not insignificant sum directly to a humanitarian organization?
53. "Marketplace," accessed on May 23, 2014, toms.com/marketplace.
54. "Introducing the TOMS Animal Initiative," TOMS Press Release, May 13, 2014, ac-cessed May 20, 2014, toms.com/stories/movement/introducing-the-toms-animal-initiative. See also toms.com/the-toms-animal-initiative.
55. "The Gift of Water," accessed May 27, 2014, toms.com/gift-of-water.
56. "Direct Trade," accessed May 27, 2014, toms.com/coffee#direct-trade-coffee.
57. "Every Stripe Tells a Story," retail outlet page for TOMS eyewear, accessed on May 27, 2014, pinterest.com/tomscanada/every-stripe-tells-a-story.
58. "TOMS Eyewear—Nepal Giving Trip," accessed on June 22, 2011, youtube.com/watch?v=sz7-iwmNkRA.
59. "TOMS What's Your Next Chapter," accessed on June 22, 2011, youtube.com/watch?v=EesOoKSbc4A.
60. "TOMS: Next Chapter—Ben Affleck's One for One," accessed on June 22, 2011, youtube.com/watch?v=OeS4S5ufl6o.

61. "The Dove Campaign for Real Beauty," accessed on May 28, 2014, dove.us/Social-Mission/campaign-for-real-beauty.aspx.

62. Award for Excellence in Public Relations, 2005, given to WHPR, accessed November 9, 2011, prca.ie/download/consumermore20k.pdf.

63. See, also, banda.ie/maket-research-company/who-we-are/company-overview.html, accessed May 28, 2014.

64. "The Real Truth About Beauty: A Global Report," accessed May 28, 2014, clubofamsterdam.com/contentarticles/52%20Beauty/dove_white_paper_final.pdf. StrategyOne is a global market research and opinion polling firm owned by Edelman, the world's largest independent public relations firm.

65. Lauren Dye, "Consuming Constructions: A Critique of Dove's Campaign for Real Beauty," *Canadian Journal of Media Studies* 5 (2009): 114-128.

66. "The Real Truth About Beauty: Revisited," cited on Dove's Mission webpage, accessed May 28, 2014, dove.us/Social-Mission/campaign-for-real-beauty.aspx.

67. "Our Vision," accessed May 28, 2014, dove.us/Our-Mission/Girls-Self-Esteem/Vision/default.aspx.

68. These videos are widely available for viewing. "Little Girls" may be found at adland.tv/commercials/dove-true-colors-2006-45-usa; "Daughters" on the Vimeo channel of its director, Yael Staav, vimeo.com/15858914; "Evolution" on the YouTube channel of its director, Tim Piper, youtube.com/watch?v=iYhCn0jf46U&feature=kp; "Onslaught" on the Vimeo channel of its creative director, David Hayman, who also produced a video for Brita, vimeo.com/4097693; and "Amy" on Dove's YouTube channel, youtube.com/watch?v=RWbtaj5kSUk. A less well-known video, specifically featuring older women in order to promote Dove's "Pro-Age" lotion, can be viewed on Experimenta Design's Vimeo page, vimeo.com/17210728.

69. If one visits campaignforrealbeauty.com today, one arrives at a website for Medifast diet products.

70. "Your Purchase Counts," accessed May 29, 2014, dove.us/Social-Mission/Your-Purchase-Counts/default.aspx.

71. "Self Esteem Toolkit & Resources," accessed on May 29, 2014, dove.us/Our-Mission/Girls-Self-Esteem/Get-Involved/default.aspx.

72. "Beauty is . . .," accessed on May 29, 2014, dove.us/Our-Mission/Real-Beauty/default.aspx. The remainder of the page is an invitation to twitter #beautyis... with some of the submissions presented on the page, and an archive of past years' videos and submissions.

73. There are several versions of this video. On Dove's main site, you can view this one: realbeautysketches.dove.us. On Dove's YouTube page, you can view a longer version: youtube.com/watch?v=litXW91UauE. The longer version is the one that went viral. See Tanzina Vega, "Ad About Women's Self-Image Creates a Sensation," *New York Times*, April 18, 2013. An insightful blog analysis of this video, prompted by the "sharing" of the video by several friends, can be found here: jazzylittledrops.tumblr.com/post/48118645174/why-doves-real-beauty-sketches-video-makes-me.

74. "Little Drops," accessed on October 13, 2013, jazzylittledrops.tumblr.com/post/48118645174/why-doves-real-beauty-sketches-video-makes-me.

75. Rob Walker, *Buying In: The Secret Dialogue Between What We Buy and Who We Are* (New York: Random House, 2008).

76. Luc Boltanski, *Distant Suffering: Morality, Media, and Politics* (Cambridge: Cambridge University Press, 1999), 17.

77. Chouliaraki, 2.

78. Chouliaraki, 11, and Chapter 8.

79. Chouliaraki, 12.

Chapter Eight

Morality as Propaganda

"Stories enmesh people in a single society by transmitting pictures of how the world is or ought to be."[1]

These are the stories we consume and inhabit. They surround us, constantly talking about the same things, urging the same activity, uttering the same magic words, and promising largely the same dream world just at the end of our fingertips (the ones cradling the credit card). They speak to us about what matters, about what moves us, about our desires and hopes. They configure us in particular ways, as consumer and consumable, mirroring but reshaping and reorienting our desires and dreams, presenting quite particular and limited possibilities for what kind of person to be and how to become that person. They gather us into tribes, imagined and hyperreal communities, (re)orienting us toward duty and obligation exercised through some material and consumer good. But as de Certeau has cogently argued, it is not only, and perhaps not even primarily what the producers of these representations intend that matters, but the uses to which the consumer puts them.[2] The question is not only, at least, and perhaps not primarily what it is the marketers desire to accomplish, but what it is we *do* with what they give us, how it is that we inhabit their stories, or re-story them as our own. This is particularly important to ask, I believe, since I have argued that marketing is largely in the re-storying business itself.

It is reasonable to ask what these stories do to the elements they repurpose, whoever tells them, to ask how the values, meanings, emotions, and dreams are configured and re-configured, to ask what it does to moral lessons to be taught by banks or fast food restaurants or car manufacturers in order to sell us things. The answer is rather obvious, however. As I have argued, it makes them commodities. The values, the life ways, the family and relational dynamics these dominant stories speak of become as much the commodities we are invited to acquire as any material good on display in the marketing; and they are acquired not through practice or habit, hard work or self-development, but in the marketplace, almost without effort, but for a price.

Whatever is commodity, or has become commodity, has, in some ways, a radically different ontological character. First, of course, a commodity is an economic entity. It is bought and sold. It is fungible, both in the sense that it has an exchange value and in the sense that its instances are treated as equivalent without regard both to origin and final user except as differentiated through branding. A commodity is, therefore, a market entity which satisfies market desires or needs (primarily desires), and so is integrally connected to marketing and advertising (which almost exclusively addresses desires, even if configured *as* needs under the name of "convenience"). Its exchange value is determined on that basis by the market as a whole.

Further, a commodity always expresses a mass character. Commodities are usually mass-produced, and so homogeneous and interchangeable for that reason as well. Ultimately, though, even if crafted by hand, a commodity is a "product," and so "produced," manufactured through some process rather than organic or inherent to other ontological conditions. That process is both accepted and then dismissed as occurring at some epistemic distance. We don't usually know how any of our "products" are made, and so we can comfortably remain ignorant of the structure and genealogy of these new commodities as well, when otherwise, experienced not as commodities, such properties or histories might seem to be important to understand.

Since a commodity is interchangeable, its value is grounded in its *use*, not in itself as an end, which gives it "use value" in addition to an exchange value. The original term, *commoditas*, means the fitness or adaptation of something for a particular use, from the root, *commod-*, which means "advantage" or "benefit" and includes the notion of "appropriate" and "proper," but primarily in a utile rather than moral sense. When morality or emotions or other human dynamics become commodities, they are transformed from something with at least some intrinsic value, something organic and grounded in a particular history about which it is important to know if we are to fully understand them, to something whose value is determined by their largely symbolic use in an economic market. Because such commodified human dynamics are fungible, the illusion of "freedom" and "choice" is enhanced, particularly in the sense of freely choosing between competing alternatives (brands). They become something we *can* but need not "have," but always "have" even if we are also invited by them to "be."

Of course, our human dynamics are *not* in fact "produced" in some manufacturing process, not, in fact, fungible, not mass. They are, if they are anything other than a hyperrealized abstraction of human dynamics, concrete, contextual, situated, and particular, whose value exists in their being, and not in their being possessed. Such a transformation is radical indeed, and worth giving very careful and critical attention, something a number of thinkers have provided over the past several decades. There is another quite interesting question, however, as I have noted, that has received significantly less critical attention. That is the question of what morality already has to be for us for it to be commodified and so readily adapted to market use. My response to that question is that morality has to have already become for us, primarily, a kind of moralism. I want to conclude this book by further developing a distinction I began making at its beginning, the distinction between morality and moralizing. I want to acknowledge and use a general term for the popular engagement with morality that largely consists of the latter practice and which recognizes a severely conventional and exaggerated emphasis on morality: moralism. In contemporary mass culture, there is a great deal more moralism than there is morality.

We recognize, of course, that marketing narratives are a kind of propaganda, urging particular (consumer) activity and trying to persuade us to look at the world and ourselves in particular ways. Morality, as moralism, is also a kind of propaganda and lends itself to market use so readily because it shares with marketing, to a considerable extent, structures and dynamics exhibited by what Jacques Ellul calls "sociological propaganda." Marketing didn't turn morality into moralism. We did that already. Marketing just uses the instrument we provided already adapted to its uses. Moralism and marketing, as sociological propaganda, collaborate and feed each other in ways that enhance their propaganda power. I would argue that it would be very difficult at this point to disentangle their narrative threads and myth dynamics, that we can't really understand either without at least attempting to understand both and their relations, as I have attempted over the course of this book.

As I explained at the beginning, the term "moral" refers to principles, behavior, actions, character, rules, values, codes, judgments, and decisions we each and all of us make or perform or express on a daily basis, either with the aim of making ourselves or the world better in some way or engaged as a critical practice of living. Moralism is about the same things, but hyperrealized, abstract and symbolic and exaggerated, often invoked in quasi- or even more direct religious tones. Moralism is hyper-morality. In this chapter I want to explain and briefly discuss Ellul's notion of "sociological propaganda" as something we inhabit and in which we fully participate rather than, as we usually understand propaganda, something someone else does *to* us. For Ellul, sociological propaganda is a *culture*, our modern mass culture. I want to show how the structures and dynamics of sociological propaganda rely upon and mirror the structures and dynamics of mass media, particularly marketing. I then want to discuss how morality has become moralism and what that means in our culture in terms of practice and in terms of how we story ourselves and our possibilities. Finally, I want to invite inquiry into what is problematic in this transformation and these uses, to ask how else we might be able or wish to story ourselves and why.

SOCIOLOGICAL PROPAGANDA

Jacques Ellul pioneered the sociological analysis of propaganda in the early 1960s, departing significantly from the largely psychological approach practiced before, and offering a sophisticated new understanding of propaganda as enmeshed in our larger cultures.[3] For Ellul, the most important kind of propaganda was not manufactured by an individual or group in order to sway opinions or spur action in some particular public; but inhabited by individuals in mass as a culture in which they fully participate, and which no person or group alone can control or substantially shape. The central work of such sociological propaganda is always to integrate and adapt the individual to society through the inner control exerted by social forces. Ellul distinguishes sociological propaganda from psychological propaganda, explaining that the former exists primarily within the various methods of communication "by which any society seeks to integrate the maximum number of individuals into itself, to unify its members' behavior according to a pattern, to spread its style of life abroad, and thus to impose itself on other groups."[4] Ellul calls this "sociological" first to indicate that the entire group expresses itself through this function and practice, whether consciously or not, and secondly to indicate that it aims at an entire way of living rather than primarily at opinions or actions.

This aim and practice make sociological propaganda much more difficult to notice and analyze than political propaganda. The term propaganda generally signifies political propaganda in the popular mind, a state organ that speaks for and from the state in obvious ways. In sociological propaganda, unlike its political counterpart, the various means of mass communication are not marshaled to the task of spreading an ideology or leading a public to accept some structure or practice as a discrete element of their life; but, rather, the existing ideological, economic, political, and broader cultural environment is progressively structured so as to allow an ideology to penetrate individuals or groups in order for it to be experienced as a life way, as what we are as a whole. It feels spontaneous, because in an important sense it is, since one cannot generate sociological propaganda as a pre-conceived strategy, but only participate in its development.

Such a propaganda is diffused throughout social structure and practice and produces a general "climate" rather than targeted and specific communications, influencing the individual slowly, but progressively and powerfully, because through custom or habit. It is, in an important sense, persuasion from within, as one adopts, as if freely and from oneself, new criteria of judgment and choice, producing an inexorable adaptation "to a certain order of things, a certain concept of human relations."[5] In sociological propaganda, the individual participates willingly, even if unknowingly, by virtue of his or her participation in the structures of society. In a very important sense, we are all propagandists in this way, not because we choose to actively propagandize, but because we are permeated with a "way of life" that we cannot help but communicate any time we express ourselves. Such propaganda expresses itself constantly in many ways in society, as Ellul notes: "in advertising, the movies . . . , in technology in general, in education . . . all these influences are in basic accord with each other and lead spontaneously in the same direction."[6]

Ellul believes that the United States, at the end of the nineteenth century, was faced with the particular problem of bringing together a disparate population originating from all the countries of Europe and beyond, inhabiting diverse traditions and cultures that created, in many ways, different worlds for each of them. The "solution" to this "problem" was to champion an "American way of life" as a basis of unification and standardization. Further, the US became a manufacturing nation, and mass production requires mass consumption, which is not possible unless there is mass agreement as to what is necessary or desirable, which requires mass marketing constantly valorizing the ideal which it does not generate, but rather finds and uses as a natural and even inevitable function of its practice and structure.

Ellul acknowledges that it can be difficult to recognize such broad phenomena as propaganda as we usually use that term; and he believes the failure to recognize it enhances its power. He insists that it is propaganda because the combination of advertising, public relations, and the various other mass media produces a "certain conception of society," expressing the same basic notions and fostering the same basic ways of life.[7] This is facilitated by the fact that many mass media voices are owned by a few large corporations, but the primary factor is that they all tell largely the same stories. Even if every mass media voice were independent, as long as each of them borrows the primary motifs and larger narratives from each other, as they do, then any imagined distinction flowing from plurality and independence is for the most part negated. Ellul's analysis is comprehensive and complex, but there are several primary elements that are important to highlight to both understand his notion more fully and see the connections to marketing and moralism more clearly. These include the mass and totalizing character of sociological propaganda, its connections to pre-existing myths and ideals, and the necessity for it to speak to our needs and desires.

Sociological propaganda always configures the individual in relation to and as an instance of some mass entity. That mass entity, what Kierkegaard called the "public," is constructed and exists as an abstraction, as the "phantom" subject addressed through each concrete individual. If the individual can be led to listen to mass address as that mass subject, in terms of what he or she has in common with others, then the individual configures him or herself in concrete and material terms as an instance of some larger entity, as constituting it, but nonetheless sublimated within it.[8] Sociological propaganda aims first and foremost to perform such an integrating function in which all the activities, sentiments, perspectives and ideas of an individual are presented as meaningful and fulfilled within the collective community *while at the same time* presenting the individual as having higher value, as being the ultimate source for these values and meanings, yet as *equal* (not more or less valuable) to all others, thus valorizing the ideal of the free or independent individual while reinforcing the actual and innumerable bonds and forces to which each individual is subject.

This integration is accomplished through constant mass address, breaking the individual free from his or her actual local and organic groups—family, local community, work or school—and connecting him or her directly to society as a whole through newly imagined "local," yet universal, groups—tribes. Even at work and at school, even while we express and inhabit rhetoric designed to highlight and relatively valuate the distinctiveness of each local group—this school or employer as better than another—we are addressed and treated as standardized entities, as "worker" or "student," and measured against wholly abstract and universal standards. Such abstracted "local" groups are not understood to be truly distinctive, but rather in a competitive sense as better or worse at expressing or performing the universal good than another. Even our rebellious rhetoric that seeks to recognize and respond to this mass character, our talk of "breaking free from the box," constructs new and still universal "boxes" which we must inhabit and to which we are expected (because we expect ourselves) to conform.

Ellul remarks: "When individuals are not held together by local structures, the only form in which they can live together is in an unstructured mass society. Similarly, a mass society can only be based on individuals—that is, on [individuals] in their isolation, whose identities are determined by their relationships with one another."[9] As is typical with binaries, one polar term requires the other for either to exist. A society that remains organically local can be neither individualistic nor mass, and thus is much more resistant to propaganda of any sort. In mass society, the individual largely moves in and through crowds rather than in actual communal groups, both physically and heuristically, since even when we find ourselves in an actual local community, such as family, we are still addressed by mass narratives as interchangeable instances of a type, a fact which reinforces our mass character. As social psychology has repeatedly shown, the individual in the crowd is more available, credulous, suggestible and excitable, because more anonymous and isolated. Mass media is then able to provoke and provide the isolated individual an identity in the group, to enable him or her to "communicate" with the group (even though most communication is from the group to the individual addressed as member).

To accomplish this simultaneously isolating and integrating function, propaganda must ground itself in the pre-existing fundamental currents of the society it seeks to influence. Dominant myths and stereotypes are taken up from society, transformed into mass variants, and represented as "public opinion." Such activity requires a mass society which understands itself abstractly. Concrete individuals, particularly in large numbers, cannot of course experience any concrete event or fact in the same fashion. Therefore, a "public" opinion can be formed and held by individuals only upon the basis that what actually separates them from each other is ignored and the concrete is replaced by the abstract symbol that represents it, the more remote from reality the more effective.

Such symbols must be total and totalizing. They must and do speak to every aspect of us, to our dreams and emotions and ideas, to both our individual and private and our collective and public lives. To accomplish such broad application, they must necessarily be ambiguous, even vapid. These are the "magic" terms and ideas with which we pepper our mass talk, invoking something accepted as powerful or even sacred without question, and usually without clear or definitive signification. These terms and symbols speak through myths, organized narratives that offer a complete explanation for the world. As Ellul points out, sociological propaganda, and, I would add, marketing and moralism as well, create or at least seek to colonize myths within and by which we already do happily live, which respond to and sacralize our sense of ourselves and the world through all-encompassing and activating images that condition us such that certain words, signs, or symbols provoke particular reactions. Such myths include all that we feel to be good, just, and true, and it is, of course, those feelings that are the point and what matter.[10]

Ellul lists "four great collective sociological presuppositions" in the modern world that express and encapsulate what we believe to be true and important about ourselves and the world: that our aim in life is happiness, that we are naturally good, that history develops in endless progress, and that what is material is decisive and what "matters." At least the first three of these, are, of course, central presuppositions in all moralisms. There are, in addition, he argues, a certain number of "collective myths" that provide those presuppositions with narrative power, with stories within which they live and which we inhabit: the myths of "work," "happiness," "nation," "youth," and the "hero."[11] All of these presuppositions and myths are, of course, connected. That we are good is the justification for the aim of happiness. The drumbeat of progress is the promise of its achievement. The material is decisive because it is how we measure both our progress and imagine our end concretely. The myth of youth is the promise of progress embodied, accomplished through work which aims at happiness within and through the community but particularly enabled by a courage and tenacity expressive of the heroic.

Ellul argues that propaganda, and, I would add, marketing and moralism, must build upon and pay respect to these presuppositions and their accompanying myths or no one would listen to them. They must, therefore, echo and reinforce society, however much they may also seek and actually accomplish whatever modification furthers their ends. Ultimately, their ends are the same, the reinforcing of a society particularly suited for integrating as many as possible. Yet it must always at the same time look ahead to the imaginary future, the hyperrealized dream possibilities that glitter in front of us. If it rehearses past structures or ideals, it must do so with nostalgia and with reference to their usefulness for continued progress, or with lamentation over interrupted progress in need of revitalization.

Thus, all propaganda must respond to a need, real or felt, concrete or psychological. If the individual or group does not need what propaganda offers, it is ineffective at best, or simply ignored. What propaganda always offers is coherence and meaning. We cannot live in an absurd or incoherent world. The need to feel good about ourselves, for a sense of security and purpose, for the world to make sense and it and our lives to have meaning, these are the needs that both marketing and moralism address as well, and offer to resolve, by assuring us that we are important, even heroic, that what we think and do matters, makes a difference, is needed. Ironically, the more the individual is subsumed into the mass, the more pressing is this need felt, the more urgent is the need for propaganda to address it, since, in a mass society, only this propaganda can reassure us that everyone is a free individual who matters *because* of his or her importance to the whole.

Where I differ from Ellul is that he believes that propaganda, or at least its political form, "does not aim to elevate" but to condition us "to serve." It therefore uses, according to Ellul, what is most common and widespread, the crudest patterns of thought and feeling.[12] I would argue, rather, that sociological propaganda works, like marketing and moralism, by harnessing our common ideas and feelings to symbols it evokes as noblest and most precious. We can be motivated by the base, but so much more so when we clothe what is common in the most elevated rhetoric, to present "service," for instance, as one's noblest possible occupation.

The relation to marketing of these primary characteristics of sociological propaganda, its mass character, its adoption and adaptation of our most powerful cultural myths, its focus on addressing our "needs," should be fairly obvious. Their relation to moralism may be less apparent, but is no less profound. Once certain stories become dominant, once particular notions about ourselves and the world and particular ways of life are adopted, they are taken as good and right, and those who reject them or adopt other ways are bad or wrong. Just as with ordinary political propaganda, the choice is binary and moral, and championed as definitive by those inhabiting it. There is a smooth and largely unnoticed transition from "a spontaneous affirmation of a way of life to the deliberate affirmation of a truth."[13]

MASS PROPAGANDA VOICES

Sut Jhally has called twentieth century marketing the "most powerful and sustained system of propaganda in human history."[14] He understands that it achieves this status not by being propaganda in the way political propaganda is usually viewed as working, by seeking to impose a common opinion or agitate for particular activities from the "outside" through means often viewed as ultimately manipulative or coercive, but by being sociological in Ellul's sense, by insinuating itself into our lives as a part of our "way of life." The surface mechanisms of marketing that make it propaganda in this specifically sociological sense are obvious, or should be from our analysis in the past several chapters.

Marketing obviously practices mass address and works by creating and maintaining mass identities. Marketing, as propaganda, always speaks as if it is speaking to the individual, even though it is always and only speaking to the mass, and must do so to perform its function effectively, as we have noted. Marketing clearly draws from our dominant cultural myths and stereotypes, grounding itself in the same collective presuppositions and inhabiting the same collective myths of our cultures as a whole. The goal of happiness, our natural goodness, even our inevitable progress toward perfection are all accepted, without question, as fundamental truths in all marketing. The material is even more decisive in marketing since the material is what we must ultimately buy and provides the context for the symbolic power offered, even though that power is largely free-floating. In marketing, mass entities are created and exist through their material accoutrement. Indeed, image supplants the thing itself because image collapses into and is configured by the material symbols of identity. Marketing, as we have clearly shown, speaks directly and almost exclusively to our needs and desires by addressing our dream selves. As a form of sociological propaganda, it addresses our need to make sense of ourselves and our worlds, to find meaning, to have purpose, to matter.

Marketing exhibits these characteristics, in large part, because marketing is not something *in addition* to our culture or our "way of life," but inextricably part of it. Ellul argues forcefully that sociological propaganda, addressing us as a whole and itself to the whole of us, to every aspect of our individual and collective lives, requires mass media, requires a mass-mediated world in which our way of life is mirrored at us in terms that allow for its integrating and conforming force, its propaganda force. Marketing is simply a primary part of that mass-mediated, propaganda world. Sociological propaganda "sells" a way of life by expressing its value in every communication, in large part *through* marketing that literally sells a way of life by commoditizing it and offering it as the consumer product we may in fact purchase through market exchange. Indeed, all propaganda seeks and accomplishes the transformation of way of life into commodity, by route of myth and symbolism, and thus provides marketing with its content ready to use.

In other words, marketing is simply an indispensable and central part of our current, and heavily propagandized, way of life. Marketing has not for some time been primarily an industry whose function is simply getting the populace to consume the commodities of industrial capitalism. The roughly $175 billion a year spent on marketing (the largest share, over one third, in TV ads alone) is not even some tangential or intermediary force with respect to whatever it is we believe the parent companies primarily do.[15] That money is largely spent, as we have seen, on what marketers think of as strategies for connecting to consumer's lives at an emotional level in order to instill or cement brand loyalty and interweave the company (brand, really, rather than product) more and more deeply into each individual's sense of themselves. We often speak as if we believe marketing works to accomplish these goals through manipulation, trying to get the consumer to behave in some consumer way whether he wants to or not. This is not really the primary dynamic at work, however.

The industry is itself a product. Marketing is a kind of production, not merely or even primarily the shilling of objects produced by some other process. The industry of selling needs to sell itself, needs to be sold. It needs to insinuate itself, not the stuff it ostensibly advertises, but *itself* into our communal lives so deeply that we can't imagine life without it, that it appears as just life to us, or at least as some inevitable part of life. It must do this to survive. And it has done this. Perhaps, at some level, accidentally, looking for some way to break through the clutter, looking for some new avenue of entry into our psyches, it stumbled upon identity, emotion, values, and self- and world-image. It had to wind up there, though, since those elements of our lives are simply what matter to us the most, or at least are the focus of our communal talk, our cultural narratives. Marketing has infiltrated our experiences of these aspects of our lives—self-creation, self-knowledge, emotionality—and borrowed from and shaped our experiences of them. We see ourselves differently, experience ourselves and the world differently, act, feel, think, and speak differently than before largely due to the shared discourses about these things across the various narratives of our collective and mass-mediated lives.

Marketing is an integral element of sociological propaganda because it is central to the ways we see and think, and thus able to shape much about who and what we are, an integral partner in self-formation, self-understanding, and our daily activity. One of the most important ways that contemporary marketing has shaped us is that we now view marketing as a regular component of our lives, even if we view it as something we must tolerate, if we cannot ignore. So much marketing now models the ideal consumer relationship to marketing for us, presenting not only itself as providing us with useful information about products we might need or want, but us as desiring that information, or at least desiring to be entertained. It is not wrong about that.

Marketing, fortunately for itself as an industry and as a commodity, has made us feel as if it can be, if done well, not the medium, but the point. It has become, *if done well* (and that's such a crucial element in the formula) a thing we need, even seek out, as entertainment at least, but also as offering helpful categories of interpretation, creative and desirable frameworks for understanding ourselves and our world, tools for living. It is conventional wisdom that the public is cynical and skeptical, that it feels only contempt for marketing, that its dominant impulse is to avoid all advertising at all costs. It is a frequent truism that people don't even really watch or pay attention to advertising. There are many that argue otherwise, of course, that remark the number of ads at least marginally viewed by each person each day, that show how much advertising affects public attitudes and behavior. I would argue that in western popular cultures, at least, while we love to hate advertising, it is actually more than tolerated; it actively interests people. We seek it out, look for the well-done, catchy, humorous, or emotionally cathartic ad, share those with each other, refer to them as touchstones for meaning and value. We do not hate advertising; we hate boring, overtly manipulative, irrelevant advertising. We *love* clever, striking, unusual, unexpected, creative advertising.

According to one report, even those who watch TV primarily by means of the now almost ubiquitous digital video recorders still watch, on average, two-thirds of the ads to which they are exposed during television programming. The author of that article reports that "people who have DVRs often insist that they never watch commercials, as if skipping commercials is a badge of honor."[16] There is a cultural narrative at work that insists that nobody likes commercials, and so nobody admits to liking commercials, but the research into what people *do* instead of what they *say* suggests otherwise. As one person reported in the study cited, it's about being captured by the commercial. People have their favorites. Nielsen studies and others suggest (in part based on data that such devices are able to gather about what viewers watch down to the second) that mascots, like the Geico gecko, are one key to capturing an audience. Viewers that find the ads amusing or otherwise engaging form at least a superficial connection to the mascot. When they see the mascot, they watch the ad. Another response to the "problem" of DVRs is that the advertising industry has worked to develop techniques that connect emotionally with viewers at double speed.

You say you don't look at ads, don't watch TV or pay attention to the ads you encounter while browsing, and so don't really consume mass media marketing. Perhaps. Unlikely, but perhaps. Look around you, however. Most of the people you encounter and interact with do. It is extremely difficult not to. Most of us are happy to do so, despite the conventional wisdom. We may fuss about and try to avoid the traditional television advertisement, but mostly we don't, and even if we do, that leaves a world full of mass media marketing for us to engage (or, at least, not attempt to avoid, as if that were even possible).

Mass marketing is simply a central part of our lives which we have accepted and through which we story ourselves, and it is thus a central part of sociological propaganda working to shape us into a culture, a specific kind of community with a specific way of life. It is joined in this process by our other mass storytellers, such as journalism and education. These, too, are essential voices in the construction of a unified story about who and what we are. When we are young, it is the schools that are the primary storytellers presenting a unified picture of the world and our place in it as a force of sociological propaganda. Religion and family are voices as well, but it is our schools, particularly in the western world, where that voice is increasingly universal and standardized, both in its practices and increasingly homogeneous content. That is why in states or groups in which political propaganda is particularly active, there is either sharp antipathy toward education or a concerted effort to control it.

As we grow older, however, it is the news that must take over the role of "informing" us about what is happening or has happened in the world. As we go about our daily lives, the news in its various mass-mediated forms is really the only source of such "information" we have that will connect us to and ground us in our mass society. What we learn from experience we take as local and anecdotal, or as a concrete instance of larger dynamics which we must learn and have learned elsewhere, mostly also from the news informing us about our larger collective self, offering a panoramic view of the whole to which we belong. In both journalism and education, that information is frequently offered primarily as a kind of evidence or witness for pre-determined ideological world views rather than an invitation to participate in anything like research into the conditions and structures that have generated "events."

Personality journalism (journalism's current dominant form) and most educational content work as propaganda for most viewers in precisely the way that Ellul posits, by making people feel informed about complex issues without challenging them. Repeating the same explanations and causes, evidenced anew by each current event or historical or scientific example, these narratives reassure people that they are informed indeed, that they need not worry that events outstrip their understanding, that they remain grounded in the mass through which they understand themselves. Ellul expresses a rather pejorative view of our "need" for being "informed" in this way:

> The majority prefers expressing stupidities to not expressing any opinion: this gives them the feeling of participation. For this they need simple thoughts, elementary explanations, a "key" that will permit them to take a position, and even ready-made opinions. As most people have the desire and at the same time the incapacity to participate, they are ready to accept a propaganda that will permit them to participate, and which hides their incapacity beneath explanations, judgments, and news, enabling them to satisfy their desire without eliminating their incompetence. [17]

Journalism, education, and marketing work together, whether intentionally or not, to depict how the world is and ought to be, what *we* are and ought to be. In the past half-century, marketing has become perhaps the most dominant storyteller, inflecting and altering the others, not only journalism and education, but also reshaping the stories told by and about religion and family and the other central institutions of our social lives, about what they are and how they work. All of those voices are increasingly moralistic, which is simply a natural aspect of the effort to construct a mass, unified identity. Every gathering involves a separating off. The propaganda effort to unify is strengthened by the specter of a threat to one's identity and meaning and purpose. As noted above, the acceptance of a "way of life" is always simultaneously a positing of value, including moral value; and what is understood as "good" must necessarily be in constant relation to what is not, to what poses a threat to it and to unity. Thus, a key theme that has emerged in most of these narratives, even in many marketing narratives, as we have seen, is the theme of moral decay, how events and actors in our world betray our values and threaten our way of life.

MORALITY AS MORALISM

A central dynamic of moralism as sociological propaganda is that once one accepts a "way of life" as best or "true," it becomes a criterion of judgment and value. All actions and attitudes, all perspectives, opinions and beliefs, all structures and practices are measured against these "values." From that point on, we work to perfectly adapt ourselves to the idealized cultural environment, and that environment to these values. As both Nietzsche and Ellul recognized, whatever conforms to and confirms those, whatever expresses that ideal way of life and its ideal values, reinforces or improves them, is "good," and whatever disturbs, interrupts, departs from or critiques that way of life or values is "bad." Such an attitude is a hallmark of moralism.

It is, further, a natural impulse in propagandistic narratives to seek to frame the central elements and dynamics of the shared worldview it proffers. That is why we tell stories about the kind of thing morality itself is, stories which lead to varied and sometimes conflicting understandings. As an element of sociological propaganda that seeks to integrate us into a way of life together, morality has to be specifically configured to work to that end, which is why we so often speak of morality as based in rules or character, since morality so configured lends itself more fully to the goal of conformity. When we speak of the emotional quality of our moral impulses, our emotionally driven impulses to care or sympathize, to feel shame or pride, we do so emphasizing their universal rather than subjective and variable character, as something we all share and which we can appeal to or rely upon because shared. We configure these as we do any kind of idealized moral character, as desirable and inherent communal traits we should foster and protect. We do not speak much about the role of systems and social and material structures as influencing our decisions and actions though, since such talk does not lend itself very well to standardization except in the grossest caricatured terms, in which hyperrealized systems and structures are posed as threats to our way of life. Such talk may also raise troubling doubts about our innate goodness and threaten our more general faith in the truth of our collective presuppositions.

Moralism is morality expressed as sociological propaganda. It is the form of morality we almost exclusively encounter in marketing, in journalism, in education, and in our public discourses, such as in religion and politics. It takes that form in those discourses, in part, because of the structures of their practices, as we have discussed, and because of the stories they tell. Moreover, those stories are told by voices that are increasingly interconnected in the convergence of mass media, wherein large, sometimes global networks of companies own pieces of many mass media outlets, frequently even parts of each others' networks. What the consumer experiences as independent media outlets offering web, film, television or radio content, books, music, movies, or magazines and journalism, even PR and marketing, are often, and increasingly, parts of single multi-national companies, thus giving narrative control, the ability to shape and constrain the message, into a very few hands who have fairly focused interests. The result is that the motifs we encounter are increasingly fewer in kind while greater in number, simpler, perhaps shallower, but certainly more narrowly focused.

As Eco has noted, the artifacts that populate these moralized stories must be complete and comprehensive, must present themselves as the equipment for living.[18] They need not be well-made or coherent. Indeed, the story is often received more readily and taken as "true" if it reflects the fragmentary and multivalent character of our lived experiences, while pointing symbolically and always self-referentially at the moral of the story, its "meaning" and "truth." Even the dialogue in such stories is made to be quoted because it is made of quotes, of archetypes and allusions. Such stories seek to evoke rather than illuminate, far less to invite analysis; they seek to spark an emotional reaction and a comforting sense of *déjà vu*. As Eco notes, in our mass mediated age, there are no innocent eyes or experiences. We all read what we experience against other mediated experiences, even if most of those are vicarious.

Moralism as sociological propaganda shares the structures and orientations of that propaganda. Moralistic values and norms always posit an individual caught up in the mass, inseparable from it, measured by it. As Kierkegaard clearly saw, the ethical simply *is* the commensurable.[19] Morality is the ruler by which each individual, in relation to the whole, is measured. To engage ourselves or each other along a moral register requires the "universal," in his terms, against and in front of which we necessarily stand to be judged and by which we can be understood. In moralism, that universal is the "mass" and we both stand before it and are subsumed in it as spectacle. In moralism, we must view ourselves as an other to ourselves, the subject measured against the legislation of the sovereign, which we, through the mass, also are. Moralizing seeks to ensure that we see ourselves always in light of this communal measurement and ideal, that we tie our fates together and use our communal vision as guide for our individual actions and attitudes. It therefore exaggerates the aspect of "judgment" in morality, of moral praise and blame, of self- and other-oriented critique over internal or structural critique.

Ellul remarks that all modern propaganda profits from the mass identity structures generated by mass media while exploiting the individual's need for affirmation, even self-affirmation, to feel that they measure up: "Of course, this operation is greatly facilitated by the existence of the modern mass media of communication, which have precisely this remarkable effect of reaching the whole crowd all at once, and yet reaching each one in that crowd."[20] As he emphasized, the structure of modern society, realized in important part through mass communication, places each individual where he or she can be most readily reached and affected by propaganda, such that modern propaganda cannot exist without these structures.

Morality has been reshaped as moralism due in no small part to this newly enhanced public voice, speaking, as do our textbooks, from nowhere and everywhere, with an authority enhanced by that apparent objectivity, and speaking to everyone everywhere, while seeming to speak to each of us individually since it is always each of us that is listening. It is an ineluctable structure of mass communication, however, that it speaks to each of us solely *as a member* of the mass. Each of us understands ourselves to be a part of something bigger merely by means of this mode of address. By listening we become more than we are alone. Moralism works in the same way, integrating us into the mass as a way of elevating us.

Moralizing expresses lessons as if to each individual about what is important and what must be done, but only in terms of how that individual is best integrated into the whole, best enabled to work *with* the whole in order to achieve the moral goals or perfection highlighted as the desired outcome in each moral lesson. Our political, religious, community, and even educational rhetoric constantly and pointedly harps on the moral values we are to hold and enact that will unify us, help us make progress together, ensure our well-being and the well-being of future generations. In addition, cut off from our local and organic communities, we become part of the mass, but in such a way as to become ourselves the measure of all things. We must judge for ourselves, rely upon our own resources, find the criteria for judgment within ourselves; or we must abdicate this responsibility, if we find it too much a burden, by sublimating ourselves to the mass, as Kierkegaard or Heidegger explains, saying what "they" say, thinking what "they" think, and acting as "they" act.

Propaganda is most effective when the life of the group which it targets is vital, and its feelings and beliefs intense. Moralism, then, prepares the ground for propaganda, including marketing, by intensifying the beliefs and feelings of those who subscribe, helping to provide for a more effective and malleable consumption. It is only because the experience of being a mom is so intense that a Cheerios commercial can be so effective at mirroring it. A collective life is most intense when it revolves around a limited number of clear, simple, and profoundly felt ideas. Moralism provides those ideas, and presents them with precisely this character. Indeed, much moralism is usually not much more than the valorization of the fundamental currents of the society in which it is practiced.

The main task of propaganda, as we have noted, is to repurpose the conditioned symbols that serve to transmit our culture to the end of integrating the individual into society, to the conformation or adaptation of his or her goals and desires to the group. Marketing, of course, does this as well, for its own ends. It is the very heart of moralism, in that while most moralizing does not so much "repurpose" our cultural symbols to separate and distinct ends, it seeks to imbue those symbols with moral character, apotheosizing them, conferring an authority on them that they cannot attain or maintain merely as cultural symbols, no matter how powerful. Moralism works to integrate us fully by elevating what is in question in morality to the status of unquestionable. Answers to problems are clear-cut and simple: black or white, right or wrong, good or bad. The "truths" pronounced by moralism do not bear discussion. They are to be believed or not, accepted or rejected, but never engaged critically. They are perfectly suited to mass rather than interpersonal communication. Those who hold a particular moralistic "position" mostly cannot even speak with those who do not, and cannot speak *to* them except to denounce or demand conversion.

Moralistic discourse does not address itself to deliberative audiences, but to niche audiences who have been pre-configured as audience precisely for the worldviews the moralisms inhabit and communicate. The message is customized to unify these audiences, to build a coalition, almost always, as is perhaps inevitable, by means of a frequently demonized out-group, usually presented as a threat to the in-group and its values. It addresses these audiences as "publics" but seeks, as with marketing, to divide and colonize, to garner market-share and brand loyalty. As Randal Marlin cites, Hitler intuitively recognized that the first task of propaganda is to win people for the organization, but the first task of the organization is to win people for propaganda.[21]

As any brand manager will tell you: meaning systems don't maintain themselves. A primary task of brand marketing is to win loyalty for the brand, yes, but it does so by creating a brand identity, a tribal identity whose main task is to orient people toward the brand marketing, to seek it out, to inhabit it, and in many cases, to *be* it; not just in the sense of the facile invitation to #beSouthwestern, but also in the sense that we actually see ourselves as instantiating the brand, willingly, even eagerly become walking billboards for brand advertising and model brand behavior.

Moralistic narratives are like this as well. Moral lessons, explicitly constructed to teach values, if not also the values themselves such lessons teach, work to integrate individuals into societal and moral norms configured as what we all share, or should share, at least. In moralism, a moral lesson aims not primarily to shape behavior or action (as Ellul would say most popular notions of propaganda emphasize), but to integrate the individual into the group, the group of "good" people who do what is "right" and so belong together in a society which unquestioningly takes its aim to be happiness and well-being. A moralistic lesson aims at winning an individual for the "kingdom," but the "kingdom of ends" exists to propagate and confirm the moral maxims that are instrumental to its ends, no matter how we might prefer to characterize them as categorical.

It is quite interesting to note, for instance, that for the most part we don't question that what we think says something important, even essential, about who we are. This is, in a way, both a little strange and also problematic. If what we think says something important about who we are, then we cannot change what we think without changing who we are. Therefore what we think needs to remain stable if identity is to remain stable; and there is virtually no more dogmatically held view than that *who* we are is some core and grounding reality that *should*, even *must*, remain constant. Thus, ideological identity politics entrenches resistance to genuine dialogical/dialectical engagement; and moralism presents our attitudes, beliefs, values, and ideas as necessarily and existentially static.

One of the main points I wish to make is that marketing moralism interacts with an inherent tendency of moralism generally, and that is the tendency, according to Barthes, for mythic speech to exhibit a buttonholing character, as speaking forcefully and directly to each of us as individuals in order to "put us in our place" while at the same time assuming the look of generality, neutral and innocent.[22] As Barthes says, this kind of interpellant speech is at the same time a frozen speech, always locked into saying the same thing. Moralistic talk, in ads and journalism and in our public discourse, in politics and religion, is a kind of zombie talk. It speaks of the same moral ideas and judgments and values, familiar but horrifically disfigured because divorced from and emptied of concrete significance in the exercise of life. Moralistic talk is a kind of "walking dead" talk, missing the deeply situated contexts of actually choosing how to act that distinguish live moral questions. It is morality frozen into abstraction and universality.

Moralistic talk is a signifier, in Barthes' terms, which always signifies the same things, the same largely empty, deeply abstract things: well-being, power, progress, goodness, and truth. The exact same things that the world, mythologized in ads, signifies. Unlike the actual world of experience and interaction, where personalities are complex, motives are unclear, and outcomes are ambiguous, moralism presents a world of clarity and simplicity, where personalities are caricatured, motives are transparent, and outcomes straightforwardly flow from actions as directly as any market transaction. Conflicts are personal and solved by action, rather than systemic or structural and resistant to "solutions." In the stories we most frequently encounter and consume, plot lines follow the most widely accepted hyperrealized notions of morality, however remotely they bear upon our lived complexities of choice and interaction.

In the face of such categorical disjunctives, however, it is perhaps not surprising that we sometimes work to introduce what I'll call the semi-excluded middle (the morally exhausted negation of extremism). In other words, in the face of such zombie speech, we call out the disjunctions as extreme, and extremely undesirable, and seek to inhabit a kind of normative moderate position that makes a virtue out of its non-identification with the polarities. Such a position is negative and negating, reactive but not reflective, lethargic and largely hopeless. It is passive at its core. It is a shrugging of our shoulders in the face of the radicalization of "taking a stand." Such a response is the abdication of morality to moralism, its rejection in the place of its reclamation.

Moralism as a form of sociological propaganda is inextricable from its consumerist, market incarnations. The question of what kind of person to be or to whom we owe some obligation cannot live in some separate, pure realm. Our possibilities are framed by the metaphysical structures of our stories, which are themselves framed within our social and material structures and conditions, which are dominated in western societies, at least, by consumerism and mass media marketing. Marketing has worked to configure our ethical options and choices in consumerist terms, but it has not had to work very hard at it. Most of the primary elements remain, largely unchanged, the mostly unquestioned goal of happiness perhaps the most salient among them, while the face of the possibility of "character" has become, arguably, more explicitly material while remaining thoroughly symbolic. Or, to put that another way, the material, generally, has become much more symbolic in our consumerist culture. It is worth asking whether what we really want or need is so much moralizing, particularly as a substitute for a more complex morality that can perhaps better serve to critique our actions, structures, choices, and desires rather than primarily mirror them back at us, normalized and valorized, and always hyperrealized.

OTHER STORIES

In a world in which everything has a price, everything is a commodity, nothing has dignity, as Kant would put it, nothing stands apart, non-fungible, and nothing, therefore, exists as an end in itself. I do not say this to invoke some possible or necessary categorical imperative. I suppose I do not have much faith in such things. But in such a world, everything is instrumental, and in marketing and morality, the ends to which things serve as instruments are frequently unclear, often simplistic, and usually hopelessly abstract when not configured as material, or as a general well-being grounded in the material. I *am* interested in the possibility of dignity, the possibility that things, particularly but not only human beings, can be ends and not merely means. I think such a possibility is at the heart of a more complex sense of morality than the one we mostly encounter.

In arguing that morality already has to have become moralism, a kind of sociological propaganda, in order to lend itself so fully and neatly to its employment in marketing (or journalism or education), I am not arguing that morality is merely propaganda, that it has no real substance. Morality's character as social integrator, no matter how fundamental or grounded in its cultural and even evolutionary genealogies, is only one aspect of it as a phenomenon. It is that dimension that is most useful to marketing, and so most dominant in our consumerist culture, and for that reason alone needs to be more fully and clearly understood. It is but one dimension, however. Just as is the case with any feature of human being under an evolutionary frame of reference, the fact that it has evolved as adaptive in particular ways need not limit or determine its complete character for us now. We are the storytellers, not just characters in the story. We can decide what some aspect of our nature means for us now and how or why to nurture or employ it in some ways rather than others. If nothing else, the employment of morality in marketing is ample proof of that ability.

Morality matters to us. It matters in many ways on many levels. That is in part why it is so useful and effective in marketing. We simply do care about what is right and good. We do experience sympathy and care for others. We do want our own lives, the lives of those we care for and about, and the world in general to have meaning, to be good. It is both inevitable, given the kind of thing we are, that we do, and it is, in any moral sense, good that we do. At any rate, it is frankly impossible to imagine any story in which we, as a whole, do not. All our stories about failure or some threat to our way of life assume, and must assume, a moral frame, or they make no sense whatsoever. Morality is always glorified in the breach, else there is no breach.

This fact will not change. What will change, what has always changed, is how we inflect and ground and narrate these dynamics, by means of the integrating and world-crafting stories we tell and are told. This book offers its analysis in the desire to foster further analysis, in the hope that such critical analysis can become more common, a part of our regular consumption practices; because only by attending carefully and critically to the stories, and how they are told, how we participate in telling them, how they work on us and in us and through us and why, can we regain or retain agency as consumers *and* as storytellers, with the ability to shape the story as we desire for our own purposes.

As Nietzsche argued, that the world may be largely a lie is no complaint against it. Life may be essentially lie, or, to put it more politely, as he sometimes did, art. We are artist and work of art both at the same time. We are material and maker. The challenge is not to break free from the lie to some essential and absolute truth, to break free from the story and spectacle to the underlying real. If we tell ourselves a story in which that is the goal, we simply get in our own way and frustrate what is possible. The challenge is to tell powerful stories in which we are agents of world-making, not victims, in which we "lie" creatively and productively and are better for it. A large part of why marketing works so well is because it understands that goal and possibility. It offers us the chance to possess and employ that power, albeit channeled through quite particular pathways of material consumption.

I'm not saying that we shouldn't want the things we want that marketing and moralism offer us, a sense of purpose and meaning, a sense that we matter and can make a difference. I am wondering, like Kierkegaard in his preface to *The Present Age*, whether we want those things on the cheap, with such deep discounts, as it were, for very little cost in critical thought or considered discussion with each other, for a little money, actually, which buys us the hyperreal version of meaning and value. As Plato argues through

Socrates in the *Gorgias*, general rules are always of somewhat limited in concrete situations. What is often necessary and best is simply for the interested parties, those who will be affected by a decision or action, to talk and listen to each other and together work out what is "better" in a given situation.[23]

My point of departure from theorizing our world and consumer culture as spectacle and hyperreality is that I am not necessarily positing something else, some true reality which is harmed or forgotten or occluded by the spectacle. The world, and we in it, make sense and work in the ways it and we do by means of the stories we tell. But not all stories are the same, of course, or tell about the same worlds with the same relations and possibilities. Some stories are more powerful than others, allow for different engagements with each other and the world. I am merely suggesting that there are better stories to tell, inhabited by fuller, more complex selves, in richer and more complicated worlds, with different, and ultimately more productive relations to each other than those we mostly consume and inhabit in the course of our daily mass-mediated lives.

If I must offer some specific alternative at the end of my analysis, I would suggest, along with thinkers as remote from each other as Thucydides and Nietzsche and Patricia Williams, that an important key to richer understanding of ourselves and our world is the ability to see the world in more than one way.[24] Williams illustrates this point powerfully in a story she tells:

> One summer when I was about six, my family drove to Maine. The highway was very straight and hot and shimmered darkly in the sun. My sister and I sat in the back seat of the Studebaker and argued about what color the road was. I said black. My sister said purple. After I had harangued her into admitting that it was indeed black, my father gently pointed out that my sister still saw it as purple. I was unimpressed with the relevance of that at the time; but with the passage of years, and much more observation, I have come to see endless highways as slightly more purple than black. My sister and I will probably argue about the hue of life's roads forever. But the lesson I learned from listening to her wild perceptions is that it really is possible to see things--even the most concrete things--simultaneously yet differently; and that seeing simultaneously yet differently is more easily done by two people than one, but that one person can get the hang of it with lots of time and effort.[25]

Of course, all propaganda, including marketing and moralism, works to ensure that we see the world in only one way.

I believe there is substantial interest in pluralistic stories, however. Witness the popularity of satirical "news" programs such as Jon Stewart's *The Daily Show* or Stephen Colbert's *The Colbert Report*, which, because they inhabit the genre of satire, *demand* the ability to look at things in more than one way. Not all of us want the cartoonish moralistic binaries of the Tea

Party. Many of us, apparently, appreciate the clever lampooning and decon-struction of such cartoons. I believe there is room and interest in a morality that is itself less cartoonish, less binary, that doesn't insist on abstracted, polarizing "values" that must be accepted or rejected wholesale, a morality that has room for multiple vectors of interest and desire, that acknowledges the importance of the concrete and situated over the absolute, that makes room for self-critique, and simply is more critical as a whole.

Such communication opens the possibility of understanding not some other, but ourselves in relation to what isn't ourselves. Such communication, necessarily complex and multivalent, matters in a world where we are so neatly divided and grouped into tribes that can't speak to or understand each other. If we learn to tell stories that open themselves up to others, that explore the relations between worlds we know and inhabit and those we don't and never have, then we grow up better able to listen across worlds, perhaps move between them, or at least inhabit richer worlds.

Those who grow up in dominant cultures in which they don't fully be-long, those whose race, ethnicity, religious identity, gender or some other central feature of their identity is marginalized, have no real choice in this matter. They must live in two worlds, at least, the world they know from their own genealogies, and the world they must inhabit because it simply is the dominant world. They have no choice but to see the world as purple and black at the same time, or at the very least to be constantly aware that others see it as black, even though they see it as purple. But if all one ever inhabits is the dominant narratives, and narrowly focused, univalent narratives at that, then the road is black. You see it as black. The dominant narrative says it's black. It's black. If you become aware of anyone else suggesting it might be purple, then you perceive that possibility as inane, erroneous, anathema. It is an irrational perspective.

This is part of the danger presented by the dominant mass-mediated nar-ratives of our cultures and their moralisms. These stories are not multivalent in productive ways. They do not really open to multiple meanings or inter-pretations, except as a result of an inherent emptiness that sometimes allows for almost any interpretation. Like all propaganda, the message can be for-mulated in many ways, but in the end, all those formulations must say the same thing. Almost all marketing, as moralistic stories, tells us we are all the same, all want to be the same, all want the same things. It tells us the whole world is the same, or would like to be, indeed, dreams of being the same. All the stories, in all their various forms, with all the differences of details, all present the same possibilities of being. There is only one way to see things, because there is only one way to be.

Thus, the advantage achieved unintentionally by those who are marginal-ized is suppressed. Even these are brought into the univocal world of market-ing, as emblems of the exotic, as fetishized "styles," but never as serious alternatives to "how things are." Like the images of the broader non-commercial world (if there still is one) that marketing co-opts, those who are marginalized or "othered" are reduced to image and used to sell things.[26] If the key to understanding more richly, to living in a larger and more potent world, a world with more possibility for agency, is the ability to see, as Nietzsche said, from multiple perspectives, to look at our experiences and surroundings from different vantage points, then marketing narratives and moralisms are not harmless. They are precisely antithetical to understanding. They narrow the world down to one way of seeing, in which every element of the narrative says the same. Further, any narrative that stands outside that monolithic and ubiquitous framing is always in danger of being incoherent, or else taken up and recast within the dominant narrative, attenuated to a kind of tokenism. We set such narratives aside as meaningless, or take them up merely as elements in our own.

I am not equipped, nor do I wish, to pass judgment on superior or inferior modes of thinking about good and bad, right and wrong, as accomplished by various agents and practices of moral storytelling, but I do think it is important for all of us to work to clearly recognize the epistemic and metaphysical shifts inherent in those practices. I, myself, would prefer a morality less focused on agents and their "values" or "character" and more focused on systems and structures, how we participate in those, and how those work to shape our actions and reactions in ways of which we usually aren't terribly aware. I am less interested in the question of whether an individual is a "good" person, than I am in the question of whether a given social or political structure fosters the kind of actions we prefer or works against our best intentions. Such structures are both engendered and maintained in and through the stories we tell, and how we tell them.

One may argue that eschewing moralism, understood as the quest for knowledge about or the teaching of what is simply right, *per se*, what is universal and absolute, means that we abandon our moral practice to the winds of context and change. I would respond with a question as to what was ever our real alternative. What methods have we ever had of either knowing or propagating universal principles other than the vehicle of contextualized, i.e., historically and culturally situated, rhetorical persuasion? There are no absolute criteria I can find for assessing the value of particular practices or goals, merely the test of intersubjective judgment with respect to the consequences of our practice and experiments. I would rather that our collective moral storytelling be guided by educated communal judgments than by profit motive and the goal of corporate well-being, of course, but I accept that they will be guided by something other than access to the "truth." The goal of this analysis is not to call for moral theory or judgment to return to some more rational or absolute foundation; rather it is to illuminate the mechanisms that simply are at work in distinction to the narratives about how it all works that are currently being bought and sold (and that often hide the actual working). My hope is that we can retain significant agency in the practice of storytelling, and perhaps even wrest that practice away from its primarily consumerist employment to resuscitate it in a broader public discourse informed by far more pluralistic voices as well as more varied and complex visions of the good.

NOTES

1. Kwame Appiah, "Into the Woods," *New York Review of Books* (2003): 46.
2. de Certeau, xii–xiii.
3. Jacques Ellul, *Propaganda: The Formation of Men's Attitudes* (New York: Alfred A. Knopf, 1965).
4. Ellul, 62.
5. Ellul, 64.
6. Ellul, 64.
7. Ellul, 65.
8. Ellul, 7.
9. Ellul, 90.
10. Ellul, 31.
11. Ellul, 39–40.
12. Ellul, 38.
13. Ellul, 66.
14. Jhally, "Advertising at the Edge of the Apocalypse." To read about the history of propaganda in the US as a market instrument in particular, see especially Walter Lippmann, *Public Opinion* (London: George Allen & Unwin Ltd., 1922); Edward Bernays, *Propaganda* (New York: H. Liveright, 1928), a particularly candid exposition; and Stuart Ewen, *PR!: A Social History of Spin* (New York: Basic Books, 1996).
15. Louise Story, "Viewers Fast-Forwarding Past Ads? Not Always," *New York Times*, February 16, 2007. See also "US Total Media Ad Spend Inches Up, Pushed by Digital," *eMarketer*, accessed June 9, 2014, emarketer.com/Article/US-Total-Media-Ad-Spend-Inches-Up-Pushed-by-Digital/1010154.
16. Story, "Viewers Fast-Forwarding Past Ads? Not Always."
17. Ellul, 140.
18. Umberto Eco, "Casablanca: Cult Movies and Intertextual Collage," in *Travels in Hyperreality* (New York: Harcourt Brace, 1986), 198–210.
19. Søren Kierkegaard, *Fear and Trembling*, (New York: Penguin, 1985), *passim*.
20. Ellul, 8.
21. Randal Marlin, *Propaganda & the Ethics of Persuasion* (Peterborough, ON: Broadview Press, 2002), 81. He is citing "Propaganda and Organization," *Mein Kampf*, Volume 2, chapter 11. Accessed on May 30, 2008, mondopolitico.com/library/meinkampf/v2c11.htm.
22. Barthes, *Mythologies*, 123–24.
23. I am not invoking some general theory of ethics or morality here along the lines of Habermas or Rawls. I understand the many social and political structures that create and maintain power differentials that stand in the way of real "dialogue" in our world. I am simply pointing to the fact that actual decisions and actions, unlike their theorized abstract counterparts, always take place in a concrete situation with concrete participants and would usually benefit from concrete efforts to communicate the various concrete interests involved to the extent that is possible.
24. See Thucydides, *The Peloponnesian War*, trs. by Steven Lattimore (Indianapolis: Hackett Publishing, 1988) and my own chapter, "'To Say What is Most Necessary:' Expositional and Philosophical Practice in Thucydides and Plato," in *Philosophy in Dialogue: Plato's Many Devices*, ed. By Gary Alan Scott (Evanston, IL: Northwestern University Press, 2007), 15–40. I

have argued that Thucydides presents much of his history in the form of paired speeches precisely because no single account can provide a rich understanding either of events or the motivations of the actors within them.

25. Patricia Williams, *Alchemy of Race and Rights* (Cambridge, MA: Harvard University Press, 1992), 149–50.

26. Patricia Williams tells a story about a chic store in the Village that sells shabby "homeless" coats, advertising them with signs on the windows that also prohibit the homeless from entering. Thus, a real and marginalized group is transformed into a style and marketed to the affluent as urban grunge in ways that exclude and further marginalize the group.

Appendix: List of Advertising Sources

Figure 1.1 American Century website ad, online.wsj.com/media/mf03-amercent2.pdf.

Figure 1.2 McDonald's website ad, mcdonalds.com.au/#/families.

Figure 3.1 "Soldier," United Colors of Benetton campaign image, adforum.com/creative-work/ad/player/21466.

Figure 3.2 "AIDS patient," United Colors of Benetton campaign image, benettongroup.com/media-press.

Figure 3.3 "Bosnian soldier clothes," United Colors of Benetton campaign image, benettongroup.com/media-press.

Figure 3.4 Kenneth Cole Fall 2004 Campaign, archive.kennethcole.com/timeline/2004-fall-campaign/1122.

Figure 3.5 Kenneth Cole Fall 2004 Campaign, archive.kennethcole.com/timeline/2004-fall-campaign/1122.

Figure 3.6 Kenneth Cole Fall 2011 Campaign, archive.kennethcole.com/timeline/2011-fall-campaign-1/1791.

Figure 3.7 "Starlet," magazine ad for Skyy Vodka, richarddirk.com/blog/article/skyy-vodka-starlet.

Other ads referenced in chapter 3:

"Naomi," David Yurman ad, naomi-watts.org/2013/09/05/old-david-yurman-advert-video.

Figure 4.1 "Drivers Wanted – Jetta," Volkswagen Jetta ad, 2001-2. Image retrieved from *Advocate*, December 10, 2002.

Figure 4.2   Screen capture from "Always One of a Kind," commercial for
              Dr. Pepper, youtube.com/watch?v=0Ix7T_XIA28.

Figure 4.3   Screen capture from "Always One of a Kind," commercial for
              Dr. Pepper, youtube.com/watch?v=0Ix7T_XIA28.

Figures   "Make your own ad," Curve perfume ad, retrieved from
4.4–4.7   *Seventeen*, April 2007.

              Other ads referenced in chapter 4:

              "Reality," produced by GlobalHue for Jeep, youtube.com/
              watch?v=MbcVr1nRDms.

              "Always One of a Kind," commercial for Dr. Pepper's "One of
              a Kind" campaign, youtube.com/watch?v=0Ix7T_XIA28.

              "Brighter," Discover Card ad in "Life Takes Visa" ad campaign
              from 2008, adforum.com/creative-work/ad/player/12657333/
              sxi:5834033.

Figure 5.1   Screen capture from "It's a Beautiful Life," Lancôme
              commercial, ispot.tv/ad/7L1q/lancome-la-vie-est-belle-
              featuring-julia-roberts.

              Other ads referenced in chapter 5:

              Acura commercial, adland.tv/commercials/acura-rsx-life-
              perfect-2002-030-usa.

              "Favorites Bucket Family Time," KFC commercial, ispot.tv/ad/
              7fbK/kfc-favorites-bucket-family-time.

              "Target: Santa's Job," Target commercial, youtube.com/
              watch?v=GwcMuHsvvYY.

              "Coca-Cola Stories," website, coca-colacompany.com/stories/
              coca-cola-stories.

              "Anna Clark – Jif Peanut Butter," Jif commercial,
              youtube.com/watch?v=S3UeS8RJqNk.

              "LivingSocial: It'll Change Your Life," LivingSocial.com
              commercial, ailymotion.com/video/xoaw8s_adzone-living-
              social-it-ll-change-your-life_shortfilms.

              "It's a Beautiful Life," Lancôme commercial, ispot.tv/ad/7L1q/
              lancome-la-vie-est-belle-featuring-julia-roberts.

              "Father-Daughter," Subaru commercial, youtube.com/
              watch?v=6F3-InOdMP4.

              "Keepsake," Subaru commercial, streetfire.net/video/
              keepsakesubaru-commercial_748699.htm.

Ads referenced in chapter 6:

"The Day You Became Mine," Carter's commercial, youtube.com/watch?v=Gza-yfENn_4.

"Nana," Cheerios commercial, youtube.com/watch?v=CSNAdo9Czns#t=17.

"Childhood is Calling," Rice Krispies commercial, splendad.com/ads/show/3134-Rice-Krispies-Childhood-is-Calling-Speak-Their-Language.

"Live Better," Wal-Mart commercial, adage.com/article/ad-review/long-awaited-wal-mart-ads-obvious-brilliant/120476.

"Journey," Louis Vuitton video, youtube.com/watch?v=QPzxmIWWep0.

"We Agree: Profits Help Create Growth and Jobs," Chevron commercial, youtube.com/watch?v=lEazYJkzjMg.

"Together," Honda Insight commercial, youtube.com/watch?v=pEuei5gvtqg.

"What Matters," Buick commercial, youtube.com/watch?v=OrviER_pGws.

"Powered by Pizza," Domino's Pizza commercial, ispot.tv/ad/71WM/dominos-pizza-powered-by-pizza.

"Security Cameras," Coca-Cola commercial, youtube.com/watch?v=DKy4utFUN-k.

"Coca-Cola Security Cameras: Big Game Commercial 2013," Coca-Cola, 2014, coca-colacompany.com/videos/coca-cola-security-cameras-big-game-commercial-2013-yte8m5d6xenwa.

"Rule the Air," Verizon Wireless commercial, youtube.com/watch?v=QNSDbkBG_IY.

"Hyundai – Commitment," Hyundai commercial, splendad.com/ads/show/1602-Hyundai-Commitment.

"Piñata," Skittles commercial, adweek.com/video/advertising-branding/funniest-commercials-skittles-pi-ata-132704.

"Mobsters," produced by BBDO San Francisco, adforum.com/agency/9575/creative-work/6696848/mobsters/keep-california-beautiful-keep-california-beautiful.

"Transgender Apology," Banco Provincia commercial, *The Financial Brand* (thefinancialbrand.com), youtube.com/ watch?v=Wu7nKR0t5zQ.

"Come As You Are," McDonald's commercial, huffingtonpost.com/2010/06/01/gay-mcdonalds-ad-in-franc_n_596361.html.

Figure 7.1 "Every Stripe Tells a Story," blurppy.files.wordpress.com/ 2011/06/page_2.jpg.

Figure 7.2 "Real Women Have Real Curves,"ad-review.co.uk/view/ image/item/doves_campaign_for_r/1287.

Figures 7.3–7.5 "Campaign for Real Beauty," archive.epica-awards.com/pages/ results/2005/winners/results2005-cat16.html.

Other ads referenced in chapter 7:

"Dawn Animals Commercial," commercial for Dawn Dish Detergent, schooltube.com/video/249f1df7bd72a1887cc8.
"Open," Dawn dish detergent commercial, dawn-dish.com/us/ dawn/commercials.
"Saving Wildlife," Dawn commercial, ispot.tv/ad/7Vq3/dawn-saving-wildlife.
"2009 Brita Climate Ride: My Hope for the Future," Brita PR video, dailymotion.com/BritaFilterForGood.
"Feed USA: Kate," Target TV commercial, http:// www.ispot.tv/ad/7toS/target-feed-usa-kate.
"TOMS – Change One Decision to Help Change a Life," youtube.com/watch?v=LGO1TFH1seo& list=PLvSoqFwcrRNi-Vh01q0YDfWPLlLHW_rkJ.
"TOMS Campus Clubs," youtube.com/ watch?v=G9DVVyBKlYs.
"TOMS Employee" video, youtube.com/ watch?v=Ojs2VPQlZR8&feature=kp.
"TOMS Eyewear – Nepal Giving Trip," accessed on June 22, 2011, youtube.com/watch?v=sz7-iwmNkRA.
"TOMS What's Your Next Chapter," youtube.com/ watch?v=EesOoKSbc4A.
"TOMS: Next Chapter – Ben Affleck's One for One," youtube.com/watch?v=OeS4S5ufl6o.
"Little Girls," Dove Campaign for Real Beauty, adland.tv/ commercials/dove-true-colors-2006-45-usa.
"Daughters," Dove Campaign for Real Beauty, vimeo.com/ 15858914.

"Evolution," Dove Campaign for Real Beauty, youtube.com/watch?v=iYhCn0jf46U&feature=kp.

"Onslaught," Dove Campaign for Real Beauty, vimeo.com/4097693.

"Amy," Dove Campaign for Real Beauty, youtube.com/watch?v=RWbtaj5kSUk.

"Pro-Age" Dove Campaign for Real Beauty, vimeo.com/17210728.

"Beauty Sketches," Dove Campaign for Real Beauty, realbeautysketches.dove.us.

Bibliography

Adler, Richard, ed. *Understanding Television*. Santa Barbara, CA: Praeger, 1981.

Adorno, Theodor. *The Culture Industry*. New York: Routledge, 1991.

Alfano, Mark. *Character as Moral Fiction*. Cambridge: Cambridge University Press, 2013.

Alsever, Jennifer. "In the Computer Dating Game, Room for a Coach." *New York Times*, March 11, 2007.

Anscombe, G. E. M. *Intention*. Oxford: Basil Blackwell, 1957.

Appiah, Kwame Anthony. *Experiments in Ethics*. Cambridge, MA: Harvard University Press, 2008.

————. "Into the Woods." *New York Review of Books*, December 18, 2003.

Atkins, Douglas. *The Culting of Brands: When Customers Become True Believers*. New York: Portfolio, 2004.

————. "Interview: Douglas Atkins." *Frontline: The Persuaders*. Accessed August 13, 2009, pbs.org/wgbh/pages/frontline/shows/persuaders/interviews/atkin.html.

Atkins, Kim. *Narrative Identity and Moral Identity*. London: Routledge, 2008.

Bagnoli, Carla, ed. *Morality and the Emotions*. Oxford: Oxford University Press, 2012.

Bakhtin, Mikhail. *Problems of Dostoevsky's Poetics*. Minneapolis: University of Minnesota Press, 1984.

Baldwin, Clive. "Narrative, Ethics and People with Severe Mental Illness." *Australian & New Zealand Journal of Psychiatry* 39 (2005).

Barkow, Jerome, Leda Cosmides, and John Tooby. *The Adapted Mind*. Oxford: Oxford University Press, 1992.

Barthes, Roland. *Mythologies*. Translated by Annette Lavers. New York: Hill and Wang, 1972.

————. "The Rhetoric of the Image." In *Image, Music, Text*. Translated by Stephen Heath. New York: Hill and Wang, 1977.

Baudrillard, Jean. *The Consumer Society: Myths and Structures*. London: Sage Publications, 1998.

————. *The Gulf War Did Not Take Place*. Bloomington: Indiana University Press, 1995.

————. *Simulations*. New York: Semiotext(e), 1983.

————. *Symbolic Exchange and Death*. New York: Sage, 1993.

Bauman, Zygmunt. *Consuming Life*. Cambridge: Polity Press, 2007.

Bellah, Robert. "Education: Technical and Moral." In *The Good Society*, Robert Bellah, Richard Madsen, William M. Sullivan, Ann Swidler, and Steven M. Tipton. New York: Knopf, 1991.

Benjamin, Walter. "The Storyteller." In *Illuminations*. New York: Schocken Books, 1969.

————. "The Work of Art in the Age of Mechanical Reproduction." In *Illuminations*.

Berger, John. *Ways of Seeing*. London: Penguin Books Ltd, 1972.

Bernays, Edward. *Propaganda*. New York: H. Liveright, 1928.

Besley, Tina. "Foucault and the Turn to Narrative Therapy." *British Journal of Guidance & Counseling* 30 (2002).

Blair, James, and Katherine Fowler. "Moral Emotions and Moral Reasoning from the Perspective of Affective Cognitive Neuroscience: A Selective Review." *European Journal of Developmental Science* 2 (2008): 303–23.

Boltanski, Luc. *Distant Suffering: Morality, Media, and Politics*. Translated by Graham Burchell. Cambridge: Cambridge University Press, 1999.

Boorstin, Daniel. *The Image: A Guide to Pseudo-Events in America*. New York: Vintage, 1961.

Booth, Wayne. *The Company We Keep: An Ethics of Fiction*. Berkeley: University of California Press, 1982.

———. "Knowledge and Opinion." In *Now Don't Try to Reason With Me*. Chicago: University of Chicago Press, 1970.

———. "The Company We Keep: Self-Making as Imaginative Art." *Daedalus* III (1982): 56–57.

Borges, Jorge Luis. *Ficciones*. New York: Grove Press, 1962.

Botstein, Leon. *Jefferson's Children: Education and the Promise of American Culture*. New York: Doubleday, 1997.

Bourdieu, Pierre. *On Television*. New York: New Press, 1998.

Bruner, Jerome. *Actual Minds, Possible Worlds*. Cambridge: Harvard University Press, 1986.

———. *Acts of Meaning*. Cambridge: Harvard University Press, 1990.

———. "The Narrative Construction of Reality." *Critical Inquiry* 18 (1991): 1–21.

———. *Making Stories: Law, Literature, Life*. Cambridge, MA: Harvard University Press, 2003.

Caliskan, Karay, and Michel Callon, "Economization, part 1: Shifting Attention from the Economy Towards Processes of Economization." *Economy and Society* 38, (2009): 369–98.

Carr, David. *Time, Narrative, and History*. Bloomington: Indiana University Press, 1986.

"Cause Marketing Remains Strong: 2010 Cone Cause Evolution Study." Cone Communications PR release. Accessed on May 11, 2013, conecomm.com/cause-marketing-remains-strong.

Chouliaraki, Lilie. *The Spectatorship of Suffering*. London: Sage, 2006.

———. *The Ironic Spectator*. Cambridge: Polity, 2013.

Clark, William, and Michael Grunstein, *Are We Hardwired?: The Role of Genes in Human Behavior*. Oxford: Oxford University Press, 2000.

Crane, Andrew, and John Desmond. "Societal marketing and morality." *European Journal of Marketing* 36 (2002): 548–69.

Cronin, Jr., J. Joseph, et al. "Green marketing strategies: an examination of stakeholders and the opportunities they present." *Journal of the Academy of Marketing Science* 30 (2010).

Cullers, Rebecca. "Ad casts Verizon as cure for Racism, Sexism." *Adweek*. Accessed August 18, 2010, adweek.com/adfreak/ad-casts-verizon-cure-racism-sexism-12343.

Dahl, Richard. "Green Washing: Do You Know What You're Buying?" *Environmental Health Perspectives*, 118 (2010): 246–52.

Damasio, Antonio. *Descartes' Error: Emotion, Reason, and the Human Brain*. New York: Penguin, 1994.

Daum, Kevin . "Define Your Personal Core Values: 5 Steps." *Inc*. Accessed May 2, 2014, inc.com/kevin-daum/define-your-personal-core-values-5-steps.html.

Dawkins, Richard. *The Selfish Gene*. Oxford: Oxford University Press, 1989.

Dawlabani, Said Elias. "The Psychosocial DNA of Capitalism," *Huffington Post*. Accessed September 6, 2013, huffingtonpost.com/said-elias-dawlabani/the-psychosocial-dna-of-capitalism_b_3882188.html.

Debord, Guy. *Society of the Spectacle*. Detroit, MI: Black & Red, 2000.

de Certeau, Michel. *The Practice of Everyday Life*. Berkeley: University of California Press, 1984.

de Man, Paul. "Autobiography as De-facement." *MLN* 94 (1979).

De Waal, Frans. *Primates and Philosophers*. Princeton, NJ: Princeton University Press, 2006.

———. *The Age of Empathy*. New York: Random House, 2009.

Disney, Walt. *The Listener*, 16 February 1984.

Donzel, Maxime. "McDonald's dit ne pas cibler les gays avec sa nouvelle publicité," *Yagg.com*. Accessed May 8, 2014, yagg.com/2010/05/28/29999.

Doris, John M. *Lack of Character: Personality and Moral Behavior*. Cambridge: Cambridge University Press, 2002.

Dostoevsky, Fyodor. *Notes from Underground*. Translated by Richard Pevear and Larissa Volokhonsky. New York: Alfred A. Knopf, 1993.

Douglas, Norman. *South Wind*. London: Martin Secker, 1917.

Dye, Lauren. "Consuming Constructions: A Critique of Dove's Campaign for Real Beauty." *Canadian Journal of Media Studies* 5 (2009): 114–28.

Eakin, Paul John. *Fictions in Autobiography: Studies in the Art of Self-Invention*. Princeton, NJ: Princeton University Press, 1985.

———. *How Our Lives Become Stories: Making Selves*. Ithaca: Cornell University Press, 1999.

Eco, Umberto. *Travels in Hyperreality*. New York: Harcourt, 1986.

———. "Can Television Teach?" *Screen Education* 31 (1979).

Edmondson, Brad. *Ice Cream Social: The Struggle for the Soul of Ben & Jerry's*. San Francisco: Berrett-Koehler Publishers, 2014.

Elliott, Stuart. "A Brand Tries to Invite Thought." *New York Times*, September 7, 2007.

Ellul, Jacques. *Propaganda: The Formation of Men's Attitudes*. New York: Alfred A. Knopf, 1965.

Ewen, Stuart. *PR!: A Social History of Spin*. New York: Basic Books, 1996.

Foucault, Michel. *Discipline and Punish: The Birth of the Prison*. New York: Vintage, 1977.

Fournier, Ron, Douglas B. Sosnik, and Matthew Dowd. *Applebee's America: How Successful Political, Business and Religious Leaders Connect with the New American Community*. New York: Simon & Schuster, 2006.

Frank, Robert. *Passions Within Reason*. New York: Norton, 1988.

Freedman, Jill. *Narrative Therapy: The Social Construction of Preferred Realities*. New York: W. W. Norton, 1996.

Friere, Paulo. *Pedagogy of the Oppressed*. New York: Continuum, 2000.

Gaski, John. "Does Marketing Ethics Really Have Anything to Say? A Critical Inventory of the Literature." *Journal of Business Ethics* 18 (1999): 315–34.

Gazzaniga, Michael. *The Ethical Brain: The Science of our Moral Dilemmas*. New York: Harper Collins, 2005.

Godin, Seth. *Tribes*. New York: Portfolio, 2008.

Goffman, Erving. *The Presentation of Self in Everyday Life*. New York: Doubleday, 1959.

Goodman, Nelson. *Of Mind and Other Matters*. Cambridge, MA: Harvard University Press, 1984.

Gould, Stephen Jay. "On Heroes and Fools in Science." In *Ever Since Darwin*. New York: Norton, 1977.

Graves, Clare W. "Levels of Existence: An Open System Theory of Values." *Journal of Humanistic Psychology*, 10 (1970): 131–55.

Hacking, Ian. "Making Up People." *London Review of Books* 28 (2006).

Haidt, Jonathan. "The Moral Emotions." In *Handbook of Affective Sciences*, edited by Davidson, R. J., K. R. Scherer, & H. H. Goldsmith. Oxford: Oxford University Press, 2003.

Hailes, Julia. *The New Green Consumer Guide*. New York: Simon and Schuster, 2007.

Hauser, Marc. *Moral Minds*. New York: Harper Collins, 2006.

Heidegger, Martin. *Being and Time*. Translated by John Macquarrie and Edward Robinson. London: Harper & Row, 1962.

Henderson, David. *Misguided Virtue: False Notions of Corporate Social Responsibility*. London: Institute of Economic Affairs, 2001.

Heyer, Steven. "Keynote Remarks: *Advertising Age* Madison + Vine Conference." Beverly Hills Hotel, Beverly Hills, Calif., Feb. 5, 2003, adage.com/article/news/steve-heyer-s-manifesto-a-age-marketing/36777.

Hill, Adam. "Ethical Analysis in Counseling: A Case for Narrative Ethics, Moral Visions, and Virtue Ethics." *Counseling and Values* 48 (2004).

Hirsch, E. D. *Cultural Literacy*. Boston: Houghton Mifflin, 1987.

Holmes, Oliver Wendell. "The Stereoscope and the Stereograph." *The Atlantic Monthly* 3 (1859): 738–48.

Holstein, James, and Jaber Gubrium, *The Self We Live By: Narrative Identity in a Post-Modern World*. Oxford: Oxford University Press, 2000.

Holt, Douglas. *How Brands Become Icons: The Principles of Cultural Branding*. Cambridge, MA: Harvard University Press, 2004.

Hopkins, Phil. "'To Say What is Most Necessary:' Expositional and Philosophical Practice in Thucydides and Plato." In *Philosophy in Dialogue: Plato's Many Devices*, edited by Gary Alan Scott. Evanston, IL: Northwestern University Press, 2007.

Horberg, Elizabeth, Christopher Oveis, and Dacher Keltner. "Emotions as Moral Amplifiers: An Appraisal Tendency Approach to the Influences of Distinct Emotions upon Moral Judgment." *Emotion Review* 3 (2011): 237–44.

Jamieson, Kathleen Hall, and Karlyn Kohrs Campbell. *The Interplay of Influence: News, Advertising, Politics and the Internet*. 6th ed. Belmont, CA: Thomson Wadsworth, 2006.

Jenkins, Henry. *Convergence Culture: Where Old and New Media Collide*. New York: New York University Press, 2008.

Jhally, Sut. "Advertising at the Edge of the Apocalypse." Accessed January 28, 2007, sutjhally.com/articles/advertisingattheed.

Kant, Immanuel. *Grounding for a Metaphysics of Morals*. Translated by James W. Ellington. Indianapolis: Hackett Publishing, 1993.

Katz, Leonard, ed. *Evolutionary Origins of Morality*. Bowling Green, OH: Imprint Academic, 2002.

Kaufman, Leslie. "Ad for Dish Detergent Becomes Part of a Story." *New York Times*, June 15, 2010.

Kelly, Francis, and Barry Silverstein, *The Breakaway Brand: How Great Brands Stand Out*. New York: McGraw-Hill, 2005.

Kerby, Anthony Paul. *Narrative and the Self*. Bloomington: Indiana University Press, 1991.

Kierkegaard, Søren. *The Present Age*. Translated by Alexander Dru. New York: Harper & Row, 1962.

———. *Fear and Trembling*. Translated by Alastair Hannay. New York: Penguin, 1985.

Klein, Naomi. *No Logo*. New York: Picador, 2000.

Koehn, Nancy. "A Brief History of Doing Well by Doing Good." *Harvard Business Review*. Accessed June 25, 2012, blogs.hbr.org/2012/06/a-brief-history-of-doing-well.

Kundera, Milan "The Hitchhiking Game." In *Laughable Loves*. New York: Alfred A. Knopf, 1974.

Latour, Bruno. *Pandora's Hope: Essays on the Reality of Science Studies*. Cambridge, MA: Harvard University Press, 1999.

Leigh, Jr, E. G. "The Group Selection Controversy." *Journal of Evolutionary Biology* 23 (2010): 6–19.

Lemann, Nicholas. *The Big Test: The Secret History of the American Meritocracy*. New York: Farrar, Straus and Giroux, 1999.

Lippmann, Walter. *Public Opinion*. London: George Allen & Unwin Ltd., 1922.

Loewen, James. *Lies My Teacher Told Me: Everything Your American History Textbook Got Wrong*. New York: Simon & Schuster, 1995.

Lull, James, and Stephen Hinerman, *Media Scandals*. New York: Columbia University Press, 1998.

MacIntyre, Alasdair. *After Virtue*. Notre Dame, IN: University of Notre Dame Press, 1981.

Malcolm, Hadley. "Target Partners with Lauren Bush," *USA Today*. Accessed on May 11, 2013, usatoday.com/story/money/business/2013/03/11/target-lauren-bush-feed-partnership/1967139.

Marlin, Randal. *Propaganda & the Ethics of Persuasion*. Peterborough, ON: Broadview Press, 2002.

McKay, Brett & Kate. "30 Days to a Better Man Day 1: Define Your Core Values." *The Art of Manliness*. Accessed on May 2, 2014, artofmanliness.com/2009/05/31/30-days-to-a-better-man-day-1-define-your-core-values.

McLuhan, Marshall. *Understanding Media: The Extensions of Man.* London: Routledge and Kegan Paul, 1964.

McMurtry, John. *Unequal Freedoms: The Global Market as an Ethical System.* West Hartford, CT: Kumarian, 1998.

Mead, George Herbert. *Mind, Self, and Society.* Chicago: University of Chicago Press, 1934.

Merleau-Ponty, Maurice. *Phenomenology of Perception.* London: Routledge & Kegan Paul, 1962.

Mitchell, W. J. T., ed. *On Narrative.* Chicago: University of Chicago Press, 1980.

Motavalli, Jim. "A History of Greenwashing: How Dirty Towels Impacted the Green Movement." *AOL Daily Finance.* Accessed February 15, 2011, dailyfinance.com/2011/02/12/the-history-of-greenwashing-how-dirty-towels-impacted-the-green.

Murdoch, Iris. *The Sovereignty of Good.* New York: Routledge & Kegan Paul, 1970.

Neff, Jack. "Brita's Marketing Grows from Grassroots Efforts," *AdvertisingAge.* Accessed November 20, 2009, adage.com/article/cmo-interviews/brita-s-marketing-flows-grassroots-effort/140519.

Nelson, Hilde Lindemann. *Damaged Identities, Narrative Repair.* Ithaca, NY: Cornell University Press, 2001.

Nelson, Joyce. "As the Brain Tunes Out, the TV Admen Tune In." *Globe and Mail,* April 16, 1983.

Nietzsche, Friedrich. *Beyond Good and Evil.* Translated by Walter Kaufmann. New York: Vintage, 1966.

———. *On the Genealogy of Morals.* Translated by Walter Kaufmann. New York: Vintage, 1989.

Okasha, Samir. *Evolution and the Levels of Selection.* Oxford: Oxford University Press, 2006.

Pew Research Center's Journalism Project. "The State of the News Media." Accessed February 13, 2008, http://stateofthemedia.org/2004/cable-tv-intro/content-analysis/

Pont, Simon. *The Better Mousetrap: Brand Invention in a Media Democracy.* London: Kogan Page, 2013.

Prinz, Jesse. "The Emotional Basis of Moral Judgments." *Philosophical Explorations* 9 (2006).

Rampton, Sheldon, and John Stauber. *Trust Us, We're Experts: How Industry Manipulates Science and Gambles with Your Future.* New York: Penguin, 2002.

Rivera-Camino, Jaime. "Re-evaluating green marketing strategy: a stakeholder perspective." *European Journal of Marketing* 41 (2007): 1328–1358.

Ricoeur, Paul. *The Rule of Metaphor: Multi-Disciplinary Studies in the Creation of Meaning in Language.* Translate by R. Czerny with K. McLaughlin and J. Costello. Toronto: University of Toronto Press, 1977.

———. *Oneself as Another.* Chicago: University of Chicago, 1992.

Ridley, Matt. *The Origins of Virtue.* New York: Penguin, 1996.

Roberts, Robert C. *Emotions in the Moral Life.* Cambridge: Cambridge University Press, 2013.

Rorty, Richard. *Contingency, Irony, and Solidarity.* Cambridge: Cambridge University Press, 1989.

Rosenwald, George, and Richard Ochberg, *Storied Lives.* New Haven, CT: Yale University Press, 1992.

Rudd, Anthony. *Self, Value, and Narrative.* Oxford: Oxford University Press, 2012.

Sacks, Oliver. *The Man Who Mistook His Wife for a Hat.* New York: Simon & Schuster, 1970.

Sandel, Michael. *What Money Can't Buy: The Moral Limits of Markets.* New York: Farrar, Straus, and Giroux, 2012.

Schechtman, Marya. *The Constitution of Selves.* Ithaca, NY: Cornell University Press, 1996.

Scheuer, Jeffrey. *The Sound Bite Society: Television and the American Mind.* New York: Four Walls Eight Windows Press, 1999.

Schwartz, David. *Consuming Choices: Ethics in a Global Consumer Age.* New York: Rowman & Littlefield, 2010.

Segestrale, Ulliga. *Defenders of the Truth: the Battle for Science in the Sociobiology Debate and Beyond.* Oxford: Oxford University Press, 2000.

Selbin, Eric. *Revolution, Rebellion, Resistance: The Power of Story.* London: Zed Books, 2010.

Sherif, Muzafer, O. J. Harvey, Jack White, William Hood, and Carolyn Sherif. *The Robber's Cave Experiment: Intergroup Conflict and Cooperation.* Middletown, CT: Wesleyan University Press, 1988.

Silko, Leslie Marmon. *Storyteller.* New York: Penguin, 1981.

Silverstone, Roger. *Media and Morality: On the Rise of the Mediapolis.* Cambridge: Polity, 2007.

Sluzki, Carlos. "Transformations: A Blueprint for Narrative Changes in Therapy." *Family Process* 31 (1992).

Smith, Paul. *Discerning the Subject.* Minneapolis: University of Minnesota Press, 1988.

Smith, Toby. *The Myth of Green Marketing.* Toronto: University of Toronto Press, 1998.

Sober, Elliott, and David Sloan Wilson, *Unto Others: The Evolution and Psychology of Unselfish Behavior.* Cambridge, MA: Harvard University Press, 1998.

Sokolowski, Robert. "The Method of Philosophy: Making Distinctions." *The Review of Metaphysics* 51 (1998): 515–32.

Stanley, Alessandra. "Amid Chaos, One Notably Restrained Voice." *New York Times.* April 19, 2007, TV Watch.

Stengers, Isabelle. *Power and Invention: Situating Science.* Minneapolis: University of Minnesota Press, 1997.

———. *Invention of Modern Science.* Minneapolis: University of Minnesota Press, 2000.

Story, Louise. "Anywhere the Eye Can See, It's Likely to See an Ad." *New York Times* , January 15, 2007.

———. "Viewers Fast-Forwarding Past Ads? Not Always." *New York Times*, February 16, 2007.

Strawson, Galen. "Against Narrativity." *Ratio* XVII (2004): 428–52.

Tangney, June Price, Jeff Stuewig, and Debra Mashek. "Moral Emotions and Moral Behavior." *Annual Review of Psychology* 58 (2007): 345–72.

Taylor, Charles. *Sources of the Self: The Making of the Modern Identity.* Cambridge, MA: Harvard University Press, 1992.

Tester, Keith. *Compassion, Morality, and Media.* Maidenhead, UK: Open University Press, 2001.

Thucydides. *The Peloponnesian War.* Translated by Steven Lattimore. Indianapolis: Hackett Publishing, 1988.

Tillich, Paul. *The Dynamics of Faith.* New York: Harper Collins, 1957.

Tomlinson, John. "'And Besides, the Wench is Dead': Media Scandals and the Globalization of Communication." in Lull and Hinerman.

"US Total Media Ad Spend Inches Up, Pushed by Digital." *eMarketer.* Accessed June 9, 2014, emarketer.com/Article/US-Total-Media-Ad-Spend-Inches-Up-Pushed-by-Digital/1010154.

Vega, Tanzina. "Ad About Women's Self-Image Creates a Sensation." *New York Times*, April 18, 2013.

Walker, Rob. *Buying In: The Secret Dialogue Between What We Buy and Who We Are.* New York: Random House, 2008.

Walton, Douglas. *Media Argumentation: Dialectic, Persuasion and Rhetoric.* Cambridge: Cambridge University Press, 2007.

Watson, Jamie Carlin, and Robert Arp. *What's Good on TV?: Understanding Ethics Through Television.* Hoboken, NJ: Wiley-Blackwell, 2011.

"What are Core Values?" National Park Service. Accessed on May 2, 2014, nps.gov/training/uc/whcv.htm.

White, E. B. "Truth in Advertising." *The New Yorker*, July 11, 1936.

Wilks, Tom. "Social Work and Narrative Ethics." *British Journal of Social Work* 35 (2005).

Williams, Bernard. *Problems of the Self.* Cambridge: Cambridge University Press, 1973.

Williams, Patricia. *The Alchemy of Race and Rights.* Cambridge, MA: Harvard University Press, 1992.

Wilson, James Q. *The Moral Sense.* New York: Simon & Schuster, 1997.

Wright, Richard. *The Moral Animal: Why We Are the Way We Are: The New Science of Evolutionary Psychology.* New York: Vintage, 1995.

Žižek, Slavoj, Ernesto Laclau, and Judith Butler, *Contingency, Hegemony, Universality: Contemporary Dialogues on the Left*. London: Verso, 2000.
Žižek, Slavoj. *First as Tragedy, Then as Farce*. London: Verso, 2009.
———. "10/7/01 – Reflections on WTC – Third Version." Accessed on November 28, 2013, egs.edu/faculty/slavoj-zizek/articles/welcome-to-the-desert-of-the-real.
———. "A Cup of Decaf Reality." Accessed on November 28, 2013, lacan.com/zizekdecaf.htm.

Index

Adler, Richard, 2
advertisements, analysis of: Acura, 124; American Century, 12–14, 13, 38n6; AT&T, 137; Banco Provencia (in Argentina), 156–157; Benetton Group, 74, 74–75, 75, 76, 119; Buick, 147–148, 149; Carter's (baby clothes), 137–138, 160n3; Cheerios, 138–141, 216; Chevron, 145–146, 151; Coca-Cola, 150–152; Curve Perfume, 101, 101–105, 102, 103, 104, 120; DirecTV, 137; Discover Card, 107–108; Domino's Pizza, 148–149; Dove, 185, 185–186; Dr Pepper, 98, 98–101, 100, 114–115, 120; Honda, 146; Hyundai, 153–154; Jack in the Box, 144–145; Jeep, 97, 120; Jif, 127–128, 141; Jimmy Johns, 125, 126, 128; Keep California Beautiful (PSA), 155–156, 164; Kenneth Cole, 75–76, 77, 78, 79, 119; KFC (Kentucky Fried Chicken), 124; Lancôme, 129, 129–130, 154; LivingSocial, 128; Louis Vuitton, 142, 150; McDonald's, 12, 14, 130–131, 133, 157–158; Rice Krispies, 139–140, 141; Skittles, 155; Skyy Vodka, 79, 80; Subaru, 131–132, 141; Target, 125–126, 141–142, 176–177; Toyota, 146–147; Verizon Wireless, 152–153; Volkswagen (Jetta), 93–95, 94, 119; Wal-Mart, 140, 141

advertising: DVR (digital video recorders), impact on, 211; families (parenting), use of, 14–15, 124–128, 130–133, 137–142, 148–150; and life lessons, 139–142; mirroring "real" life, 75–77, 107, 119, 127–128, 132; nostalgia, use of, 12, 15, 99, 110, 126–127, 140, 172; humor in, 124, 128, 137, 144–145, 155–156. *See also* marketing narratives
Affleck, Ben, 183
American Marketing Association, 96
anonymity/impartiality as authority, 50–52, 54, 60, 64, 191
Anscombe, Elizabeth, 20
appearance vs. reality, 1, 25, 29–30, 61, 105–106, 191–192
Appiah, Kwame Anthony, 31, 34, 62, 71
argument, 33, 43, 50, 55–58, 60, 119, 154–155
Aristotle, 20, 29
Atkins, Douglas, 96–97, 110, 114
authority: of anonymity/impartiality, 50–52, 54, 60, 64, 191; of experts, 52–54, 55–56, 59; of images, 6, 67, 70, 122; of witnesses, 59–60; of truth-telling narratives, 5, 46, 50, 55–56

Barthes, Roland, 15, 67, 105–106, 107–108, 218
Baudrillard, Jean, 7n2, 71, 77, 79, 83, 85–86, 87, 105, 115

About the Author

Phil Hopkins is professor of philosophy at Southwestern University and Holder of the Lurlyn and Durwood Fleming Professorship in Religion and Philosophy. He has published on early Greek philosophy, with a focus on rhetoric and the centrality of language in shaping how we see the world, and on the intersections of moral philosophy and mass media discourse.